W9-AFQ-753

ETHICS IN HARD TIMES

THE HASTINGS CENTER SERIES IN ETHICS

A Continuation Order Plan is available for this series. A continuation order will bring delivery of each new volume immediately upon publication. Volumes are billed only upon actual shipment. For further information please contact the publisher.

ETHICS IN HARD TIMES

Edited by
Arthur L. Caplan
and
Daniel Callahan

The Hastings Center, Hastings-on-Hudson, New York

PLENUM PRESS • NEW YORK AND LONDON

Library of Congress Cataloging in Publication Data

Main entry under title:

Ethics in hard times.

(The Hastings Center series in ethics)
Includes bibliographies and index.
1. Political ethics—Addresses, essays, lectures. 2. Social ethics—Addresses, essays,
lectures. 3. Social justice—Addresses, essays, lectures. I. Caplan, Arthur L. II. Callahan,
Daniel, 1930   . III. Series.
JA79.E825   172   81-17728
ISBN 0-306-40790-6   AACR2

© 1981 The Hastings Center
Institute of Society, Ethics, and the Life Sciences
360 Broadway
Hastings-on-Hudson, New York 10706

Plenum Press, New York
A Division of Plenum Publishing Corporation
233 Spring Street, New York, N.Y. 10013

Printed in the United States of America

CONTRIBUTORS

DANIEL CALLAHAN, Director, The Hastings Center, Institute of Society, Ethics, and the Life Sciences, 360 Broadway, Hastings-on-Hudson, New York

ARTHUR L. CAPLAN, Associate for the Humanities, The Hastings Center, Institute of Society, Ethics, and the Life Sciences, 360 Broadway, Hastings-on-Hudson, New York

ROBERT A. GOLDWIN, American Enterprise Institute for Public Policy Research, 1150 17th Street, Northwest, Washington, D.C.

ROBERT LEKACHMAN, Department of Economics, Herbert H. Lehman College, City University of New York, Bronx, New York

JONATHAN LIEBERSON, Center for Policy Studies, The Population Council, 1 Dag Hammarskjold Plaza, New York, New York

JAMES RACHELS, Office of the Dean, School of Humanities, University of Alabama in Birmingham, Birmingham, Alabama

THOMAS C. SCHELLING, John F. Kennedy School of Government, 79 Boylston Street, Harvard University, Cambridge, Massachusetts

PETER SINGER, Department of Philosophy, Monash University, Clayton, Victoria, Australia

SHELDON S. WOLIN, Department of Politics, 206 Corwin Hall, Princeton University, Princeton, New Jersey

A.D. WOOZLEY, University Professor of Philosophy and Law, 521 Cabell Hall, University of Virginia, Charlottesville, Virginia

CONTENTS

INTRODUCTION

There is widespread agreement among large segments of western society that we are living in a period of hard times. At first glance such a belief might seem exceedingly odd. After all, persons in western society find themselves living in a time of unprecedented material abundance. Hunger and disease, evils all too familiar to the members of earlier generations, although far from eradicated from modern life, are plainly on the wane. Persons alive today can look forward to healthier, longer, and more comfortable lives than those of their grandparents. Nevertheless, the feeling that life today is especially difficult is rampant in government, in the media, in popular books, and in academic circles. Western society is perceived in many quarters as wracked by crises of all sorts—of faith, of power, of authority, of social turmoil, of declining quality in workmanship and products, and of a general intellectual malaise afflicting both those on the Left and the Right. A tone of crisis permeates the language of public life. Editorials in major newspapers are full of dire warnings about the dangers of unbridled egoism, avarice and greed, and the risks and horrors of pollution, overpopulation, the arms race, crime, and indulgent lifestyles.

Many of the social institutions that have historically served as the glue of modern social existence—the church, the family, local government, the schools, the armed forces,

the police—have been diagnosed as seriously ailing or certi
fied as dead by countless publications, studies, commissions,
and panels. Science, medicine, and technology, once the hope
of an entire generation of young idealists, are now viewed as
pernicious practices whose fruits are bitter and toxic. The
quality of life in large urban centers today has led many cultural commentators to recall Hobbesian descriptions of life
grown brutish, nasty, and short. The language of triage, of
lifeboat ethics, of belt tightening, of conservation, of battening
down the hatches is now the argot of policy makers, bureau-
crats, and politicians. Quality not quantity has become the
criterion by which life in advanced modern society is measured. Although no single indicator has gained universal as-
sent as the appropriate index of the quality of personal life,
there seems to be a universal consensus that most of the
available signs and indices are pointing in a negative direction.

Ironically, one symptom of the view that we are living
in a period of hard times is the frequency with which contemporary debates about public and private matters are pep-
pered with references to ethics and morality. Many of the
debates and disputes current in contemporary society are conducted in the language of ethics. Talk of rights, justice, virtue,
freedom, duties, and liberty is widespread. Indeed, it would
not be unfair to sum up the popular opinion about why these
are hard times with the phrase "moral crisis." We have an
abundance of knowledge and material goods, yet we seem
uncertain about how to use these goods, about who should
benefit from them, even about whether these goods are really
goods at all.

Talk of ethics is not a new phenomenon in periods of
hard times. In nineteenth-century England legislators and
academicians, appalled by the hard times brought on for

many by rapid industrialization, turned to ethics for answers. The 1834 Royal Poor Law Commission for Inquiring into the Administration and Practical Operation of the Poor Laws concluded that poverty was a condition that resulted from the moral inferiority of afflicted individuals. Similarly, in the United States during the 1840s and 1850s, waves of German and Irish immigrants were divided into the morally "worthy" rich and "unworthy" poor. The hard life borne by these new immigrants was diagnosed as resulting from a failure of moral nerve and congenital defects in moral character. New immigrants simply lacked the necessary moral resources to raise themselves from poverty, unemployment, and hard times. This tendency to attribute the new immigrant's harsh life to defects in moral character is still manifest today in editorial complaints about crime and poverty among Haitians, Cubans, and Vietnamese in America, and among Pakistanis, Trinidadians, and Surinamese in Europe.

In hard times ethics is often thought to be useful not only in diagnosis but also in therapy. Utilitarianism, for example, clearly arose as a nineteenth-century moral response to hard times. Social welfare efforts for the poor and the disabled were closely tied to moral theorizing about benefiting the greatest number. Prisons and asylums were also defended on these same moral grounds.

Those who do work in the humanities are often quick to scold those in other fields, professions, and walks of life for ignoring their social and political roots. Indeed, entire scholarly industries have arisen in the humanities to chart the history and social context of the sciences. Unfortunately, humanists in general and moral philosophers in particular have not been as quick to look at the historical and social roots of their own theories and views. When one looks in this direction, it becomes obvious that ethical theorizing is not at all immune to hard times. As the case of utilitarianism shows, war, poverty, and economic vicissitudes are powerful motives to philosophizing about morality.

This book represents an effort to see what the current perception of hard times means for ethical inquiry. Is ethics a place to turn for answers to hard questions of the sort now confronting technologically advanced societies? Is the current perception of hard times fueled by a perceived failure in modern morals, and, if so, is the perception valid? And if cultures, as they have in the past, turn in hard times to ethics for help, what has contemporary inquiry into morality to offer in the way of diagnoses and solutions? The essays assembled here are intended to illustrate that inquiry into moral issues can provide some relief for hard times.

The essays fall into three general categories. Rachels, Singer, and Lieberson concern themselves with the scope, content, and purpose of ethics. Rachels argues that ethics ought to be conceived as an autonomous subject matter, related to but not reducible to psychology, sociology, or anthropology. The strict exercise of what he terms "rational methods" will improve the quality and, more importantly, the efficacy of moral argument. Ethics can give answers if we realize that these answers are only useful in proportion to the information and self-understanding available to anyone who formulates them. Rachels maintains that the methods of ethics are only as valid as the factual evidence on which they depend.

Singer argues that certain plain facts about sentience and suffering must force a reevaluation of our current thinking about moral standing. According to Singer, the ability to feel and suffer is sufficient for conferring moral standing on an entity. If this is so, since we now use such a criterion for conferring moral status upon children, the retarded, the mentally ill, and the senile, then we must include most animals in the sphere of our moral concerns as well. If, as Rachels notes, consistency is a central norm of ethical method, then babies and baboons deserve equal consideration as, and only as, sentient beings. Ironically, whereas Singer's sentience standard leads him to argue for extending our traditional sphere of moral concern, Lieberson finds himself arguing against those who would limit the boundary of moral concern to our own bodies. Lieberson argues that current fascinations with egoism and self-advantage are conceptually muddled. The notions of self used by those who preach the glories of raw egoism are petty and static. Lieberson is in agreement with Rachels and Singer that the demands of morality in good times and bad require us to do more rather than less in overcoming our desires for short-term personal security and comfort.

Lekachman, Goldwin, and Woozley address themselves to the issue of the role of the state vis-à-vis the citizen in hard times. Lekachman notes that American society is currently divided as to the optimal mode for achieving justice for its citizens between providing equal opportunity for all and strict equality in the resources and goods that all persons in fact possess. He argues that libertarian minimalism in the distribution of goods is not likely to nourish the desires and hopes of the general population for long. On Lekachman's view of equality we must not settle for anything less than an economic system that promises to provide more to the poor and disadvantaged at the expense of the rich—no matter what the opinion of the rich might be.

Goldwin addresses himself to an issue of central moral importance to any society—the duties of citizenship. Goldwin cautions that the hope of helping others, of benefiting the poor and the disadvantaged, should not fool us into undercutting our notion of civic duty by claims about individual rights. In contrast to Lekachman, he argues that the protection of liberty and the recognition of civic duty are the best prophylactics against the totalitarian impulses present in government during hard times.

Woozley addresses himself to another issue of vital importance in citizen–state relations: the role of law in regulating personal and public behavior. Woozley argues that the law should be coextensive in its concern with the immoral. If morality tries, as Rachels, Singer, and Lieberson all suggest, to protect and advance interests, then the state has no choice but to enforce sanctions against immorality. The law must serve as a societal standard of minimally acceptable and maximally desirable conduct. Woozley concurs with Goldwin that the law should not be a vehicle for moral change, but rather is dependent on moral motives for its existence. Both Goldwin and Woozley trust to individual good sense and sensitivity as the ultimate guardians of civility and stability in hard times. Lekachman, although less sanguine about the overlap of readings among individual moral barometers, believes that the sentiment for equity in the distribution of resources will ultimately prevail over all others.

The essays by Schelling, Wolin, and Callahan address themselves to a particularly timely concern in hard times: How should a society as pluralistic as America's come to grips with the need to establish unanimity concerning moral choices in a period of hard times? Schelling addresses the question of how the supposedly neutral or "disinterested" policy sciences can grapple with a broad range of ethical opinions about divisive social issues. He notes the unexpected pernicious effects meliorative social programs have had and can have in rewarding risky personal behaviors. He argues that those involved in the policy sciences can best protect the greatest number of human interests by honestly attempting to calculate the relative costs to individuals of following various policy alternatives, and by leaving the ultimate policy choice to those concerned enough to care.

Wolin worries about the power implicit in obeisance to a principle of the inviolability of pluralism. Powerful groups within society are able to get their way, he warns, both by maintaining the illusion of pluralism—that no common interests exist—and by defending the morality of tolerating pluralism. Unlike Schelling, Wolin believes that "disinterested" expertise is not to be trusted since technical solutions are most attractive to those well placed enough to utilize them.

Callahan argues that current popular conceptions of morality that tout the virtues of liberty and autonomy are not sufficient to glue together a society faced with hard times. Like Goldwin, he looks toward the articulation of a communitarian or civic ethic based on duty, obligation, and trust to rectify the "moral anemia" of contemporary society. Callahan agrees with Wolin that mere tolerance for tolerance's sake is not the optimal solution for a pluralistic society looking for solutions and options in hard times. And, like Rachels, Callahan believes that morality and pluralism could better be reconciled with less attention to tolerance and more attention to common interests.

The disposition to philosophize may show itself most in hard times. But in times such as these, that disposition cannot flourish without financial aid and support. Thus we must warmly thank the Rockefeller Foundation for their generous support of the Humanities Program at the Hastings Center, under whose auspices these essays were produced. We must also thank Elizabeth Bartelme, Mary Gualandi, and Bonnie Baya whose editorial and typing skills contributed mightily to making the production of this volume a pleasant task despite the rigors of the times.

ARTHUR L. CAPLAN
DANIEL CALLAHAN

Chapter 1 / CAN ETHICS PROVIDE ANSWERS?

JAMES RACHELS

ETHICS AND ETHICAL THEORY

No great powers of observation are needed to see that the American people are not as optimistic or confident as they once were. Even as the Vietnam War and the Watergate scandals recede into memory, other concerns take their place. The energy crisis and a growing rate of inflation are the visible signs of an uncertain economy—an economy which, in addition to creating a general sense of insecurity makes it harder than ever to satisfy demands for social justice. Technology, which was supposed to save us, now presents as many problems as solutions—witness the controversy over nuclear energy, for example. Pessimism seems not only understandable, but rational.

In this bleak situation the study of ethics flourishes. Perhaps moral guidance is most needed when times are hardest,

JAMES RACHELS ● Office of the Dean, School of Humanities, University of Alabama in Birmingham, Birmingham, Alabama 35294.

because then temptation is greatest. But there is a curious pessimism even about ethics itself. Recently I saw a proposal, written by a distinguished professor of buisness, to add a course in ethics to his department's curriculum. It was an enthusiastic statement, in which the benefits of such an offering were set forth in detail. But it concluded with the remark that "since there are no definite answers in ethics, the course should be offered on a pass-fail basis." I do not know why he thought that lacking definite answers it would be any easier to distinguish passing from failing work than "B" from "C' work, but what struck me most was the casual, offhand manner in which the remark was made—as though it were *obvious* that no matter how important ethical questions might be, no "definite answers" are possible.

Philosophers have given a great deal of attention to this issue, but the result, unfortunately, has been a great deal of disagreement. There are generally two schools of thought. On one side there are those who believe that ethics is a subject, like history or physics or mathematics, with its own distinctive problems and its own methods of solving them. The fundamental questions of ethics are questions of conduct—what, in particular cases, should we do?—and the study of ethics provides the answers. On the other side are those who, like the professor of business, deny that ethics is a proper subject at all. There are ethical questions, to be sure, and they are important; but since they do not have definite answers, there cannot be a subject whose business it is to discover them.

In this chapter I shall discuss whether, in fact, ethics can provide answers. As a preliminary to that discussion, however, I need to say something about the relation between ethics and ethical theory. Ethics is the subject that attempts to provide directions for conduct: Should a manufacturer advertise a product as being better than it is? Should a lawyer suppress evidence that tends to show that his client is guilty? Should a physician help a dying patient who, because of constant misery, wishes to end his life sooner? And so on—endlessly.

Ethical theory, on the other hand, concerns itself with questions *about* ethics. These questions divide naturally into two categories. First, ethical theorists want to know about the relations between the various principles that are used in justifying particular moral judgments. Can they be fitted together into a unifed theory? Can these diverse principles be reduced to one ultimate principle that underlies and explains all the rest? Much of modern moral philosophy has consisted of the elaboration of such theories: egoism, Kantianism, and utilitarianism, each purporting to have discovered *the* ultimate principle of ethics, are the most familiar. Second, there are questions about the *status* of ethics. Are there any objective truths in ethics that our moral judgments may correctly or incorrectly represent? Or are our moral judgments nothing more than the expression of personal feelings, or perhaps the codes of the societies in which we live? Often it is helpful in dealing with such issues to analyze the meaning of moral concepts—to examine what is meant by such words as "good," "right," and "ought."[1]

Twenty years ago the prevailing orthodoxy among English-speaking philosophers was that ethical theory, but not

[1]William Frankena, *Ethics*, 2nd ed. (Englewood Cliffs, N.J.: Prentice-Hall, 1973) is a helpful introduction to ethical theory. For information about particular topics and theories, various articles in the *Encyclopedia of Philosophy*, ed. Paul Edwards, 8 vols. (New York: Macmillan & Free Press, 1967) are useful. The reader should not be put off by the fact that this source is "merely" an encyclopedia; it is a splendid work with which everyone should be familiar.

ethics itself, was the proper concern of philosophy. Philosophers, it was said, are theoreticians, not ministers or guidance counselors. The more radical philosophers even excluded what I have called the first part of ethical theory from their purview; they restricted their attention entirely to the analysis of moral language. The result was a body of literature that seemed to those outside academic circles curiously empty and sterile.

Today this attitude has been almost completely abandoned; the best writing by moral philosophers combines ethical theory with a concern for concrete ethical issues. Part of the reason for this change is that the traumas of the past two decades—especially the protest movements against racism, sexism, and the Vietnam War—forced philosophers to rethink their role in society. But there is a deeper reason, internal to philosophy itself. The rejection of ethics was the result of a preoccupation among philosophers during the first half of this century with understanding the different kinds of inquiry. Science, mathematics, religion, and ethics are very different from one another, and as philosophers tried to sort out the differences, the idea took hold that philosophy's distinctive contribution is to analyze and clarify the concepts used in each area. It was an appealing idea with ample historical precedent. After all, the patron saint of philosophy, Socrates, had conceived of his work mainly as an investigation of definitions; and the great figures such as Aristotle and Kant had appealed, at key points in their work, to linguistic considerations for support. Philosophers, then, were not to study ethics but only the language of ethics. That philosophers are not ethicists seemed as natural a conclusion as that philosophers are not scientists or mathematicians.

By the mid-1960s, however, it was becoming clear that the recognition of differences between kinds of inquiry does not require that they be pursued in isolation from one another. Indeed, separation may not be desirable or even possible—one cannot do physics without mathematics. Today philosophers generally do not recognize sharp boundaries between their own work and work in other areas. Thus W. V. Quine, whom many consider the most eminent living American philosopher, regards his work as continuous with that of theoretical science. Although Quine's writings can be read with only a layman's knowledge of science, much contemporary philosophy of science cannot. The reuniting of ethical theory with ethics, then, is merely a part of a larger movement within philosophy, bringing back into proper relation the disparate inquiries.

THE CASE AGAINST ETHICS

The professor of business whose statement I quoted is not unusual; a great many people, including many philosophers, believe that there are no "answers" in ethics. It is a remarkable situation: people make judgments every day about what should or should not be done; they feel strongly about those views, and sometimes they become angry and indignant with those who disagree. Yet when they reflect on what they are doing, they profess that their judgments are no more "true" than the contrary ones they reject so vehemently. The explanation of this puzzling situation goes deep into our history, and into our understanding of the world and our place in it.

Throughout most of western history there was thought to be a close connection between ethics and religion. In Plato's *Euthyphro* Socrates offers powerful arguments for separating the two, but this point of view did not prevail. (Socrates, it will be remembered, was tried and convicted of impiety.)

Right and wrong continued to be defined by reference to God's will, and human life came to be regarded as meaningful only because of its place in God's plan. The church, therefore, was the guardian of the moral community and its main authority. By the eighteenth century these ideas had begun to lose their grip on people's minds, largely because of changes that had taken place in the conception of the physical world. The physical sciences had successfully challenged the ancient belief that the earth is the center of the cosmos; instead, it was recognized to be a relatively insignificant speck. The next step would be the realization that, from a cosmic point of view, human beings are themselves insignificant. In his famous essay on suicide, published posthumously in 1783, Hume took that step, declaring that "The life of a man is of no greater importance to the universe than that of an oyster."[2] The aim of this essay was to defend the permissibility of suicide; in doing that, Hume was particularly eager to separate religious from moral notions, and to dispel the idea that human life is a gift from God that can rightly be taken only by God. This belief he considered to be a compound of "superstition and false religion," and he held that the purpose of our thinking should be to replace superstition and false religion with reason and understanding. The truth, in his view, is that *we* care about human life, because we are human, and that is all there is to it. Our lives have no more, and no less, importance than that. Hume would no doubt have felt vindicated by the second great modern change in our conception of the world and our place in it, which came after his death from the biological

---

[2]The essay on suicide, together with other relevant works, is conveniently reprinted in Alasdair MacIntyre, ed. *Hume's Ethical Writings*, (New York: Collier Books, 1965). Of the many commentaries on Hume, Rachel Kydd's *Reason and Conduct in Hume's Treatise* (New York: Russell & Russell, 1964) is especially recommended.

sciences. The thought that we are the products of an evolutionary history much like that of all the other animals has further eroded confidence about any special place for humanity in the scheme of things.

In our own time, however, it has been the social sciences that have presented the greatest challenge to traditional ideas about human beings. In particular, the understanding of human nature derived from contemporary sociology and psychology has seemed to many people incompatible with a belief in the objectivity of ethics—that is, with a belief in objective standards of right and wrong.

The sociologists have impressed upon us that moral standards differ from culture to culture; what the "natural light of reason" reveals to one people may be radically different from what seems obvious to another. This fact, of course, has been known for a long time. Herodotus made the point very clearly in the fifth century B.C.:

> Darius, after he had got the Kindgom, called into his presence certain Greeks who were at hand, and asked—"What he should pay them to eat the bodies of their fathers when they died?" To which they answered, that there was no sum that would tempt them to do such a thing. He than sent for certain Indians, of the race called Callatians, men who eat their fathers, and asked them, while the Greeks stood by, and knew by the help of an interpreter all that was said—"What he should give them to burn the bodies of their fathers at their decease?" The Indians exclaimed aloud, and bade him forbear such language. Such is men's wont herein; and Pindar was right, in my judgment, when he said, "Custom is the king o'er all."[3]

[3]*The History of Herodotus,* trans. George Rawlinson, adapted by John Ladd in *Ethical Relativism* (Belmont, Calif.: Wadsworth, 1973), p. 12. *Ethical Relativism* is a good collection of articles on the relation of ethics to culture.

Today any educated person could list countless other examples: the Eskimos allow firstborn daughters to die of exposure; the Moslems practice polygamy; The Jains will not eat meat. With the communications media providing constant contact with other parts of the world, it may now seem simply naïve to think that our moral views are anything more than one particular cultural product.

Psychological studies tend to undermine confidence in the objectivity of ethics in a different way, by making us aware of the nonrational ways in which moral beliefs are formed in the individual. The general picture remains remarkably constant even when we consider radically different psychological theories. Freud and Skinner, for example, tell much the same story. The key idea in Freud's account is that of the "pleasure principle." The child learns from an early age that certain types of behavior will be followed by pleasure, often in the form of parental approval, and that other actions produce unpleasant consequences. Thus he learns to behave in some ways and to avoid others, and when his vocabulary has become sufficiently rich he calls the former acts "right" and the latter "wrong." Skinnerian psychology could hardly be more different from Freudian thought; nevertheless, their fundamental ideas concerning moral development are almost identical. Where Freud speaks of pleasure, Skinner speaks of "positive reinforcement": the individual is positively reinforced (rewarded) when he performs certain acts, and so tends to repeat such behavior; he is negatively reinforced (punished) for other acts, which he subsequently tends not to repeat. The concepts of good and evil become attached to the two kinds of behavior. Indeed, Skinner goes so far as to suggest that "good" may be *defined* as "positively reinforcing." On both theories, a person who has been raised differently will have different values. The suggested conclusion is that the belief that one's values are anything more than the result of this conditioning is, again, simply naïve. Thus in many people's minds sociology and psychology swallow up ethics. They do not simply explain ethics; they explain it *away*. Ethics can no longer exist as a subject having as its aim the discovery of what is right and what is wrong, for this supposes, naïvely, that there *is* a right and wrong independent of what people already happen to believe. And that is precisely what has been brought into doubt. Ethics as a subject must disappear, to be replaced, perhaps, by something like "values clarification." We can try to become clearer about what our values are, and about the possible alternatives. But we can no longer ask questions about the truth of our convictions.

With such impressive intellectual forces behind it, it is not surprising that this way of thinking about ethics has been tremendously influential. However, most contemporary philosophers have, with good reason, taken a dim view of these arguments. In the first place, the fact that different societies have different moral codes proves nothing. There is also disagreement from society to society about scientific matters: in some cultures it is believed that the earth is flat, and that disease is caused by evil spirits. We do not on that account conclude that there is no truth in geography or in medicine. Instead we conclude that in some cultures people are better informed than in others. Similarly, disagreement in ethics might signal nothing more than that some people are less enlightened than others. At the very least, the fact of disagreement does not by itself *entail* that truth does not exist. Why should we assume that, if ethical truth exists, everyone must know it?

Moreover, it may be that some values are merely relative to culture whereas others are not. Herodotus was probably right in thinking that the treatment of the dead—whether to eat or to burn them—is not a matter governed by objectively true standards. It may be simply a matter of convention that respect is shown in one way rather than another. If so, the Callatians and the Greeks were equally naïve to be horrified at each other's customs. Alternative sexual customs—another favorite example of relativists—might also be equally acceptable. But this does not mean that there are *no* practices that are objectively wrong: torture, slavery, and lying, for example, could still be wrong, independently of cultural standards, even if those other types of behavior are not. It is a mistake to think that because some standards are relative to culture, all must be.

The psychological facts are equally irrelevant to the status of ethics as an autonomous subject. Psychology may tell us that beliefs are acquired in a certain way—perhaps as the result of positive and negative reinforcements—but nothing follows from this fact about the nature of those beliefs. After all, *every* belief is acquired through the operation of some psychological mechanism or other, including the simplest factual beliefs. A child may learn to respond "George Washington" when asked the name of the first president because she fears the disapproval of the teacher should she say anything else. And, we might add, if she were reinforced differently she might grow up believing that someone else first held that office. Yet it remains a matter of objective fact that Washington was the first president. The same goes for one's moral beliefs: the manner of their acquisition is logically independent of their status as objectively true or false.

Thus the outcome of the psychological account of ethics is reminiscent of the fate of nineteenth-century attempts to reduce mathematics to psychology. In the late 1800s there was considerable interest in explaining mathematics by reference to psychological theories of human thought—but that interest waned when it was realized that little light was being shed on mathematics itself. Regardless of how it might be related to our thought processes, mathematics remained a subject with its own integrity—its own internal rules, procedures, problems, and solutions; in short, its own standards of truth and falsity. The reason ethics resists explanation by sociology or psychology or, for that matter, the most recent pretender, sociobiology, is that like mathematics it is a subject with its own integrity.

Although contemporary philosophers have not been impressed by the social-scientific arguments concerning ethics, they have nevertheless found certain other arguments against ethics to be plausible. Those arguments go back to Hume, who maintained that belief in the very possibility of an objectively correct ethical system is part of the old "superstition and false religion." Stripped of false theology, Hume said, we should come to see our morality as nothing more than the expression of our feelings.

But Hume did not merely assert this; he attempted to prove it with arguments. His most influential argument was based on the idea that there is a necessary connection between moral belief and conduct. The test of whether we sincerely believe that we ought to do something is whether in fact we are motivated to do it; if I say that I believe I ought to do such-and-such but have not the slightest inclination to do it, my statement is not to be believed. Thus having a moral belief is at least in part a matter of being motivated to act, or, as Hume put it, of having a sentiment. On the other hand, a person's capacity to discern truth and falsehood—in Hume's terms, his reason—has no necessary connection with his conduct at all: "Morals move men to act; reason alone is utterly impotent in this particular." The point is that if moral belief is conceived as the perception of truth or falsity, its connection

with conduct remains mysterious; whereas if it is regarded
as an expression of sentiment, this connection is definitely
made clear.

In our own time Hume's thoughts have been adapted to
support a theory according to which moral judgments are not
really judgments at all, but disguised imperatives. According
to this theory, known as emotivism, when one makes a moral
judgment such as "It is wrong to make someone the subject
of an experiment without his permission," one is actually
saying no more than *"Don't* make someone the subject of an
experiment without his permission." Alternately, as it was
sometimes said, one is doing nothing more in making these
judgments than expressing one's attitude, and urging others
to adopt that attitude. Even though they may be sincere or
insincere, imperatives and expressions of attitude are neither
true nor false—and thus moral judgments are neither true
nor false.[4]

If *this* is what moral judgments are, then once again ethics
has lost its status as a subject. There are no truths for it to
investigate. It cannot even be a branch of pyschology, for
although psychology is concerned with attitudes, it is only
concerned with nonmoral truths *about* attitudes, which, unlike
expessions *of* attitude, are true or false.

Among English-speaking philosophers, emotivism has
been the most influential theory of ethics in the twentieth
century. Earlier I remarked on some of the reasons that led
philosophers to reject normative ethics as part of their subject.
Clearly, the influence of emotivism was another important
element in this rejection, and little was written by philosophers on concrete moral issues until fairly recently—the mid-
1960s—when emotivist ideas had begun to lose their influ-

---

[4]The classic defense of emotivism is Charles L. Stevenson, *Ethics and Language*
(New Haven: Yale University Press, 1944). J. O. Urmson, *The Emotive Theory
of Ethics* (London: Hutchinson, 1968) provides a critical assessment.

ence. Until then the literature on moral issues was mainly the work of the theologians who, standing firmly against the trends of thought I have been describing, never lost confidence in the integrity of ethics as a subject.

There is now an extensive philosophical literature cataloging the deficiencies of emotivism. One of the main problems with the theory was its failure to account for the place of reason in ethics. It is a point of logic that moral judgments, if they are to be acceptable, must be founded on good reasons: if I tell you that such-and-such action is wrong, you are entitled to ask *why* it is wrong; and if I have no adequate reply, you may reject the advice as unwarranted. The emotivists were able to give only the most anemic account of the relation between moral judgments and the reasons that support them. Moral reasoning, on this theory, turned out to be indistinguishable from propaganda. If moral judgments are merely expressions of attitude, then reasons are merely considerations that influence attitudes. It was a natural outcome of this theory that *any* fact which influences attitudes counts as a reason for the attitude produced; thus if the thought that Jones is black causes you to think badly of him, then "Jones is black" becomes a reason in support of your judgment that he is a bad man.

Obviously, something had gone wrong. Not just any fact can count as a reason in support of just any judgment. For one thing, the fact must be relevant to the judgment, and psychological influence does not necessarily bring relevance with it. But this is only the tip of the iceberg. Arguments in support of moral judgments can be criticized, and found adequate or inadequate, on any number of other grounds. Once this is realized, however, we have taken a big step away from emotivism, and all the other trends of thought I have been describing, toward the recognition of ethics as an autonomous subject.

ETHICS AND RATIONALITY

Ultimately the case against ethics can be answered only by demonstrating how moral problems are amenable to solution by rational methods. In any particular case the right course of action is the one that is backed by the best reasons. Consider, for example, euthanasia. We may determine whether mercy killing is right or wrong by formulating and assessing the arguments that can be given for and against it.[5] This is at bottom what is wrong with psychological and cultural relativism: if we can produce good reasons for thinking that this practice is wrong, and show that the arguments in its support are unsound, then we have proven it wrong regardless of what belief one has been conditioned to have, or what one's cultural code might say. And emotivism runs afoul of the same fact: if a stronger case can be made for euthanasia than against it, then mercy killing *is* permissible, no matter what one's attitude might be.

The first and most obvious way that a moral argument can go wrong is by misrepresenting the facts. A rational case for or against a course of conduct must rest on some understanding of the facts of the case—minimally, facts about the nature of the action, the circumstances in which it would be done, and its likely consequences. Even the most skeptical thinkers agree that reason has this role to play in moral judgment: reason establishes the facts. Unfortunately, however, attaining a rational view of the facts is not always a simple matter. In the first place, we often need to know what the consequences of a course of action will be, and this may be impossible to

---

[5]A survey of the relevant arguments may be found in James Rachels, "Euthanasia," in *Matters of Life and Death,* ed. Tom Regan (New York: Random House, 1980), pp. 28–66.

determine with any precision or certainty. Opponents of euthanasia sometimes claim that if it were legalized, it would lead to a diminished respect for life throughout the society, and we would end up caring less about the elderly, the mentally retarded, and so forth. Defenders of euthanasia, on the other hand, heatedly deny this claim. What separates the two camps is a disagreement about "the facts"; but we cannot settle the issue in the same easy way we could settle an argument about what would happen if Coca-Cola were boiled. We seem to be stuck with different *estimates* of what would happen if euthanasia were legalized, which may be more or less reasonable but which we cannot definitely adjudicate.

Moreover, it is often difficult to determine the facts because the facts are distressingly *complex*. Take, for example, the question of whether the government of South Vietnam, which the United States supported during the late war, was democratic. This question figured prominently in some of the debates of the time. I take it to be primarily a matter of fact, but it was not a *simple* matter of fact. In order to decide the matter one had to fit together into a pattern all sorts of other facts about the operation of that government and its relation to its citizens. Whether the government was or was not democratic was a kind of conclusion resting on those other facts; it was a matter of what the simpler facts added up to.

Suppose, though, that we have a clear view of the relevant facts, so that our arguments cannot be faulted on that ground. Is there any other test of rationality that the arguments must pass? Hume's official view was that at this point reason has done all it can do, and the rest is up to our "sentiments." Reason sets out the facts; then sentiment takes over and the choice is made. This is a tempting idea, but it only illustrates a common trap into which people fall. Philosophical theses may seduce with their beautiful simplicity; an idea may be accepted because of its appeal at a high level of generality even though it does not conform to what we know to be the case at a lower level. In fact, when Hume was considering concrete ethical issues and not busy overemphasizing the role of sentiment, he knew very well that appeals to reason are often decisive in other ways. In the essay on suicide to which I have already referred he produced a number of powerful arguments in support of his view that a person has the right to take his own life, for example, when he is suffering without hope from a painful illness. Hume specifically opposed the traditional religious view that since life is a gift from God, only God has the right to decide when it shall end. He made the simple but devastating observation that we "play God" as much when we save life as when we take it. Each time a doctor treats an illness and thereby prolongs a life, he has decreed that the patient's life shall not end *now*. Thus if we take seriously that only God may determine the length of a life, we would have to renounce not only killing but saving life as well.

This point has force because of the general requirement that our arguments be consistent, and consistency, of course, is the prime requirement of rationality. Hume did *not* argue that the religious opponent of suicide has got his facts wrong—he did not insist that there is no God, or that God's will has been misunderstood. If Hume's objection were no more than that, then no religious person need be bothered by it. Hume's objection was much stronger; for he was pointing out that we may appeal to a general principle (such as "Only God has the right to decide when a life shall end") only if we are willing to accept *all* its consequences. If we accept some of them (the prohibition of suicide and euthanasia) but not others (the abandonment of medicine), then we are inconsistent. This point, which has fundamental importance, will be missed if we are blinded by overly simple doctrines such as "Reason establishes the facts; sentiment makes the choice."

There are other ways in which an ethical view may fail to pass the test of consistency. A person may base his ethical position on his "intuitions"—his prereflective hunches about what is right or wrong in particular cases—and, on examination, these may turn out to be incompatible with one another. Consider the difference between killing someone and "merely" allowing someone to die. Many people feel intuitively that there is a big moral difference between these two. The thought of actively killing someone has a kind of visceral repulsiveness about it that is missing from the more passive (but still unpleasant) act of standing by and doing nothing while someone dies. Thus it may be held that although euthanasia is wrong because it involves direct killing, nevertheless it is sometimes permissible to allow death by refraining from life-prolonging treatment.

To be sure, if we do nothing more than consult our "intuitions" there seems to be an important difference here. However, it is easy to describe other cases of killing and letting die in which there does *not* seem to be such a difference. Suppose a patient is brought into an emergency room and turned over to a doctor who recognizes him as a man against whom he has a grudge. A quick diagnosis reveals that the patient is about to die but can be saved by a simple procedure—say, an appendectomy. The doctor, seeing his chance, deliberately stalls until it is too late to perform the lifesaving procedure, and the patient dies. Now most of us would think intuitively that the doctor is no better than a murderer, and the fact that he did not directly kill the patient but merely let him die would make no difference whatever.

In the euthanasia case, the difference between killing and letting die seems important. In the grudge case, the difference seems unimportant. Is the difference important or isn't it?

Such cases show that unexamined intuitions cannot be relied on. Our intuitions may be nothing more than the product of prejudice, selfishness, or cultural conditioning; we have no guarantee that they are perceptions of the truth. And when they are not compatible with one another, we can be sure that one or the other of them is mistaken. In the case of killing and letting die we need to ask *why* the distinction does or does not make a moral difference. It certainly does not matter from the patient's point of view whether he is killed or allowed to die: either way he ends up dead. (In the euthanasia case, it may matter to the patient that he die sooner rather than later because he is suffering—therefore, it may be preferable that he be killed because it is quicker. But what governs choice here is an argument about suffering, not the importance of killing versus letting die *as such*.) Perhaps the reason why there *seems* to be a difference is that killings are so often accompanied by bad motives, whereas acts of letting die are usually done from acceptable motives. Thus it is the difference between the motives and not the difference between the acts themselves that is morally significant.

Recently there has been much discussion of this distinction in the philosophical literature. At first it was largely a matter of different writers citing their intuitions, with each one producing cases in which the favored intuition "seemed" correct. Now, however, the debate has reached a more profitable stage in which the emphasis is on investigating whatever reasons can be produced to support one view over the other.[6]

---

[6]James Rachels, "Active and Passive Euthanasia," *New England Journal of Medicine* 292 (1975): 87–80 argues that there is no morally important difference between killing and letting die. This article is reprinted, together with a response by Tom L. Beauchamp, "A Reply to Rachels on Active and Passive Euthanasia," in Tom L. Beauchamp and Seymour Perlin, eds., *Ethical*

Let me mention one other way in which the requirement of consistency can force a change in one's moral views. I have been emphasizing that a moral judgment, if it is to be acceptable, must be backed by reasons. Consistency requires, then, that if there are exactly the *same* reasons in support of one course of conduct as there are in support of another, those actions are equally right, or equally wrong. We cannot say that X is right but that Y is wrong unless there is a *relevant difference* between X and Y. This is a familiar principle in many contexts: it cannot be right for a teacher to give students different grades unless there is a relevant difference in the work that they have done; it cannot be right to pay workers different wages unless there is some relevant difference in the jobs they do; and so on. In general, it is this principle that underlies the social ideal of equality.

It has recently been noticed that this principle has even more radical implications than egalitarians have realized, for, if applied consistently, it would require that we rethink our treatment of nonhuman animals. We routinely perform experiments on chimpanzees that we would never perform on humans, but what is the difference between chimps and humans that justifies this difference in treatment? One answer might be that humans are far more intelligent and sensitive than chimpanzees; but this answer only invites a further query: Suppose the humans are mentally retarded, so that they are *less* intelligent and sensitive than the chimps? Would we then be willing to experiment on retarded humans in the

Issues in Death and Dying (Englewood Cliffs, N.J.: Prentice-Hall, 1978). Richard L. Trammell, "Saving Life and Taking Life," *Journal of Philosophy* 72 (1975): 131–137 is an excellent defense of the distinction. James Rachels, "Killing and Starving to Death," *Philosophy* 54 (1979): 159–171 continues the attack and criticizes some of Trammell's arguments.

same way? And if not, why not? What is the difference between the individuals in question which makes it all right to experiment on one but not the other? At this point the defender of the status quo may be reduced to asserting that, after all, the humans are *human,* and that is what makes the difference. This, however, is uncomfortably like asserting that, after all, women are *women,* or blacks are *black,* and that is why *they* may be treated differently. It is the announcement of a prejudice and nothing more.[7]

This example brings us back to the point at which we started. We have adjusted in many ways to the idea that the earth is not the center of the universe, and that we humans are but one race of animals among others that have developed here. But when ethics is concerned, we cling to the idea that humanity is still at the center of the cosmos. The idea that every human life is sacred has been replaced by its secular equivalent, that every human life has special value and dignity just in virtue of being human. As a plea for equality among people, the idea has merit; as a justification for our treatment of the nonhuman world, it won't do.

I have left until last a matter that many moral philosophers believe is at the heart of their subject. In many instances we cannot make progress in moral deliberation until we become clearer about the meaning of the concepts that are employed in our arguments; and the analysis of concepts has always been the philosopher's special concern. The most important concepts for ethics in general are the concepts of rightness, goodness, and obligation. We want first to be clear about what they mean—and this is not merely a matter of idle curiosity, but a necessity for making progress in our thinking. In this chapter I have, without announcing the fact, made a

---

[7]These arguments are advanced with great vigor by Peter Singer in *Animal Liberation* (New York: New York Review Books, 1975).

number of points which depend on the analysis of these concepts: that the right thing to do is the course of action supported by the best reasons, and that in the absence of relevant differences it cannot be right to treat individuals differently, are, in my opinion, propositions that follow directly from the meaning of the moral concepts.

The importance of conceptual analysis may not be obvious, however, if we concentrate only on such general concepts. Where particular moral issues are concerned, the analysis of more specific concepts may be crucial. By now it is obvious that the argument over whether fetuses are persons and so fall under the protection of the moral rules governing the treatment of persons is not an argument over "the facts." We all know what sort of biological and psychological entity a fetus is, or we think we do, and yet disagreement persists about whether it is a person. What divides the parties on this point is their differing understandings of what it means to be a person—the analysis of the concept.

Opponents of abortion like to show photographs of fetuses to underscore the point that it is not merely a blob of tissue that is destroyed in an abortion. What makes the photographs effective is that they seem to show *people* just like you and me, albeit very tiny and helpless ones. Yet the proabortionist might point out that what the pictures show is only that the fetus has the physical characteristics normally associated with persons. In addition, persons have psychological characteristics—consciousness, beliefs, desires, hopes—which define their lives as individuals. Since fetuses do not have this complex of psychological characteristics, the proabortionist can argue plausibly that they are not persons in any morally important sense. The whole argument hinges on what is meant by "person."

In one respect I believe that the proabortionists are right. It is a person's psychological characteristics, and not the fact that the person has a certain kind of body, that is important from a moral point of view. That is why, when people have become irreversibly comatose, it seems pointless to keep them alive by artificial means. Without consciousness, with all that it involves, being alive does one no good. Indeed many are tempted to say that such unfortunate people are already dead, in recognition of the fact that their biographical lives are over even though biologically they are still alive. The case of the fetus is, however, different because although the fetus may lack the psychological characteristics of a person, it nevertheless *will* have them if it is allowed a normal development. The major unresolved question about the morality of abortion is how much, if at all, this potentiality counts. People have differing intuitions on the matter, but I am not aware that anyone has produced a convincing argument either way.

THE LIMITS OF RATIONALITY

The preceding discussion will not have dispelled all the nagging doubts about ethics. Rational methods can be used to expose factual error and inconsistency in the ways I have described; but is that enough to save ethics from the charge that, at bottom, there is no "truth" in its domain? Could not two people who are equally rational—who have all the relevant facts, whose principles are consistent, and so on—still disagree? And if "reason" were inadequate to resolve the disagreement, would this not show that, in the end, ethics really is only a matter of opinion? These questions will not go away.

There is a limit to what rational methods can achieve, which Hume described perfectly in the first appendix to his *Inquiry Concerning the Principles of Morals*, published in 1752:

Ask a man *why he uses exercise;* he will answer, *because he desires to keep his health.* If you then inquire *why he deisres health,* he will readily reply, *Because sickness is painful.* If you push your inquiries further and desire a reason *why he hates pain,* it is impossible he can ever give any. This is an ultimate end, and is never referred to any other object.

Perhaps to your second question, *why he desires health,* he may also reply that *it is necessary for the exercise of his calling.* If you ask *why he is anxious on that head,* he will answer, *because he desires to get money.* If you demand, *Why? It is the instrument of pleasure,* says he. And beyond this, it is an absurdity to ask for a reason. It is impossible there can be a progress *in infinitum,* and that one thing can always be a reason why another is desired. Something must be desirable on its own account, and because of its immediate accord or agreement with human sentiment and affection.[8]

The impossibility of an infinite regress of reasons is not peculiar to ethics; it applies in all areas. Mathematical reasoning eventually ends with axioms that are not themselves justified, and reasoning in science ultimately depends on assumptions that are not proven. At some point reasoning must always come to an end, no matter what one is reasoning about.

The difference between ethics and other subjects is in the involvement of the emotions. In order for anything to count as an ultimate reason for or against a course of conduct, one must *care* about that thing in some way. In the absence of any emotional involvement, there are no reasons for action. The fact that the building is on fire is a reason for me to leave only if I care about not being burned; the fact that children are starving is a reason for me to do something only if I care

[8]*Hume's Ethical Writings,* p. 131.

about their plight. (On this point the emotivists were right, whatever defects their overall theory might have had.) It is the possibility that people might care about different things, and so accept different ultimate principles between which "reason" cannot adjudicate, that continues to undermine confidence in the subject itself.

There is, however, one other point that needs to be considered before we reach any conclusions. What people care about is itself sensitive to pressure from the deliberative process, and can change as a result of thought. A person might not care very much about something prior to thinking it through, but come to feel differently once he has thought it over. This fact has been considered extremely important by some of the major philosophers. Aristotle, Butler, and others emphasized that responsible moral judgment must be based on a full understanding of the facts; but, they added, after the facts are established, a separate cognitive process is required for the agent to fully understand the import of what he or she knows. It is necessary not merely to know the facts, but to rehearse them carefully in one's mind, in an impartial, nonevasive way. Then one will have the kind of knowledge on which moral judgment may be based.

Aristotle even suggested that there are two distinct species of knowledge: first, knowledge had by one who is able to recite facts, "like the drunkard reciting the verses of Empedocles", but without understanding their meaning; and second, knowledge had when one has thought carefully through what one knows. An example might make this clearer. We all know, in an abstract sort of way, that many children in the world are starving; yet for most of us this information makes little difference to our conduct. We will spend money on trivial things for ourselves rather than spending it on food for them. How are we able to explain this? The Aristotelian explanation is that we "know" the children are starving only in the sense in which the drunkard knows Empedocles' verses: we simply recite the fact.[9] Suppose, however, we thought carefully about what it must be *like* to be a starving orphan. Our attitudes, our conduct, and the moral judgments we were willing to make might be substantially altered.

A few years ago a wire-service photograph of two Vietnamese orphans appeared in American newspapers. They were sleeping on a Saigon street; the younger boy, who seemed to be about four, was inside a tattered cardboard box, while his slightly older brother was curled up around the box. The caption said that as they begged for food during the day the older boy would drag the box with them because he did not want his little brother to have to sleep on the sidewalk at night. After this photograph appeared, a large number of people contacted relief agencies offering to help. What difference did the picture make? I don't believe it was a matter of people being presented with new information—it was not as though people did not "know" that starving orphans have miserable lives. Rather, the photograph brought home to people in a vivid way things that they already "knew." It is easy to think of starving children in an abstract, statistical way; the picture forced people to think of them concretely, and it made a difference in their attitudes.

In ordinary moral discussion we recognize that thinking through what one knows is a separate matter from merely knowing. Those who favor voluntary euthanasia ask us to consider what it is like, from the point of view of the dying patient, to suffer horribly. Albert Camus, in his essay on capital punishment, "Reflections on the Guillotine," argued that people tolerate the death penalty only because they think

---

[9]Aristole, *Nichomachean Ethics,* 1147b.

of it in euphemistic terms ("Pierre paid his debt to society") rather than attending the sound of the head falling into the basket.[10] And as I have already mentioned, opponents of abortion show us pictures of fetuses to force us to pay attention to what it is that is killed. Often this method of argument is dismissed as involving nothing more than a demagogic appeal to emotion, which ought to have no place in rational discussion. Sometimes the charge is true. However, such an argument may also serve as an antidote for the self-deception that Bishop Butler saw as corrupting moral thought. When we do not *want* to reach a certain conclusion about what is to be done for whatever reason—perhaps we would rather spend money on ourselves than give it for famine relief—we may refuse to face up to what we know in a clear-minded way. Facts that would have the power to move us are put out of mind, or are thought of only bloodlessly and abstractly. Rehearsing the facts in a vivid and imaginative way is a needed corrective.

Now let us return to the question of ethical disagreement. When disagreement occurs, two explanations are possible. There could be some failure of rationality on the part of one or the other person, or they could simply be different in that they care about different things. In practice, when important matters are at issue, we always proceed on the first hypothesis. We present arguments on the assumption that those who disagree have missed something: they are ignorant of relevant facts, they have not thought through what they know, they are not consistent, and so on. We do not credit the idea that they are "different."

[10]Albert Camus, *Resistance, Rebellion, and Death* (New York: Alfred A. Knopf, 1961), pp. 175–234.

Is this procedure reasonable? Are there any real-life examples of ethical disagreement where the explanation is that the people who disagree, although rational enough, simply care about different things? If there are, they are notoriously hard to find. The familiar examples of the cultural anthropologists turn out, upon analysis, to have other explanations. The Eskimos, who allow their firstborn daughters to die of exposure and who abandon feeble old people to a similar fate, do not have less respect for life than other peoples who reject such practices. They live in different circumstances, under threat of starvation in a hostile environment, and the survival of the community requires policies which otherwise they would happily renounce. The Ik, an apparently crude and callous people indifferent even to the welfare of their own children, took on those characteristics only after a prolonged period of near starvation that virtually destroyed their tribal culture. There may be some disagreements which reflect cultural variables—I have already mentioned Herodotus's Greeks and Callatians, for example—but beyond that, and barring the kind of disaster that reduced the Iks, it is plausible to think that people are enough alike to make ethical agreement possible, if only full rationality were possible.

The fact that rationality has limits does not subvert the objectivity of ethics, but it does suggest a certain modesty in what can be claimed for it. Ethics provides answers about what we ought to do given that we are the kinds of creatures we are, caring about the things we will care about when we are as reasonable as we can be, living in the sort of circumstances in which we live. This is not as much as we might want, but it is a great deal. It is as much as we can hope for in a subject which must incorporate not only our beliefs but our ideals as well.

WHO PROVIDES THE ANSWERS?

In one of Charles Schulz's *Peanuts* cartoons, Lucy wonders aloud: "Are there more bad people in the world or are there more good people?" With an expansive gesture, Charlie Brown responds: "Who is to say? Who is to say who is bad or who is good?" "I will," says Lucy.

Lucy has the right idea. Of course there is no central authority who decrees what is good and what is bad; each person must make his or her own judgments. This should come as no surprise, for exactly the same is true of ordinary factual matters. Who is to say how many books are on the shelf? The answer is, obviously, anyone who cares to count. Similarly, where moral matters are concerned, anyone who cares to think things through can "say" what is good or bad.

This parallel between factual and moral issues can be pushed one step further. We are not tempted to ask for the help of an "authority" when the issue is as simple as the number of books on a shelf. We can easily figure this out for ourselves. However, other factual issues may be so difficult or complicated that lay persons cannot figure things out for themselves; technical competence is required. In these cases we do look for help from authorities. Similarly, we are all competent to judge relatively simple moral matters: we need no expert consultants to tell us that murder, rape, and pointless lying are wrong. But some moral matters are more complicated, and here we may wish the guidance of "experts," if there are any.

As one might expect, remembering our discussion of rational choice, there are two kinds of expertise required for dealing with complicated moral issues. The first is expertise concerning relevant facts. Suppose the issue is nuclear energy: we need to know about the costs of this source of energy; the likelihood of accidents at power plants; the probable consequences of such accidents; the disposal of radioactive wastes; and so on. We also need to know about the possibilities of alternate sources of energy. These are difficult matters even for those who devote their professional lives to them, and quite beyond the comprehension of lay persons who have not bothered to do a lot of studying. It would be easy to give other examples of the same kind: to mention a different area, competent judgment in many matters of public policy requires a distressingly broad knowledge of economics. Clearly, in these matters lay persons need the guidance of the experts; and when the experts disagree, the rest of us may not know what to think.

The other area of expertise concerns more abstract matters: the critical assessment of arguments, the formulation and testing of principles, the analysis of concepts, and so on. These are the traditional skills of philosophers and theologians, and that is why it has seemed natural to look to these thinkers as moral guides—not because they are better people or because they are blessed with some kind of occult insight. I say "philosophers and theologians" although I have a certain reservation about theology. The theologian is most helpful when he is least theological. Morality concerns everyone, religious and nonreligious alike. Arguments that appeal only to the faithful will have limited value. Theologians themselves realize this, and often present their arguments entirely in secular terms. It may be emphasized that certain values are espoused within a religious tradition, but at the same time it is assumed that those values can be discussed and defended independently of that tradition.

There are, then, "experts" on ethical matters—people who have informed themselves as to the relevant facts and who have studied the arguments and concepts involved. We have already begun to make use of such people in special contexts. For example, institutions conducting research with human subjects have special review boards to consider from an ethical point of view the permissibility of particular projects. It would be foolish to think that every decision made by such boards is wise; even leaving aside political considerations, infallibility is not to be expected. Nevertheless the very existence of such panels acknowledges that there are ethical matters that cannot be dealt with responsibily apart from special knowledge and study. Egalitarian sentiments notwithstanding, one person's opinion is not always as good as another's.

This conclusion may easily be misinterpreted. Sometimes it is wise and even necessary for the rest of us to leave certain ethical decisions to experts, especially those concerning matters with which we have little experience. This does not mean, however, that moral life is a game of follow-the-leader. Lucy was right. People who are not able to spend a lot of time studying ethical questions ought to pay attention to the results of those who have. But that is a matter of where we find guidance, not where we find bosses. A slavish follower is not a moral agent. In the end, moral agents must answer the question "Who is to say?" as Lucy did. If, in the hard cases, different agents come up with different answers, that is why we need politics as well as ethics.

Chapter 2 / THE CONCEPT OF MORAL STANDING

PETER SINGER

APPROACHING THE QUESTION

What are the limits of the sphere of ethics? Or, as Christopher Stone, the author of *Should Trees Have Standing?* put it: "What are the requirements for 'having standing' in the moral sphere?"[1] Stone's terminology comes, of course, from his legal background; in the courts, to "have standing" is to be able to take legal action, to sue. In current American law, infants may have standing and can sue through guardians, but neither trees nor nonhuman animals can have standing. I am, however, concerned with ethics rather than the law—although ethics may have implications for what the law should be.

The question of moral standing is clearly a basic question

[1]Christopher Stone, *Should Trees Have Standing? Toward Legal Rights for Natural Objects* (New York: Avon Books, 1975).

PETER SINGER ● Department of Philosophy, Monash University, Clayton, Victoria, Australia 3168.

in ethics. In law, whether a party to an action has standing is the first thing the court needs to know, but it will not take the court very far along the road to its decision—unless the court rules that the party does not have standing. So, in ethics, if we decide that a being is outside the limits of ethics, we need give it no further ethical consideration; but deciding that a being is within the ethical sphere does not, of course, take us very far toward the solution of ethical issues involving it.

One way of approaching this issue is to ask: Why should ethics have any limits at all? Is there not something suspicious about excluding any being at all from ethical consideration?

In a sense, what these questions imply is right. We are not justified in excluding from the start any being at all. Yet, in another sense, the inclusion of certain beings turns out to be meaningless and thus they may justifiably be excluded, if not from the very start, at least by the time introductions are over with and we get down to business.

Let me illustrate. The right approach to ethical problems is, I believe, that which can be traced back to the Golden Rule of Moses: "Do unto others as you would have them do unto you." Obviously this dictum is only one possible formulation of a principle that can also be found in the Christian commandment that we love our neighbor as ourself, in the Stoic idea of a universal natural law, in Kant's categorical imperative ("Act only on that maxim through which you can at the same time will that it should become a universal law"), and more recently in R. M. Hare's notion of the universalizability of moral judgments. Hare's account is the most philosophically refined of these, but it lacks vividness; and he himself has recently suggested that the essence of his view can be captured by a formulation used by C. I. Lewis: to decide whether an action is right, imagine yourself living, one after another, the lives of all those affected by the action. If, under those conditions, you still want the action done, you have satisfied the universalizability requirement.[2]

Suppose we accept that this idea of imagining ourselves living the lives of all those affected by our action is central to ethics. Our initial question about the limits of ethical concern then reappears as: Which lives—perhaps "existences" would be a more neutral term at this stage of the argument—do I have to imagine myself as living? And now it becomes clear what I meant by saying that we are not justified in excluding, from the start, anything at all; and yet the inclusion of certain beings turns out to be meaningless. For whereas I have no difficulty in imagining myself living the lives of other people—no profound philosophical difficulty, at any rate—when I imagine myself existing as a rock, I imagine nothing but a complete blank. No matter how much I attempt to take the point of view of a rock and imagine whether I would like a certain action to be done, the only answer I get is that nothing could make the least difference. Rocks are not conscious. They have no mental life, no feelings, no pleasures, no pains. For brevity, I shall use the term "sentient being" to refer to a being that has feelings, such as the ability to feel pain. Rocks are not sentient beings. Hence they cannot prefer one action to another. We cannot harm them and we cannot benefit them. However much time we spend during our ethical deliberations in imagining what it would be like from the rock's point of view, we will get nowhere. Rocks do not have a point of view. Therefore they cannot be included in the ethical sphere in a way that will make the slightest difference to our ethical decisions.

[2]R. M. Hare, "Ethical Theory and Utilitarianism," in *Contemporary British Philosophy*, 4th series, ed. H. D. Lewis (London: Allen & Unwin, 1976), p. 117; see also R. M. Hare, *Freedom and Reason* (Oxford: Oxford University Press, 1963).

In saying that rocks cannot meaningfully be included within the ethical sphere I am not, of course, saying that what we do to rocks is of no ethical concern. What we do to rocks may be of ethical concern because it may affect beings who are not themselves rocks. For instance, the Matterhorn is just a big lump of rock, and nothing we can do to the Matterhorn will make a difference to *it*. Turning the Matterhorn into gravel for roadmaking would nevertheless be wrong because there are many people who enjoy looking at or climbing upon the Matterhorn. It has a special beauty that cannot easily be found elsewhere, and no doubt it will, unless turned into gravel, be a source of inspiration and joy for generations to come. Therefore destroying the Matterhorn is wrong, but it is a wrong not to the Matterhorn itself but to those, present and future, who will benefit from the unspoiled continued existence of the Matterhorn. I shall express this point by saying that although destroying the Matterhorn would not be *intrinsically* wrong—wrong in itself—it would be *extrinsically* wrong, that is, wrong because of factors beyond the Matterhorn itself. We can also express this distinction by saying that the Matterhorn has no intrinsic values, but does have value as a means to the ends of others.

So far I have mentioned two extremes: rocks, which cannot meaningfully be treated as objects of ethical concern, and other people, who obviously can and should be. What of the categories in between these extremes? I shall work my way up from the rocks. It will be important to bear in mind that throughout what follows I am talking only of intrinsic value.

Rocks cannot meaningfully be included in the ethical sphere because to imagine oneself as a rock is to imagine a complete blank. Thus everything else with this limitation will also lack moral standing. Now which things we believe to have this limitation will obviously depend on our beliefs. A pantheist of some kind might think that the environment as a whole has some kind of conscious mind. Some people seem to believe that plants are conscious—though the evidence often put forward in support of this belief does not withstand investigation. Someone might even demur at my denial of an inner life to rocks. All things are possible, and in this credulous age most possible beliefs are actually held by somebody. But I cannot discuss every weird argument that might be proposed, and so I shall simply state that I adhere to the position, which I believe to be that of common sense as well as that of the majority of people, that the only things we have good reason to believe are conscious are living things, and among living things, only animals. I use the term "animals" broadly to include at one end human beings and at the other end insects. I am not saying that all animals are conscious, only that nothing that is not an animal is conscious.

Now we can make rapid progress. Neither rocks nor trees nor streams have intrinsic value. (They may, of course, have immense extrinsic value.) What of the environment as a whole? That question is a little more difficult, since the environment as a whole includes within it animals that are conscious. Nevertheless insofar as it is possible to distinguish the environment from those individual sentient beings that are part of it, the environment has no intrinsic value.

The case of the environment is akin to that of some other collectives. I will mention only two: species and corporate entities.

We hear a lot about the importance of saving endangered species. I do not dispute the importance of this aim. But the aim must, in my view, be defended on the grounds of the benefits of preventing extinction for sentient creatures. There are many such benefits, including the pleasures of a varied environment, the possible future benefits of a diverse gene pool, and of course—in the case of an animal species—the enjoyment of continued life by the individual animals. The species as a whole, however, has no conscious existence above and beyond that of the individual conscious beings that make it up. A species as such, therefore, cannot meaningfully be the object of ethical concern.

The same point applies to corporate entities. A corporate entity may have legal standing as if it were a person, but such standing is, of course, only a legal fiction. A corporate entity is not a person, and to harm it can only be to harm the individuals who work for it, own it, or are otherwise affected by it. To make this point is not to commit oneself to any simpleminded reduction of the interests of the corporation to the interests of a definite set of individuals. It might make sense to say that the cancellation of plans to build a nuclear reactor was bad for the corporation that had contracted to build it and yet good for all the employees and stockholders in the corporation, who would have been exposed to radiation leaks if the project had gone ahead. Still, the employees and stockholders have been harmed, in their roles as employees and stockholders, by the loss of bonuses and dividends, even though overall they may have benefited. Harm to the corporation must somehow be reducible to harm to its individuals.

ANIMAL LIFE

That is all I shall say about things that are not animals, in the broad sense of the term. Now what about animals? As I have said, not all animals are sentient. The first task, therefore, is to consider those that are not. Among these are some nonhuman animals and some humans.

We need not dwell long on the nonhuman animals that are not sentient. I assume that some microorganisms that are technically classed as animals rather than plants are not sentient. Since scientists do not use sentience as a criterion for making the distinction between plants and animals, there is no reason to suppose that all animals will be sentient. Exactly which animals are not sentient is a tricky question, but like the issue of plant sentience it is one that I do not wish to go into now since it is strictly irrelevant to the ethical issue I am discussing. My own view is that certainly all mammals and very likely all vertebrate animals are capable of feeling pain. I am less confident about invertebrates such as crustaceans, insects, mollusks, and so on. I suggested in *Animal Liberation* that somewhere between a shrimp and an oyster might be a good place to draw the line beyond which the attribution of consciousness cannot be justified; but I am open to further argument on that point.[3]

Putting aside these nonsentient—or very dubiously sentient—nonhuman animals, what can we say about the rest of the animal kingdom? Remember that we started out with the idea that central to ethical deliberation is the requirement that we imagine ourselves living the lives of all those affected by a proposed action. Then we found that trying to do so with rocks and other nonsentient things got us nowhere. No proposed action made the slightest difference to our imagined existence as a rock. But if we carry out the same thought experiment with a sentient animal, we see that some actions could make a great deal of difference to our existence as, say, a laboratory rat. For example, if the proposed act is the carrying out of an experiment in what is known as "learned helplessness" I will, after imagining myself as a rat, certainly not want the action performed. (These experiments involve repeated applications of severe and inescapable electric shock

[3]*Animal Liberation* (New York: New York Review of Books, 1975) Ch. 4.

until the animal is reduced to a state in which it ceases to struggle or resist the shock.)

I should say a little more about this idea of imagining myself as a rat. It seems to suggest something anthropomorphic, in which I imagine myself, with all my knowledge, awareness, and imagination, taking the physical shape of the rat and then being treated as if I were the rat. This is not, of course, what the phrase is intended to suggest. In imagining myself as a rat, I must try to imagine what it is really like to be a rat, with the rat's mental capacities. This is difficult, and we may never be sure that we have succeeded entirely; nevertheless, it will often be possible to say whether a particular experience is very bad, slightly bad, or not at all bad from the rat's point of view.

It is also important to understand that if, when imagining myself as a rat, I decide that I would not want a certain action performed, that does not settle the ethical question. I must place myself in the position of all those affected by the action, and it will sometimes be the case that the benefits to some will outweigh the losses to the rat and others. This issue is a separate one that cannot be pursued here, for it relates to the moral question of what one may do to a rat rather than the question of whether a rat has moral standing. A rat clearly does have moral standing, as do all those nonhuman animals capable of feeling pleasure or pain. As I argued at some length in *Animal Liberation*, the fact that a being is not a member of our species is no better a reason for excluding it from moral consideration than the fact that a being is not a member of our race.

Note that it is the possession of consciousness, not self-consciousness, that is crucial here. Kant said that "so far as animals are concerned, we have no direct duties. Animals are not self-conscious and are there merely as a means to an end.

That end is man."[4] Anyone defending Kant's view today would need to explain why the argument does not also show that we have no direct duties toward infants or human beings with such severe mental defects that they are not self-conscious. Kant himself overlooked this problem, probably because like most of us he was biased toward members of his own species, and it would never have occurred to him that his own criterion of self-consciousness would justify us in using some human beings as we now use nonhuman animals. In any case, the test of universalizability indicates that consciousness is sufficient to create moral standing. A being that is conscious can feel pain, and its attempts to escape from the painful situation can make it clear that it wants the pain to stop. That being so, there is no reason why we should insist that it be self-consciously aware of the pain before we take its want into account in our moral deliberations. No one thinks that a baby's pain is of no account because the baby is not self-conscious. We should not think any differently about the pain of an animal that is not self-conscious.

If consciousness is enough to give animals moral standing, it might be asked whether that means that animals have rights, as humans do, and whether there is not something puzzling about this idea. I find the concept of moral rights very tricky, and I prefer not to use it in moral arguments except where the context makes it a useful, shorthand way of putting the point that it is wrong to do certain things to certain beings. But I do not find the application of the concept to animals any more problematic than I find its application to infants or the gravely mentally defective. If these categories of human beings, whose mental faculties are no higher than those of

[4]Immanuel Kant, "Duties to Animals and Spirits," in *Lectures on Ethics*, trans. L. Infield (New York: Harper & Row, 1963), p. 239.

many nonhuman animals, have rights, then so must many nonhuman animals, for the fact that they are not members of our species cannot be a morally justifiable reason for denying rights to them, any more than the fact that some human beings are not members of our race can be a morally justifiable reason for denying them rights.

HUMAN RIGHTS

Finally, in our climb up the evolutionary ladder, what of human beings? In referring just now to the sentience of nonhuman animals, I had in mind normal, mature members of the species. There is no problem about the moral standing of normal, mature human beings. They qualify, as nonhuman animals do, because they are sentient. So, for the same reason, do immature or less than quite normal humans. Infants and young children are capable of feeling pleasure and pain. So are the insane and—barring the extreme cases I shall come to in a moment—the retarded. Therefore all these human beings are proper objects of ethical concern. There are, however, three categories of human beings who are not sentient. First, there are those who are so severely brain-damaged that they were never conscious, or if they were once conscious, have now irrevocably lost all consciousness. Second, there are the most immature human beings of all—fetuses up to the point at which the nervous system is sufficiently developed to make the existence of sentience a reasonable hypothesis. And third, there are future generations of human beings, not merely unborn but also unconceived. I will conclude by considering these three categories.

If a human being is so severely brain-damaged that consciousness is utterly and irrevocably lost, nothing we can do can make a difference to the welfare of that human being. In these very extreme cases, the term "human vegetable" does, for all its contemptuous overtones, make a real point. The life of such a being has no more intrinsic worth than that of a cabbage.

To many that assessment will seem too harsh. Of course there are differences between cabbages and human beings, even permanently unconscious human beings; but the differences relate to the extrinsic rather than the intrinsic value of these forms of life. Human beings have human parents, or other friends or relations, who may have views about what should be done with their child, relative, or friend. That is, of course, relevant to any moral decision we might make about permanently unconscious human beings, but it is quite distinct from saying that permanently unconscious human beings have moral standing in their own right.

There is also another complication that arises when the permanently unconscious human being was not always in that state, but was once a normal person who expressed a view about how he or she would like to be treated in the event of becoming permanently unconscious. In that case we may feel we should respect the past desires of the person whose body now lies before us. If so, however, it is the desires of the person who used to exist we are respecting. That person no longer exists. He or she may not medically be dead, but the person, as distinct from the body, is as irrevocably gone as if he or she were dead. Respecting the desires of that person is on a par with respecting the desires of the dead—which is something we often do, or feel we should do. It can most straightforwardly be defended as a way of providing reassurance for those now alive that nothing they object to will happen to their bodies should they ever irrevocably lose consciousness. (Temporary unconsciousness is of course different: if we regard a desire as a disposition to choose in a certain way when faced with a choice, it is possible to say that the temporarily unconscious person still actually has desires about the future, which should be respected.)

Let us next consider the fetus. Evidence presented to the British government advisory group on fetal research, chaired by Sir John Peel, indicated that the brain of the fetus is not sufficiently developed for consciousness until the fetus reaches a weight of about 300 grams—a weight normally reached around the eighteenth week of pregnancy.[5] Up to this point the mental life of a fetus appears to be as blank as that of a stone or a tree; from that point on, the fetus may be sentient and so should be included within the sphere of moral consideration. To err on the right side, it might be wise in practice to include the fetus at, say, fifteen weeks. And it should not be necessary to point out—although to avoid misunderstanding I shall—that to say that the fetus after fifteen weeks has moral standing is not to say that its interest in not suffering will not often be overridden by other factors, among which will be the interests of the pregnant woman.

Some will say that in making actual sentience crucial to the moral standing of the fetus, I have overlooked the most important fact about the fetus: its potential to become a full-fledged human being. What can the universalizability test I have proposed make of the potential of the fetus?

There are two possibilities. One is to say that potential is irrelevant. When I imaginatively place myself in the position of the fetus I can know nothing about its potential. Its potential is not a fact that makes any difference to what it is like

[5]The report of the Peel Committee is reprinted as Item 19 of *Research on the Fetus: Appendix*, the report of the National Commission for the Protection of Human Subjects of Biomedical and Behavioral Research (Washington, D.C.: Department of Health, Education and Welfare, OS 76-128, 1976).

to be a fetus. The aborted fetus does not know that it is missing out on a full life.

The second possibility is to look at the matter retrospectively, from the standpoint of an adult. I can say to myself: "I am glad to be alive. So I am glad that my mother did not have an abortion after I was conceived. Therefore, I must place myself in the position, not just of the fetus in the womb, but also of the person the fetus will grow into if it is not aborted. If this person is able to lead a good life, he or she will be glad not to have been aborted." In this way the potential of the fetus can be taken into account.

R. M. Hare, from whose work I have taken the device of universalizability that I have used throughout this essay, adopts this second possibility in his own application of universalizability to the abortion issue.[6] But opponents of abortion should pause before rejoicing; for Hare goes on to point out that the same argument from the fact that we are glad to be alive applies to our conception. I have as much reason to be thankful that my parents did not use a contraceptive on the night I was conceived as I have to be thankful that my mother did not have an abortion; indeed I have the same reason to be thankful that my parents decided to have sexual intercourse at that particular time. The fact that the sperm and egg have actually come together does not make any real difference if we are looking at the matter from the point of view of later existence. Not having intercourse, or using a contraceptive, is just as much a way of ensuring that there is no one around who will be glad to be alive as abortion is.

Thus so far as the argument from potential is concerned, the nonsentient fetus is on a par with unconceived potential human beings. What, then, is the moral standing of uncon-

[6]R. M. Hare, "Abortion and the Golden Rule," *Philosophy and Public Affairs* 4 (1975): 201–222.

ceived potential human beings? This category of beings is the last and also the most difficult that I shall discuss.

First we must distinguish between future human beings whose existence is not in doubt, and beings that are potential in the sense of being merely possible future beings. For instance, it seems that whatever happens to birthrates in the next few years, there will, barring catastrophe, be at least 100 million people living in the United States in the year 2100. The existence of this minimum number of people is scarcely in doubt. Nor is their moral standing. Since they will exist and will, when they exist, be sentient, they have moral standing. The fact that their existence is future rather than present is irrelevant. Thus in deciding, for example, whether to go ahead with nuclear power despite the problems of safe storage of radioactive waste, we must take their interests into account.

On the other hand there are also future beings whose existence is uncertain. A couple may be thinking about having children. Until they decide, the existence of any such children is merely possible. On a national level, a government could adopt policies designed to hold the nation's population at its present figure, or to increase it by 10 million over the next thirty years. These extra 10 million people are, at this stage, merely possible. It is here that the question of moral standing suddenly becomes murky indeed.

Is it good, other things being equal, to bring into existence beings who will lead happy lives? That is one question raised by the issue of the moral standing of beings who are potential in the sense of being merely possible. But it is not the only one. If one is impelled to answer with a firm no, one must first reflect on the opposite case. Is it bad, other things being equal, to bring into existence beings who will lead miserable lives? Most of us think it is—imagine, for example, a couple who carry a genetic defect so severe that any children they might have will suffer from a painful disease and die before the age of two. If we think the misery their child will go through is a reason against their deciding to have a child, we are in some way giving moral standing to a merely possible being, and if we are prepared to give such standing to a possible child that will, if it becomes actual, lead a miserable life, why should we not also give it to a possible child that will, if it becomes actual, lead a happy life.?

The implication is that merely possible beings can have moral standing. In practice the consequences of this decision will be affected by all sorts of other questions, especially the effects of having children on prospective parents as well as on the world population problem. I am not suggesting that we are all under an obligation to produce as many happy children as we can. Such a suggestion, especially when times are getting more difficult and we have enough trouble ensuring an adequate standard of living for the numbers we now have on our planet, would be absurd. Nevertheless, it does seem that, other things being equal, it is good to have children if they can reasonably be expected to be happy. I recognize that this conclusion sounds odd. It struck me as odd when I first considered the argument for it, and it still strikes me as odd. But I cannot see a plausible way around it.

Chapter 3 / WHY SHOULD WE BE MORAL?

JONATHAN LIEBERSON

Although it is a dramatic question, Why should we be moral? is rarely posed sincerely by anyone except philosophers and impertinent children. It is, nonetheless, an absorbing question that continues to provoke skeptical intellects, lending itself to a variety of interesting interpretations and connecting with important issues about moral knowledge, moral motivation, and the just society. Moreover, in times of social and political disorder or unrest, it may express the urgent need of a novel morality to justify itself. We live today in a period marked by conspicuous attention to self—to self-interest, self-fulfillment, self-improvement. "Leave me alone!" seems to be the cry not only of businessmen, but also of parents and children, lovers and careerists. What is the significance of this phenomenon, if it is one? More important, are present conditions hostile to the claims of morality? Are we asking ourselves why we should be moral any more often (or any more seriously) than we have in the past?

JONATHAN LIEBERSON ● Center for Policy Studies, The Population Council, 1 Dag Hammarskjold Plaza, New York, New York 10017.

WHY MIGHT "WHY BE MORAL?" BE ASKED TODAY?

Do present conditions conduce to our posing sincerely the question as to why we should be moral? It is not clear that they do; it is not evident that the question is sincerely asked more often today than it has been in earlier times. Nonetheless it might be argued that there are intellectual currents in our popular literature, especially in our popular concerns with self-realization and individualistic politics, that do furnish a ground for worry or skepticism about our supposed obligations to others. We may look in passing at some illustrations.

In his book *Looking Out for #1*, Robert Ringer recommends that we make a concerted effort "to spend as much time as possible doing those things which bring [us] the greatest pleasure and less time on those which cause pain."[1] He begins by noting that "the degree of your happiness at any given moment will depend upon the rationality of your objectives and the success you have in obtaining them." But his answer to the question whether "looking out for #1" is "right" is that morality is a "personal" matter and that we must categorically reject "absolute morality" and those who try to decide what is right or wrong "for others." Accordingly, whether looking out for #1" is "right" or not is a matter to be decided by asking whether it is "right" *for me* or not. This is an indelicate circle. But to continue, Ringer believes that both psychological and ethical egoism are correct; we must be inexorably "realistic," he says, and that involves recognizing that "we always do what we want most."[2] This principle is always true. It is true even of Mahatma Gandhi:

> Can I honestly say that I believe Gandhi was acting selfishly when he "sacrificed" himself for the freedom of the

[1]Robert Ringer, *Looking Out for #1* (New York: Fawcett Crest, 1977), p. 10.
[2]Ibid., p. 47.

Indian people? No, I can't say that I believe it. It would
be more proper to say that I know it for a fact. . . .
Whatever Gandhi did, out of rational or irrational choice,
he did because he chose to do it. . . . Martyrs are selfish
people—the same as you and me—but with insatiable
egos.[3]

As this passage indicates, Ringer accompanies his notion of
psychological egoism with the view that we can be rational
or irrational in our egoism—the "irrational" kind is based on
a position that is not truly in one's own "self-interest" (a
conception not explained further by Ringer). Morality is deciding what principles are right for me—and since the choice
of a morality is a choice that falls under the domain of Ringer's
egoism, it too is presumably egoistically motivated. Ringer's
book asks us to accept these views and gives a procedure for
further realizing ourselves with their aid. We must recognize,
he writes, that "absolutely everything in life has a price: love,
friendship, material gain, a relaxed mind, the freedom to
come and go as you please—anything which adds pleasure
to your existence."[4] Life is a market, and if we are to succeed
in it, we must, according to Ringer, avoid neurotics, "buy"
appropriate friends and lovers, get away with as much as
possible in the case of Uncle Sam, not allow others to hurt
us (because it would only mean that we "allowed" them to),
and not "help" others if by this term is meant doing something for nothing in return.[5]

Ringer's book is refreshing in that it pursues to the bitter
end principles that most people would be ashamed to profess
openly at all. But his advice and his theory are little more

[3]Ibid., p. 50. Compare the extended analysis of the philosophy of Ayn Rand
in William O'Neill, *With Charity towards None* (Totowa, N.J.: Littlefield,
Adams, 1977).
[4]Ibid., p. 26.
[5]Ibid., p. 266; on buying friends, p. 70.

than a colorful and occasionally contradictory expression of views that rest on false assumptions about the self and fail to recognize the claims of others to our sympathy and co-operation.

It has become common to dismiss views like Ringer's as instances of "me-ism" and extravagantly narcissistic indulgence. But this view overlooks the urgency of our popular concern for self-expression and authentic individuality, properly the preoccupation of a culture that has lately failed to realize these desiderata of a satisfactory life. If it is unclear why the generous moral sentiments and ideals held by the young a decade ago should have lapsed into silence or else have been canalized in the present direction, it is perhaps because the new self-improvement movements (egoistic though some of them might be) are the sole decently articulated contenders for retaining the impulses that were organized by those earlier ideals. If this suggestion is correct, what is needed is new and better popular theory as well as newer and more adequate forms of moral individuals—and not, for example, a view that looks on life as a market, friendship as an exchange of services, and love as the mutual lease of sexual organs.

SOME INTERPRETATIONS OF THE QUESTION

The question, Why should we be moral? is radically ambiguous and as such has occasioned much discussion among moral philosophers, however infrequently it has been asked in other circles. Initially the question might appear to be either silly or senseless. It is certainly silly if by asking it we mean to inquire why we should do that which we ought to do; that would be akin to asking why a red sparrow is red or A identical with A. The query seems to be senseless because it demands moral grounds for being moral. How are we to discover grounds *within* morality for justifying all of morality? This interpretation of the question would seem to demand a justification of an entire practice or activity which (impossibly) presupposes that which is to be justified. Moreover, even assuming such a justification were possible, reason and experience would no doubt support it less than the moral convictions it would purportedly legitimate.[6]

These interpretations are now, however, the only ones that have been or can be offered. For example, the question has also been construed as inquiring why we should do that which is *said* or *claimed* to be moral; it has been posed as a skeptical question about our claim to possession of moral *knowledge*. How does anyone *know* what is good or bad, right or wrong, independently of how he learns it or is indoctrinated into it? Why should we blindly follow the opinions of those who claim to have such knowledge, whether they be cautious sages or dominant rulers or energetic prophets? If we do not know what moral knowledge is, why should we conform to that which is merely asserted to be moral knowledge? This form of the question invites one to examine the merits of the various views (in their varying formulations) that have been urged by philosophers and others concerning the sources or criteria of moral knowledge. Do we know what is moral because moral facts exist that can be understood by means of the same procedures and methods we use in understanding physical or sociological or psychological facts; or

---

[6]For criticism of the "silly" interpretation, see Marcus G. Singer, *Generalization in Ethics* (New York: Alfred A. Knopf, 1961); of the "senseless" interpretation, see Stephen E. Toulmin, *An Examination of the Place of Reason in Ethics* (Cambridge: Cambridge University Press, 1958), Section 11.9.

do we know what is moral because moral principles are no more than commands or laws laid down by an identifiable authority? Are moral rules simply behavioral traits or response patterns that characterize members of the social group to which we belong; or do we know what is moral because there are moral "facts" that, although not discoverable by experimental or scientific means, are yet discoverable through the use of "conscience" or a "moral sense" or "moral intuition," by pure (or impure) reason?[7] One celebrated philosopher had a short way with the question of a criterion of moral knowledge:[8] if a criterion of this kind were required to certify our claims to moral knowledge, we would perforce have to know *it* and that second piece of knowledge would itself have to be known, ad infinitum. Accordingly, if we are to possess any moral knowledge, which he took to be evident that we do, then we just know it, immediately and without the aid of "criteria." Thus, the question under consideration "vanishes."

The true answer probably lies in a mix of the foregoing views: moral principles are in some sense empirical, but they are not discoverable by laboratory techniques or survey methods; they are like commands in that they have the force of law, but they are not right because someone has issued them as commands; they are "social" traits, and have weight because members of society are led by them to approve or disapprove certain conduct, but they do not consist of these behavioral patterns; they are known in part through "reason," but there is no such thing as a moral "sense" or the Pure Reason of Kant which alone can inspect the realm of the

---

[7]For an overview of these different views of moral epistemology, see Richard Brandt, *Ethical Theory* (Englewood Cliffs, N.J.: Prentice-Hall, 1959) or John Hospers, *Human Conduct* (New York: Harcourt, Brace & World, 1961).

[8]Harold A. Prichard, *Moral Obligation* (Oxford: Clarendon Press, 1949), p. 1.

moral. As for "criteria" of moral knowledge, no doubt we do indeed possess such criteria if we mean "reasons that permit us to justify moral claims as true"; but it is unclear, as we shall see, that we *need* "criteria" in any stronger sense—say, one that purports to offer "certification" or "proof" of moral judgment.

PSYCHOLOGICAL EGOISM AND THE QUESTION OF MOTIVATION

Most discussion of our question has not, however, concerned itself with the epistemological question of how we know what is moral, but has rather focused on psychological and logical issues. The psychological question concerns the limits or constraints placed on moral conduct by human nature. How is it possible that man can be moral? What is it in his constitution that might serve to explain moral motivation? What are the relations among human powers, abilities, capacities, and dispositions and moral duties, between what man is (or can be) and what he ought to be and do? These queries have enjoyed a long and distinguished history; if the historical debate has been inconclusive, the vitality of the questions has been enhanced by the important fact that every moral vision adopted or projected by philosophers has been framed against a picture of human nature.

With few exceptions, the Greek thinkers regarded the close study of human nature as critical to the appraisal of moral injunctions and codes. The very earliest among them, it has been convincingly argued,[9] regarded the good as con-

---

[9]In Alaistair MacIntyre, *A Short History of Ethics* (New York: Collier Books, 1966), which also provides a good, short historical account of ethical theories.

sisting of the execution or discharge of assigned social functions; the conception of the "ought" as we now conceive it was apparently of later origin (or at any rate was only discussed and stressed in later times). The accumulation of information and communication between tribes and communities in antiquity led to awareness of the existence of radically diverse moral and social codes and customs, encouraging the formulation and articulation of the "ought," of standards and rules, of criteria for judging the merits and demerits of different customs. The debate over man—what he is like in himself, independent of society and distorting social forces—and over what social orders are conducive to his well-being has hardly diminished in intensity since that time, flourishing particularly in moments of social and political stress; the natural and "cosmological" backdrop to morality was central to the thought of Plato and Aristotle; the same questions were investigated by Machiavelli and Hobbes, and with famously different conclusions by Rousseau, by Vico and Hume, by Butler and Mandeville, by Burke and Hegel, and straight down into our own times by Dewey and Niebuhr.

One position or point of view about human nature has, perhaps more than any other factor, fueled the question as to why we should be moral: if human beings are "essentially" or "ultimately" selfish, egoistic, and amoral, then morality and politics must be seen for what they are, a means of controlling a dangerous and volatile animal, a method for channeling brutal and ferocious impulses into safer pathways. The "defense" of morality against egoism has been an obligatory chapter in the ethicist's textbook, akin to the epistemologist's defense of human knowledge against various skepticisms.

A closer look at the debate over "egoism" reveals that there are a wide variety of theories called "egoistic", but all of them would probably agree that, as a matter of psychological fact, all of our "ultimate" desires are desires to maintain, prolong, or maximize what is pleasurable to us or to avoid that which is not. The point is not that we have no other motives than to do or pursue the pleasurable or that we never do that which is not pleasurable to us, but that at bottom, beneath appearances, our ultimate motives are egoistic[10]—these motives come first. There are, of course, broader and narrower versions of pyschological egoism, some of them highly sophisticated and others crude—"everyone always acts in his own self-interest," "no one does anything unless he gets something out of it," "everyone always does in the end what he wants to do." Some popular views thought to be egoistic are in fact not egoistic without further qualification. Consider the idea that "everyone has his price" or "everyone is *just* his price," an idea as old as Hobbes.[11] This thesis is not in itself egoistic; it means that the motive of money can defeat other motives to action. But this claim, if it is true, is not inconsistent with the possibility that someone's "price" may be so high that no one could pay it, or that someone will accept a monetary price in order to do something nonegoistic with it.

It is customary to try to defeat psychological egoism by parading stories of altruists and saints. There is nothing to prevent the egoist, however, from responding that Mother Teresa or Albert Schweitzer or others who have tended to the irremediably poor and diseased are no less "egoistic" than anyone else; it is just that what is pleasurable to them—their "reward system"—is uncustomary. For example, they might

[10]See Hospers, Ch. 9–11. A good collection of articles is Ronald D. Milo, ed., *Egoism and Altruism* (Belmont, Calif.: Wadsworth, 1974).
[11]Cf. Thomas Hobbes, *Leviathan*, Pt. I, Ch. 10: "The Value or Worth of a man is, as of all other things, his Price, namely as much as would be given for the use of his Power."

derive pleasure from self-sacrifice, even self-abnegation; they
might believe in rewards that will accrue to their souls in an
afterlife; they might even derive pleasure from being described as people who derive pleasure from altruistic actions.
The man who rescues a child from a fire or an animal from
drowning, the man who loses his life by throwing himself
onto an exploding mine and thus saves others, the man who
warns others from stepping in front of a moving vehicle—all
may be equally described (or described away) by the defender
of egoism as persons who are motivated by promise of reward. Some theorists of egoism claim that in some cases it is
difficult if not practically impossible to identify what sort of
conscious egoistic motive was operative; they assert, however, that if a conscious motive of this kind is not present,
then an *un*conscious egoistic motive undoubtedly is.[12]

There are indeed egoistic theories that need not posit
either conscious or unconscious motives as necessary for explaining human action. Some sociobiologists, for example,
have recently claimed that actions that appear to be nonegoistic can be explained by evolutionary theory insofar as
such actions can be shown to involve rewards or beneficial
reciprocities for the kin or offspring of the actors, thus aiding
transmission of their genes into future generations.[13]

Clearly no single response is adequate to rebut these
theories. We might begin by distinguishing between those
that are genuinely relevant to our ordinary appraisals of conduct and those that are not. What is overlooked by the sociobiologists is the difference between the consequences of
competitive actions and the motive of competitiveness: the

[12]See Hospers.
[13]For example, Edward O. Wilson, *Sociobiology* (Cambridge: Harvard University Press, 1975), p. 120. Cf. also his remarks on the "reduction" or
"explanation" of ethics and epistemology itself (p. 3).

self-interestedness of "selfishness of the gene"—the "morality of the gene"—concerns the effects of certain behaviors (e.g., altruistic ones) on the composition of future generations of human beings; such considerations are of dubious relevance to our assessment of the motives and intentions behind these actions. The "egoism" of the gene is compatible with a whole range of human intentions, namely, the intentions of *persons*.[14]

But what of those other theories of egoism that purport to address the actual character of our motivation? What can be said against them? One charge against psychological egoism in the general way we have stated it is that it is either false or trivial. How so? It is false if there are clear examples of actions generated by dominantly nonegoistic motives that only those corrupted by theory could describe as crypto-egoistic. There are self-regarding and other-regarding motives. To be sure, some of the latter are really instances, upon inspection, of the former; but are all, or even most? Is passionate antipathy, for example, at bottom self-regarding? Is supererogatory action self-sacrifice? In both cases, probably not. But the egoist does not have to deny that there are genuine cases of other-regarding motives, only that they are dominated by other motives in contexts of choice or preference, and in *most* action. But faced with an instance of a man who devotes his life to unpublicized work for the poor or who secretly gives a fortune to a cause—cases that we have every reason to believe are motivated predominantly by nonegoistic motives—why should we hesitate to label them as they appear to be unless we are concerned to save psychological egoism? The springs of nearly every action are mixed, with certain

[14]Cf. Mary Midgley, *Beast and Man: The Roots of Human Nature* (Ithaca, N.Y.: Cornell University Press, 1978), p. 127, and Ch. 6 generally.

components that are self-regarding and others that are not, with some components that are no doubt egoistic and others that are clearly nonegoistic. As the philosopher C. D. Broad noted, the actions done in behalf of the welfare of a child by its mother are certainly in part other-regarding: "the mother is directly attracted by the thought of her child as surviving, as having good dispositions and pleasant experiences, and as being the object of love and respect to other persons." On the other hand, her desire might also be self-regarding and egoistic in part; she might desire the envy of other mothers concerning the health and happiness of her child, and she has "the desire not to be burdened with an ailing, unhappy, and unpopular child."[15]

But, granting that actions have complex motives, can we in all sincerity deny there are *many* cases of actions whose *dominant* motive is nonegoistic? When we routinely stop to pick up or toss aside a piece of jagged glass found on the beach so that others will not be harmed by it, or warn someone that there is a wasp on his hamburger,[16] is there any reason to believe we are not performing actions of this kind? We just *do* such actions all the time (and forget them when engaged in moral theorizing); they exhibit our "sympathies," the other-regarding, compassionate, benevolent impulses of human beings that have been emphasized in moral theory by writers and thinkers as diverse as Hume and Schopenhauer. To characterize them as self-regarding or deny their existence on behalf of a philosophical theory is as perverse as adopting those specious versions of altruism that would recommend

---

[15]Cf. Charlie Dunbar Broad in Milo, *Egoism and Altruism*, pp. 92–93.

[16]I take this illustration from Thomas Nagel, *The Possibility of Altruism* (Oxford: Clarendon Press, 1970). Nagel believes that ethics is a "part" of psychology and yields (or can yield, if successful) discoveries about human motivation; he believes that ethics might show us that we have reasons for directly promoting the interests of others. See pp. 5, 81.

that for reasons of equity we toss our grandmother off a life-boat in order to make room for a perfect stranger drifting nearby.

A theorist of egoism would no doubt reply that unapparent, "deep," and unconscious egoistic motives are postulated by egoism as underlying the sort of actions we have just described and are operative whether we know it or not. But such a claim trivializes the theory. It renders it immune to the kind of criticism that even philosophical theories must endure. Furthermore, it is empty; it in no way impugns or casts doubt on the kind of distinctions we draw in ordinary behavior. One is reminded of the idealist claim that everything that exists is ultimately a complex of ideas. But whether this claim is true or not is of dubious relevance for any identifiable context of discussion; we must still distinguish between the money we spend and the idea of that money, between the food we eat and the idea of that food, and so on. The theory "drops out." It hovers around us, but fails to make contact with its material.

THE MYTH OF THE FIXED SELF

Perhaps something stronger might be said against psychological egoism, namely that its most popular formulations depend upon an incorrect theory of the self. Consider the proposition that all, or most, or the most crucial actions undertaken by human beings are at bottom 'selfish." In one sense, such a proposition is true, but only trivially so; *every* act we perform is one that we perform *as* a self, *as* an agency—the self—which is composed of habits and organized impulses that demand satisfaction or successful outlet. But although we do indeed always act *as* selves, it is simply false to say that we always act *selfishly*, that is, *on behalf of a self*.

Some acts are genuinely selfish; we do sometimes just

push our way around until we get what we want; we do sometimes override other impulses and motives in order to pursue our "self-interest" (real or perceived). But many other acts are not selfish—and not because they are altruistic or self-sacrificing or benevolent (which some acts surely are), but because they are not obviously selfish *or* unselfish. They just *are*. When we are absorbed in writing a poem or reading an interesting book or eating a meal we are not being selfish or unselfish; we are absorbed, we are engrossed, we "lose ourselves," as the expression goes. We like the poem, we like the food, but it is the poem or the food, not our apprehension or sensation of them, that is our object, our *direct* object, as it were.

It is also important to note that sometimes we are not acting on behalf of any self at all, but are engaged in changing our "self" or arriving at a *new* self. We are frequently in conflict; we do not know *which* values to identify with, which self to be; we are in the *making*. In such cases, there is simply no self to be selfish or unselfish for. We do not always seek benefits *for* a fixed thing, we are not constantly looking for a prize that is to be rewarded to a fixed self; sometimes we are involved simply in altering (and possibly improving) our old self. Consider a student wondering what field of study he should enter; his great love has been sports, but he is "changing his interests" and thinking of entering psychology. Is he acting on behalf of a *particular* self? Is he "maximizing what is utile to him?" Surely not; he is engaged in the process of *altering* his appreciation of the world; he is changing his "utilities," his values, his notion of what a "gain" is—as can be seen if we ask whether it would be "useful" for him to learn about behaviorism. *After* his course of studies he might say that learning about behaviorism was highly "utile," but it was not utile to him *qua* athlete. At best, it was useful for the athlete-who-was-thinking-of-becoming-a-psychologist.

Cases like these, which we encounter quite frequently but often ignore or even suppress, can hardly be reconstructed as "egoistic" or as instances of "looking out for number 1." Indeed, if they are instances of any generalized project, they are instances of "looking out for number 2"—the next, second, self; the improved self that we have a desire to be, the self that we try to bring into being with our second-level desire not merely to have desires, but to have desires of a special, hitherto unfamiliar kind.

The egoistic theory assimilates too many of our actions to actions on behalf of a fixed self. Any significant action, the theory assumes, *must* be an action that not only is an act of a self but for a self, an action whose result is to be entered into the credit or debit side of the balance sheet of a boxed-off, fixed, inner "business." But this view, as we have seen, not only levels down all satisfactions to the satisfaction of impulse or current habit—and ignores the discriminations we in fact make—but overlooks that we are frequently selves in the making. Altruism might be hypocritical and misleading, but what could be as false as this view of the self? The point was made by Nietzsche and by Dewey some generations ago: there is no fixed self. Egoism and altruism are functional distinctions drawn within behavior and not underlying, mythical motive-causes. Both are learned and developed dispositions to action that we acquire as we grow up among others and learn or achieve the insight that our actions can affect others in beneficial or damaging ways, and thus must be framed accordingly.[17]

---

[17]For a discussion of Friedrich Nietzsche's views on the self, see Walter Kaufmann, *Neitzsche* (Princeton: Princeton University Press, 1950). For John Dewey, see John Dewey and James H. Tufts, *Ethics* (New York: Holt, 1936), Pt. II.

REFUTING ETHICAL EGOISM AND MOVING
BEYOND SELF-INTEREST

Our views of the self might be elaborated, but let us leave them for now and note that despite criticism the hold of psychological egoism—sometimes expressed in the form that men generally attempt to maximize their perceived "self-interest"—has been strong enough to motivate many celebrated ethical theorists, such as Aristotle and Spinoza and Bishop Butler, to try to "prove" that morality is in effect either justifiable by "enlightened self-interest" or "reducible" to it. Indeed, why should we be moral? has indeed been frequently seen as asking no more than, Why move beyond self-interest?; that is, Why should we adopt the so-called impartial, universal, "moral point of view"? Why is *ethical* egoism—the view that we *ought* to maximize our real or perceived self-interest—false? Why should we not accept ethical egoism and not move beyond self-interest, the maximization of our *own* pleasures and goods and the subordination of the interests of others?

A celebrated requirement on ethical thought has held that if human beings cannot—that is, causally and constitutionally—do something, then it is false to claim that they *ought* to do it: "ought implies can"; no moral rule should dictate that a man perform actions in two places at the same time, or help an old man become young. Few disagree with the principle, but the debate over human nature keeps the interpretation of the key word "can" open. If psychological egoism is true, of course, ethical egoism is redundant; since we can *only* act in our own self-interest, to say that we ought to is unnecessary.

Ethical egoism has always been a target for moral philosophers, a useful device for training graduate students and young philosophers; very few philosophers actually accept it, but it is somehow important to "refute" it or get it out of the way. Suppose that someone claims that happiness or pleasure is the only worthy, good thing in the entire universe. One variety of ethical egoism holds that this person should pursue his own interests and ignore those of others unless dealing with others and their interests was somehow instrumental to his own interests; such a person has no principled advice to give to others except to say that they should help him in "maximizing the good," that is, *his* good. But this version of egoism is too implausible to consider further. Instead we must consider the version that impersonally demands that *each* person should (morally) maximize his own interests, real or perceived, so that this person, *A*, should follow his own interests, that person, *B*, follow her own interests, and so on.

What can be said against this second form of ethical egoism? It might be said that it wholly ignores our moral duty, the sense of right and wrong we all have; but that would be a mistake, as it redefines it in terms of "self-interest." It might be said that self-interest is uncertain and that our self-interest as well as our effort to determine what our self-interest is can only be realized in cooperation with others in a way that infringes upon the dictates of ethical egoism. But that too, would be an error; ethical egoism is not incompatible with cooperation, either to determine what our self-interest is or to maximize our self-interest. No ethical egoist would deny that following my interests might involve adjusting to yours in a "cooperative" way. It might be said that ethical egoism is self-contradictory[18] as it tells businessman *A* to pur-

---

[18]Cf. Kurt Baier, *The Moral Point of View* (Ithaca, N.Y.: Cornell University Press, 1958), for this charge; also David Gauthier, *Practical Reasoning* (Oxford: Clarendon Press, 1963).

sue his self-interests by ruining businessman B, but it also tells B to ruin A, which seems, taken together, to imply that A (or B) is both ruined and not ruined. But once more the objection can be easily overcome: the two egoistic counsels are compatible, for they are directed at different persons and under different descriptions; they are no more inconsistent than to tell two card players to try to win. Another criticism is that the ethical egoist would seem of necessity to be deceitful. If he tells other people he is an ethical egoist, then he will go against his own self-interests, for they will frame their plans to involve him accordingly. But once more, that is not necessarily correct; he might derive more pleasure from honesty than he would from deceit, and his relations with others might be more efficient if they know him for what he is.

It seems, in fact, that ethical egoism is no more self-contradictory than psychological egoism. Nor does it seem to have been decisively refuted in any strict fashion that would be acceptable to moral philosophers. It might conduce to deceit, brutality, distrust, obtuseness to the interests of others, or to lack spontaneous and genuine cooperation, but it has not been shown inconsistent or false.

Only the pressure of our common moral sense can upset ethical egoism. We may, for example, examine the consequences for our lives of existence in a society of ethical egoists. We may reflect as to whether lives in such a society would conform to our notion of decency or humanity, whether its members could pursue the kind of aspirations we would prize. Ethical egoism does not entail psychological egoism, so that our earlier criticisms of the latter are not decisive against it; but if our view of the open self is correct, ethical egoism too would be challenged. For if we are open selves, in search of (and in need of) improvement and redirection, life with others construed as market relations or barter and exchange is not illuminating. Rather we seek others for mutuality of learning and growth, for acquaintance and internalization of a wider ambit, a broader perspective; these others are not instruments for our self-advantage, but interesting to us *because* they are other and we value them as different from us, *as* other than us—a point stressed by Kant in his *Groundwork of the Metaphysics of Morals*.[19] As a pattern of life, ethical egoism would produce a kind of self-cultivated version of the brutish lives that, according to generations of political theorists, prevail prior to genuinely civil association—indeed, life would be uncivil.

REASONS FOR MOVING BEYOND SELF-INTEREST

Even if ethical egoism is not adopted, it does not follow that good reasons have been provided for moving beyond self-interest. What reasons have philosophers given for thinking that we should go beyond self-interest? Apart from the view, no longer as popular as it once was, that the answer lies in the commands given us by God or some other law giver, there have been roughly three kinds of answers: (1) that we must move beyond self-interest because reason or rationality demands it, (2) that whereas brute self-interest seems to conflict with morality, "enlightened self-interest" does not, and (3) that we must recognize the claims of the "common interest" and act accordingly.

The first answer is associated with the tradition in moral philosophy issuing from the work of Kant, who argued that only those who act from a genuinely free decision of the moral

---

[19]See Ch. 3 of Bruce Aune, *Kant's Theory of Morals* (Princeton: Princeton University Press, 1979).

will to be regulated by chosen principles, perhaps adopted and acted upon brute inclination and impulse, and not from factors or "determinations" outside their control—whether these be sociopolitical or psychological or physical—are authentic moral agents or actors. "Rightness" is recognized by our reason, he argued; rightness as such can serve as a motive to action; when we are moral, we do that which is right *because* it is right, because virtue is its own reward. The good will, or the person with a good will, is always motivated by the thought of doing what "duty" enjoins—and "duty" is submission, obedience, compliance with moral laws, laws that themselves satisfy or conform to a supreme maxim of consistency, generalizability, and universalizability. Thus, in the Kantian theory duty and virtue reside in the freely acting and choosing self, not primarily in the social order and not in perceived consequences or effects of the actions we perform. What is important, in Kant's view, is that actions have value when executed for the sake of "duty"; the moral worth of an action depends on the maxim or law on which it is based rather than on some desired or emotively attractive goal or purpose it fulfills, and on the condition that the maxim or law in question can be made (or willed to be) truly universal.[20] This last point is critical; Kant broke decisively with the Humean tradition before him of regarding rationality and reason as purely calculative, a matter of figuring out means suitable to attaining preset ends. For him, reason does calculate but also does more; it also fixes ends and sets categorical aims and imperatives for action; the very nature of reason is universal and general, and that is why such imperatives must

[20]Cf. Bruce Aune, also Herbert J. Paton, *The Categorical Imperative* (Chicago: University of Chicago Press, 1948); Mary Gregor, *Laws of Freedom* (Oxford: Basil Blackwell, 1963); John Rawls, *A Theory of Justice* (Cambridge: Harvard University Press, 1971), Section 40.

be universally applicable. To take a famous example from Kant, suppose that you entertain the idea of borrowing money from a friend. You promise to pay it back, even though you really have no intention to do so. Now, if your attitude on this matter of promising became a universal law, what would happen? The very purpose of the institution of promising would collapse, "since no one would believe that he was promised anything, but would laugh at all utterances of this kind."[21] Therefore Kant argued that the tentative supposition that the "law" of promising without an accompanying intention to keep the promise would lead to self-defeat or self-frustation, to a transparent proof that such a purported "law" could not in fact be a true law of moral conduct.

Kant's achievement was a singular one: he rejected the simple view that reason is a plaything of desire, unable to motivate action on its own, and the claim that it is purely calculative. Moreover, as we have already pointed out, he emphasized the dignity and worth of human beings in themselves, as ends, and repudiated the treatment of men and women as "materials" to be "fashioned," perhaps by some dominant leader, or a revolutionary force, or the "vox populi," into what they are not. On the other hand, his picture of human reason and the rules it sanctions and obeys cannot stand critical scrutiny. He made reason into a segregated causal power of its own instead of the natural and integral harmonizing apparatus that it is; he overrigorously applied what has been aptly termed the "colonial" account of reason inherited from Plato, which views reason as an external force brought in from without to discipline and control the "lower" impulses.[22] Not only did he invent the mythology of Pure

---

[21]Cf. Herbert J. Paton, trans., *Groundwork of the Metaphysics of Morals* (New York: 1964), p. 90.
[22]Cf. Midgley, p. 260.

Reason independent of desire and habit, but his test of the rational acceptability of moral injunctions is empty, a purely formal sanction of consistency. In sum, his concern for the objective and universal features of reason led him to an exaggerated respect for formal order and to a corresponding neglect of other functions of reason and of equally significant constitutive human factors, desires, and needs.

The point is that there is no "Pure Reason"; reason is a product of interaction with social forces and other human beings and not an original, fixed faculty; it is not "outside" desires but the self-control of a human being who desires to shape and balance his desires. Of course, reason does play a central role in dealing with conflict and redirecting our projects and our lives, but although it might be useful in showing us why we move beyond self-interest in our moral life, it cannot supply us with the kind of justification the Kantian tradition has hoped for.

Turning now to enlightened self-interest, it is evident that those who have found its conception clear and firm have quite naturally tried to base morality on it or justify morality with its aid; some thinkers have advanced the idea that self-interest could play the role for a science of ethics that the fundamental particles and forces in physics play for our understanding of the natural world. One of the major claims of this tradition is that it "pays" to be moral; enlightened self-interest can understand that restricting unbridled self-interest in the here and now can yield greater benefits for self-interest at some future date. If you behave morally toward others, you can expect that they will do so in return, so that all benefit; if, as Plato asserts, you pay your debts and keep your promises, you will gain friends. Duty can be derived from interest.

Much of the difficulty with the theories that have flowed from this tradition is that it is unclear precisely what the "payoffs" of morality are. Thus much discussion has centered on whether being moral conduces to being happy, whether the lonely but morally impeccable man is happier than his libertine friends, whether crime does or does not pay, whether the undetected murderer or embezzler is "really" happy, and so on. But the real flaw in the arguments that justify morality by appeal to self-interest is that there is no rigid or decisive dilemma between duty and interest or self-interest and other-interest, so that reducing the one to the other or justifying the one on the basis of the other need not be seriously pursued. In fact, both factors figure essentially in most action, as we have already indicated; without self-interest, or an interest that is self-referential, there is no motive to action at all—this may be splendid for robots, but action without self-interest produces strained and forced human action. On the other hand, we do recognize that men do have and follow duties that override inclination, often painfully. But acting on duty is never a case of acting without self-interest (although it might be an action that is disinterested). A truer view of the self would show that self-interest and morality need not stand in the relation of either pure mutual antagonism or perfect harmony—nor does one have to ground or justify the other.

We are left with the "common interest," the interest of all, not necessarily identical with the self-interest of anyone in particular. We must, on this view, recognize the existence of mutual interests that can be promoted by everyone adopting a moral code or set of principles; morality is motivated as a system of such principles whose adoption by everyone in a given social setup or community as overriding the dictates of "self-interest" is in the interest of everyone alike.[23] This

[23]Cf. Baier.

view is not a justification of morality on the basis of self-interest; it assumes a person-independent point of view that rationality assists us in projecting and guiding; once we adopt the impartial "moral point of view," we apprehend that obeying moral rules yields a better society for all than would a social system not obeying those rules.

This view seems perfectly correct, but does it escape skeptical objections that point to the possibility of radical conflict between self-interest and morality? Does it provide a reason for actually taking "the moral point of view" in the first place? Does it justify a transition beyond self-interest? No. The objections that postulate freeloaders who derive a share of the goods provided by a society of moral persons without doing their own share, that describe possible social situations in which the immoral man might do better by not obeying the adopted principles of morality, that point to cases in which complex plans of pursuing self-advantage exclusively succeeded undetected in a moral society—all may be admitted as counterexamples.[24] But the common-interest view does not (or should not) pretend to rebut such possible counterexamples; its strength lies in reminding us of the beneficial fruits of moral community. It should give up the quest to justify itself against skeptical objections, and it should give up the need to attach profound significance to the question of justifying why we should go beyond self-interest. We just *do* go beyond self-interest. Self-interest in any case is obscure and not rigidly separable from other-interest (or common interest); the issue is how to improve and effectively channel and direct our common interests.

[24]Cf. David Gauthier, "Morality and Advantage," *Philosophical Review* 76 (1967): and more generally the collection edited by the same author, *Morality and Rational Self-Interest* (Englewood Cliffs, N.J.: Prentice-Hall, 1970). For the "freeloader" problem, see James M. Buchanan, *The Limits of Liberty* (Chicago: University of Chicago Press, 1975), p. 36.

These assumptions, however, sound like an abandonment of everything that ethics and "ethical theory" is supposed to do. What is ethical theory *for*, it might be asked, unless to provide a "foundation" for morality on such bases as reason or self-interest? What is ethical theory about unless it is about giving a justification appealing to deeper philosophical considerations of our moral convictions?

MORALITIES AND MORAL THEORIES

Before discussing these questions further, let us make some preliminary distinctions and claims: The first is to separate moralities and moral theories. Moralities are codes of conduct that are observed in a social setting; they are indeed "social" in use and in origin, generally emergent and undesigned artifacts (as Montesquieu and Adam Smith might have said) that have arisen in response to *prior* conflicts between moral beliefs or between such beliefs and altering social conditions. As such, moralities are not boxed off from ordinary life or free from the constraining and molding influence of "human nature." Insofar as we possess and submit to such moralities, which we do, we simply *are* moral and cannot escape being moral.

One reason we occasionally need to be reminded of this distinction is that we unwittingly identify morality with "moral theory," namely, the deliberate effort to identify, articulate, and design a full set of rules and principles that capture the "nature" or "essence" of our "moral life" or that give "accounts" of our "moral capacities" or of how we come to "know" the truth or falsity of our moral convictions.

But there is no ground for identifying the realm of morality with the dialectical play among theories found in our ethics textbooks, and we generally do not need to await the resolution of the truth or falsity of such theories before claiming that we are moral or answering why we are moral. Furthermore, whereas some such theories have been indispensable, others have provided little more than a "transcendental" or "ultimate" or "constitutive" way of reformulating some especially cherished common belief, dressed up in mythological, pseudological, or pseudopsychological language. Preoccupation with these moral theories has encouraged the misleading identification of the sphere of morality with that of the "final moral truths" and kept alive an equally misleading distinction between "pure" or "higher" ethics and "applied ethics" or the "lower" procedures associated with customs and moralities.

"EMPIRICAL" MORALITY AND MORAL INQUIRY

A great deal of moral theory has concentrated on whether ethics could be "natural" or "empirical" and what methods could be suitable to investigating moral phenomena. Morality is indeed "empirical" in any common sense of the word, and moral "facts" are features and properties, however complex, of human beings and their lives and interests—what else could they be? We may also note that values are assuredly not denizens of a "realm" or arena of their own so that whenever we derive satisfaction from giving money to a beggar, we must be reaching out with a special mental "organ" to "grasp" the quality of benevolence that lies outside of space and time. If it is obscure to us how "ethical" and so-called "natural" terms are related, it is surely nothing more than the obscurity that accompanies any project that is in its infancy. The task, of course, is to *forge* links among our ethical and nonethical thought and language; when we face a problem in actual life, we have no difficulty in locating or placing our values in definite empirical contexts, in conditions and consequences, yet in moral theory the *possibility* of doing so continues to preoccupy (and sometimes paralyze) us.[25]

Morality guides our conduct; we are directed most of the time by principles that are held without examination or reflection. Ordinarily we do not worry about the rightness or wrongness of what we are doing—we just do it. But the presence of conflict among our values and beliefs can lead to difficulties that occasion reflective morality. However much moral theory has been pried off the contexts in which it arose and unsympathetically and routinely applied to foreign contexts or erected into a "subject matter" of its own, it is at root a response to trouble: theory developed in response to one problem may indeed be used with clarifying effect in response to another, but it must be constantly reexamined. The general point is that moral inquiry is reasoned deliberation—the process of arriving at a compromise or harmony or balance among competing values and preferences—a unique and never-to-be-repeated event of working through materials at hand here and now, and not a matter of routine as the promise of a final, true moral theory mechanically applicable to case upon case would suggest.

These points suggest something about the content of morality. There are elements of theory and generalization in all morality. We do well to recall the Kantian emphasis on universality and generality of moral judgment; we do well to remember the weight that should be accorded the approval

---

[25]See John Dewey, *Human Nature and Conduct* (New York: Holt, 1922), and Dewey and Tufts, Pt. II, *passim.* For other relevant discussions see Rawls, Sections 4, 9, 87, and the introductory chapters of Hospers and of Brandt.

or disapproval of society or the claims of conscience; all these enter into our moral thought. But these elements serve as *principles*—which are always relevant—and not *rules*—which are not. They serve as factors that bear upon the judgment to be made, not as rules that determine an outcome.[26] In the familiar sense in which we use the term, morality is indeed concerned with the "resolution of conflict," with decisions about how to act. But it does not employ the kind of rules used in decision theory, which operate against fixed utilities to select one out of a potential set of actions that will, say, minimize our loss or gain; moral judgment is "decision theoretic" only in trivial cases where there is wide agreement on background values.[27] If there are "rules" at all in morality, they must be described as "context sensitive," as rules that state factors or types of considerations to be used in judgment with the aid of the judgment maker's discretion. Such "rules" constrain us, but there is no need to imitate the obsession some moralists have had with trying to fill the gaps in such rules by supplying codicils that cover every possible circumstance to which they might be applied. This aim is not only imposible to attain, but unwise insofar as it diminishes the spontaneity and sense of participation moral agents require in making judgments.

Morality thus far resembles a painter's palette—a collection of elements that are brought to bear on the execution of a task—more than a book of regulations or table of com-

---

[26]Dewey and Tufts. See also the editor's introduction to Sidney Morgenbesser, ed., *Dewey and His Critics* (New York: Hackett, 1978), section on "Ethics and Social Philosophy."

[27]Cf. John Harsanyi, *Essays on Ethics, Social Behavior, and Scientific Explanation* (Dordrecht, Holland: D. Reidel, 1976), Ch. 3, 4.

mandments: it is empirical and part historical; it can be upset by current problems that prompt the importation of theory and fresh ideas; its function is to assist conduct. None of these assertions implies that morality is not "objective" or "true." Moral rules, we have said, are context sensitive; they contain terms that are placeholders for further articulations of the spirit behind them. We all agree that it is wrong to murder; we all believe in social justice. But we might disagree that soldiering can be equated with murder or that state ownership of productive resources is a means toward social justice. Where disagreement arises, placeholders are bracketed and scrutinized further, retrenched and built up once more as the disagreement and the occasion dictate. Our justifications of actions and judgments are justifications *to* others who hold certain views in common with us, not wholesale, ground-up logical architectonics; "wider" and more inclusive justifications might be demanded in particular contexts, but unless discussion breaks down entirely, there does not arise the need for global validations or legitimations of our moral convictions. We need not be preoccupied with "principles of individuation" or moral contexts or problems any more than we are elsewhere, say in science. The "objectivity" of our resoltuions of contextual difficulties resides in the fittingness of our judgment to the context and to the background of assumptions shared by parties to the dispute. In this way, morality is judgment that provides critical control over present action, and it does not need to provide any sort of all-encompassing moral "system" or "ultimate" grounding. It is simply ordinary knowledge from every available source that is relevant to our present concerns, brought into play to provide guidance, control, and balance as well as to help us deliberate (and occasionally about) our present given ends and values.

ECONOMIC MAN?

To return to the relation between self-interest and ethics: there is an increasing fashion of espousing an "economic" method of interpretation of social processes and institutions.

To be sure, in recent years a number of important economic analyses of social reform, "rights," political associations, pollution control and safety hazards, childbearing, and so on have cast wanted light upon their subjects. The point that much of this preoccupation reflects our desire to glamorize existing social conditions by justifying theory and analysis is strengthened when we consider the *homo economicus* as an honorific description, not of "what we are like," but of what many have *trained* themselves to become. Given other reasons of a practical kind, it is not unattractive to look at oneself as a business; given strong motives for making money and "getting on," it is not unreasonable to describe the self as a kind of profit-seeking unit; given a fixed and stationary view of the self (of the kind we have already rejected), it is alluring to think, as the classical utilitarians did, of the self as calculating how to maximize net gain of pleasure in the way that a businessman handles his profit and loss tables. If personal advantage is seen as the object of all activities of the self, so that actions have results that either accrue to or take away from personal advantage, it is not difficult to see, for example, children as investments or as intrusive presences demanding comforts at "costs" of other items and providing an uncertain "return."

But in fact the economic picture of life reverses the true state of affairs: Life is not like a business reckoned in commensurable units; business is an abstraction from a larger social whole to which its categories have no sensible application. Cost–benefit analyses assume the clear notions of "self-advantage" which we have suggested are difficult to secure; it is far clearer that we are habitually confused as to what our "self-interest" is in the first place. Furthermore, we are too lazy and restricted to perform the calculations (on our life projects and their alternatives) that would be required to satisfy an accountant; our projects are invariably elastic and riddled with ambiguity; moreover, they depend on fortuity to a degree that diminishes the utility of calculation.[28] We enter business in order to secure instrumentalities to other items—we do not literally "consume" money; and what is *done* with profit is not a present factor in most business deliberations. Pecuniary gain is a restricted instance of satisfaction, one institution among others which, taken by itself, provides no satisfactory account of human life as a whole; one might as well model all of life on the features and rhythmic patterns observed in sexual satisfaction.

Yet it is unquestionably true that people can, under the influence of the immediate desirability and urgency of a mode of satisfaction, start to prize it no longer as an instrumentality but as an end. Like boxers who sacrifice other features of life to the cultivation of strength, we can *become* economic men; we deliberately ignore other forms of life to pursue a plan of profit and the avoidance of loss. There is currently abroad a kind of romance of the entrepreneur, the profit taker; he is identified with vigor and directness, with being hard, tough, independent, rugged, clear, not someone who is stepped on by others. If we have trained ourselves to becoming self-interested and to avert our gaze from the claims of others, it is no wonder that we might ask why we should go beyond self-interest or be moral.

[28]Cf. Bernard Williams, "Moral Luck," in *Proceedings of the Aristotelian Society,* 1968.

Perhaps the impulse behind our popular expressions of moral individualism is an admirable one; perhaps the need to be independent and self-expressive, to realize ambitious projects for self-fruition, is taking its current form to meet present economic and social stresses. Thinkers in the past have articulated programs and ideals of self-expression that do not seem far removed from some of our contemporary thinkers. Aristotle praised the great-souled man who "will be incapable of living at the will of another";[29] Nietzsche favored self-overcoming, mastery of impulse, Greek self-perfection, and wrote: "Physician, help yourself; thus, you help your patient too. Let this be his best help that he may behold with his eyes the man who heals himself."[30] But we must distinguish self-realization from exclusive self-promotion; it is simply a fallacy to suppose that the former is somehow incompatible with morality–indeed, it *involves* morality.

ECONOMIC SELF-INTEREST AND THE RIGHT

A friend of mine recently remarked that nothing has so encouraged the egoistic tendencies and self-protectionism, the freeloader mentality and the emergence of "underground economies" that defy the Internal Revenue Service, as current right-wing ideas. And, indeed, recent times have witnessed the phenomenon that many of those who, like Ringer, espouse various forms of psychological or ethical egoism link their ideals of self-realization with political programs deprecating "government" and encouraging self-reliance and self-

[29]*Nichomachean Ethics*, IV 3.
[30]Friedrich Nietzsche, *Thus Spake Zarathustra*.

interest in the economic sphere.[31] But the charge should be regarded with caution; as we shall note, political theory on the Right cannot be logically assimilated with views that exalt egoism over the claims of (nonegoistic) morality.

Of course, one outstanding difficulty of appraising any such charge against the Right is that there is no single target on which to focus. A capsule history of the Right in the past quarter-century would have to distinguish between a number of quite different movements. For example, there is the anarchistic "Old Right," which held the following kind of ideal: in the good society, each and every person would be at absolute liberty to choose his own style of life, to choose whether to work or not, to own property or not, or to trade in entirely unregulated markets or not; he would be at liberty to select the institutions that govern him, the systems of defense, education, sanitation and housing, justice and welfare; the sole punishable offense in such a society would be to harm others or their property or to defame them. Taxes, should they be needed, would be raised by common consent and in no case against a person's will. And each member of such a society could, if he so wished, opt out of the arrangement and seek alternative systems of property, justice, and defense that suited him. Much of this pattern of thought was absorbed, with some modifications, into the Libertarian Right, in recent years dominated by the writings of Ayn Rand and the economic and political work of Ludwig von Mises. Some versions of the Old Right platform were close enough to Left thinking

[31]Cf. Robert Ringer, *Restoring the American Dream* (New York: QED Books, 1979), Foreword by William Simon. Note that Ringer was not only greatly influenced by Ayn Rand, but also that Murray Rothbard, Leonard Liggio, George Reisman, Robert Hessen, Ronald Hamowy, and Ralph Raico (founders of the *New Individualist Review*) were once members of Rand's group.

in the late sixties—for example, in stressing domestic decen-
tralization and noninterventionism in foreign affairs—to merit
the suggestion of a coalition. But sharply distinguishable from
the foregoing Rightist views were those of a more traditional
conservative faction led by William Buckley (and to some
degree Frank Meyer), which argued that "temporary" abridg-
ment of liberties in the form of the draft of "confiscatory"
taxation was necessary to ensure a military and economic
state strong enough to thwart the Communist threat. To the
right (or perhaps left) of these views were a number of more
radical and extreme conservatisms.[32]

For our purposes, we may abstract from these historical
issues and focus on a popular and widely read manifesto,
William Simon's *A Time for Truth*.[33] Simon's views seem to be
based on a variety of moral and economic assumptions. There
is first the moral premise, associated with the Lockean tradition, that each and every human being has a "boundary"
around him within which no other human being or human
agency may enter unconsented to without infringement or
violation of that person's "right," whether the latter is seen
as God-given or "self-evident" or "natural." This premise is
central to what Hayek has called the English tradition of liberty, the tradition of purely negative liberty.[34] Second, Simon
also seems to hold the Lockean view that liberty and property
"go together"—property being that which one has produced

---

[32]Such as that of Buckley's brother-in-law, L. Brent Bozell, "a fanatical convert
to Catholicism who later founded the Sons of Thunder, a neo-Carlist par-
amilitary organization whose members, wearing red berets and rosary
beads, invaded hospitals to baptize aborted fetuses." Jerome Tuccille, *It
Usually Begins with Ayn Rand* (New York: Stein & Day, 1972), p. 59. Tuccille's
book contains much useful information on the recent history of the Right.
[33]William E. Simon, *A Time for Truth* (New York: Berkeley Books, 1978).
[34]Hayek, *The Constitution of Liberty* (South Bend: University of Indiana Press,
1957), p. 55.

and thus has a "right" to dispose of as one wishes. In addition to these moral premises, he holds a number of important economic theses: a "system of natural liberty" (in the sense of the classical economists) in which each is free to produce (or not produce), create, invent (or fail at invention), and exchange on a purely voluntary basis gives rise to a market that is grounded on the economic self-interests of its acting participants, none of whom necessarily intends to promote the interest of all; yet this market, in Simon's view, is spontaneously regulated by supply–demand relations, and is "the most efficient and powerful production system that is possible to [our] society."[35] This market essentially depends on the intricate interweaving of individual plans and expectations, and these are so complex that no human agent (or computer) could possibly gather enough relevant information to accurately predict its course or regulate it intelligently. Thus Simon rejects every form of *dirigisme*; he rejects every intervention on the part of government that would seek to ensure distributive (as against "commutative") justice, and believes that a structure of government larger than one limited to the enforcement of laws, minimal interference in economic life (for the purpose of restraining labor unions or monopolistic concentrations that diminish competition), and protection services is morally and prudentially unacceptable. To interfere in a nontrivial way with the market so conceived would, on Simon's view, destroy the expectations (say, of price) that are necessary for its operation; if that happens, people will cease to have the incentive to save or accumulate capital, savings will disappear, and productivity will decline with dire political and social consequences. Thus government should not "direct" the market. Nor should it, on Simon's view, "interfere"

[35]Simon, p. 25.

with productivity by progressive and discriminatory taxation and ill-conceived and burdensome regulations on industry, which can only harm the economy by diminishing incentives; nor should it print new money which "debauches" our currency, or redistribute income to the "unproductive" members of the middle class by excessive schemes of social security and social welfare; nor should it engage in controlling rents or pursue costly programs of public education that fail to accomplish a fraction of their intended aim; and so on and so on.

This position is that of classical liberalism, the Whig liberalism of natural rights and their "owner" pitted against the state and "statism." How sound is it? A number of writers have pointed out, of course, that the "free markets" postulated by its proponents would not be automatically self-equilibrating but could be "interfered" with without an accompanying breakdown of efficiency. Moreover, the linkage between economic efficiency and free markets has been challenged as a matter of history.[36] There are also a number of important questions concerning defense systems, the psychological relations between economic security and risk taking, the altering psychology of capitalism, the likelihood that voluntary donations or charity would produce an acceptable redistribution of wealth or promote unbiased scientific research, the dependence of entrepreneurial activities on the absence of excessive tax-induced reductions in reward, and so on that remain controversial elements in the position. Another important question concerns the social and economic

---

[36]By a number of economic historians. See Mark Blaug, *Economic Theory in Retrospect*, rev. ed. (Homewood, Ill.: Richard D. Irwin, 1968). See also K. Arrow's review of Milton and Rose Friedman, *Free to Choose* (New York: Harcourt Brace Jovanovich, 1980) in *The New Republic*, 22 March, 1980, pp. 25–28.

role of the massive corporations which classical economists understandably could not foresee; what precisely should their social function be? Should they at their own expense reduce safety hazards and pollution and, if so, how should infringements of this obligation be treated? Many of these questions await adequate treatment by theorists on the Right.[37]

In his book Simon offers example after example to support his view that the United States has succumbed to a vicious cycle wherein taxation curbs risk taking and supports regulations that further diminish incentive to produce wealth, and confiscates monies that are redistributed not only to the sick and poor but to the nonproductive sectors of society. His experience as secretary of the treasury convinced him that we had

> (1) a tax system that was stripping citizens of ever-increasing proportions of their wages and profits; (2) deceptive budget practices which kept citizens from grasping the full magnitude of massive federal deficits; (3) an ever-increasing national debt that was devouring the funds needed for capital investment in our productive system; (4) a federal printing press that was pouring increasingly valueless dollars into the economy, fueling both inflation and inflationary expectations; (5) a runaway "transfer" system which was compulsively redistributing the wealth from the productive citizens to the nonproductive; (6) an ever-expanding regulatory system which was wrapping increasingly tight coils around our productive institutions; (7) an entrenched profits depression; and (8) inadequate capital investment and a collapsing productivity rate that had fallen below those of the impoverished United Kingdom.[38]

[37]But see Robert Hessen, *In Defense of the Corporation* (Palo Alto: Hoover Institute Press, 1979).
[38]Simon, pp. 105–106.

But granting that there have been government waste, an entangled and inefficient bureaucracy, a deplorable system of public welfare and education and housing; granting federal regulatory agencies have occasionally (and even often) wrought havoc with economically efficient production and by virtue of size and lack of communication issued conflicting regulations;[39] granting that reduced government spending and perhaps tax incentives are desirable under present circumstances; still, shouldn't the remedy consist of improved programs and regulations?

Simon is *unfortunately* too exercised by what he regards as "antibusiness" legislation to settle for any alternative but to overhaul our entire conception of the function and purpose of government; he does not think there is an acceptable "middle ground between communism and capitalism"; like the late Ludwig von Mises, he thinks our alternatives are laissez-faire or dictatorship, and like Mises, Schumpeter, Knight, and other economists[40] he deplores the neglect of the entrepreneurial function in our economic thought, of the man who anticipates the wishes of consumers by the lure of pure profit. "For forty years," Simon writes, "those free enterprise values that made America a lusty, inventive giant have been discredited"; indeed, for him,

[39]Cf. Simon, p. 197: "A responsible meat-packing plant—Armour—was ordered by the Federal Meat Inspection Service to create an aperture in a sausage conveyor line so that inspectors could take out samples to test. The company created the aperture. Along came another federal agency, the Occupational Safety and Health Administration (OSHA), and demanded that the aperture be closed as a safety hazard. Each federal agency threatened to shut down the plant if it did not comply instantly with its order."

[40]Cf. Ludwig von Mises, *The Anti-Capitalist Mentality* (Princeton, N.J.: D. Van Nostrand, 1956). For an excellent historical treatment of the entrepreneurial role as perceived by economists, see Israel Kirzner, *Perception, Risk and Opportunity* (Chicago: University of Chicago Press, 1979).

> an American who is hostile to individualism, to the work ethic, to free enterprise, who advocates an increasing government takeover of the economy or who advocates the coercive socialization of American life is in some profound sense advocating that America cease being America.[41]

It may be admitted that the conscious pursuit of collective or social ends does considerably skew economic efficiency, apart from the just criticisms Simon may have concerning the failure of recent governmental efforts in this direction.

But intelligent pursuit of social ends is indeed the key issue. No one denies that "perfect competition is a perfect procedure with respect to efficiency."[42] When the "instability" of the market is discussed, when the need for protection from its fluctuations or recurring business cycles is argued, the point is not that the *market* can survive and recover from such downturns, but that the deleterious effects on human lives should be counterbalanced by deliberate introduction of ethical standards the market by itself cannot enforce. The entirely unregulated market—consistent with certain libertarian principles and writings—would, for example, allow human beings to sell themselves to others or rent portions of their bodies to others.[43] "Government intervention" has produced not only waste but also libraries, preservation of natural resources, laws against fraud and deception in ad-

---

[41]Simon, p. 81.

[42]Cf. Rawls, p. 272; also cf. pp. 360, 492.

[43]One wonders whether renting out one's brain would be inconsistent with the principles set down in Robert Nozick, *Anarchy, State, Utopia* (New York: Basic Books, 1972). Ethical issues arising out of slavery are regularly treated in the San Francisco homosexual magazine, *Drummer*. Compare the letter on "slave equality" (and the editor's response) in vol. 4, no. 36.

vertising or governing the suppression of inventions, corrections of inequalities of opportunity, the restraint on extravagant credit practices that we all now take for granted, the rights of labor, and many other civilizing factors.

Apart from its unbalanced perspective on social welfare, arguments from the Right (not only Simon's) have tended to rest on an overly simplified conception of human beings and their "products." We have previously noted the limits of regarding men and women as actuated by "self-interest" (or, in this case, economic self-interest). Second, there are difficulties of a familiar kind in claiming that we have a "right" to what we "produce" instead of a tentative ownership that must be balanced by considerations of the common interest. Does a tailor have an absolute right to what he earns from his clothes? Surely it was hardly by his labor alone that these clothes were made; we must also take into account the men and women who made the fabrics and thread he uses, those people who transported these fabrics from their origin of manufacture, those people who invented the means of such transport, the politicians and soldiers who have ensured that such manufacturing and trade would not be disrupted by costly wars, and so on. Although it would be an exaggeration to claim that all of society produces the tailor's clothes, it would be equally a mistake to think of the tailor as having an absolute right to their disposition. Finally, it is precisely because the arguments under consideration have so feebly addressed matters of social concerns that we *cannot* equate them with egoism or egoism-encouraging claims. For, indeed, the arguments are compatible with a full variety of views about moral conduct and moral motivation, resting as they generally do on issues relating to *economic* self-interest. It would be a disservice to the Right to find a logical connection between its economic views—views that have often been held by visionaries who foresaw a greater abundance of wealth for all through their implementation[44]—and the moral crudities of Robert Ringer. One would like to be able to say the same about the Right's view of the "self" that stands in necessary, open conflict with the reprehensible "state."

THE NEED FOR EXPERIMENTALISM

What then has attracted and continues to attract people to such arguments as those of Simon? Surely one component is found in the decline we have witnessed in recent years of trust and faith in our government, a decline that has excellent reasons behind it: an unjust war, the corruption of secret agencies like the CIA, the misuse of covert powers abroad to support morally unacceptable regimes, the persistence of high levels of taxation and unemployment, the devaluation of our currency, the deterioration of such services as transportation, the mails, police, education, and utilities, and the unsatisfactory state of our judicial system.

But the appeal of the Right seems to be primarily emotional, in that it gives a romantic projection. The images of self-reliance—that if anything is to be done, I must do it myself—amid a competitive struggle of plans and projects pursued by others; the image of unfettered, vigorous, integral, self-propagating force and strength; these are immensely powerful—even if they have been produced by underlying feelings of impotence. But the image is "emotional" insofar

[44]See the views of nineteenth-century American businessmen in Sidney Fine, *Laissez-faire and the General Welfare State* (Ann Arbor: University of Michigan Press, 1969); also Arthur M. Schlesinger, Jr. "Sources of the New Deal," in *Paths of American Thought*, ed. A. M. Schlesinger, Jr. and Morton White, (Boston: Houghton Mifflin, 1970).

as it is not congruent with conditions or anchored in identifiable contexts of reform that would serve to test its adequacy. This point becomes clear, for example, when we read in Simon's book (after over 200 pages of harsh critique of various government policies) that what is needed today are "principles" and a "counter-intelligentsia," but not "programs; one should not come up with programs of one's own. Not only would they turn out, in the current context, to be modified egalitarian-authoritarian programs, but also the very approach is itself a symptom of the interventionist disease." Simon adds:

> The *last* thing to do is to fight conventionally in the political arena, on the assumption that getting Republicans or conservatives of both parties into office is a solution. I am partisan enough to wish to see members of my party hold office, but I have learned that it solves nothing fundamental.[45]

If we adopt the customary attitude of the Right toward civil association, the state is not a servant but a force humiliating us, "confiscating" our money to feed parasites and freeloaders who do not even bother to thank us. When moral imagination is at a nadir (as it is here), when there is a lack of individuality in fact (if not in word), when our popular culture is in decay and our emotional lives standardized and uniform, it is perfectly natural to draw the inference that since cooperation (or wanting to cooperate) has not worked, therefore we may fall back on ourselves and our self-interest.

But the error in this inference is obvious: one might as well say that because today's drinking water is bad we must henceforth avoid water, or that because a national vote elected a fool henceforth we must not vote. What is signified by a

---

[45]Simon, pp. 232–233.

retreat into the mythology of the fixed self pursuing its interests against the evil machinations of the state is that we find this picture more secure, more familiar, more comfortable than the efforts required to retool institutions; what is equally signified is that our moral thought is clogged, that we are in fact unclear where our supposed "self-interest" lies, that we need new institutions and not justifications of old ones, that the cure for rotten political setups is the recanalization of energies and impulses. This is a suggestion that those veterans of the last decade who redirected their moral impulses into current forms of moral expression were *not "radical" enough then or now.*

The ideals of self-realization and moral individualism behind current popular thought might be fruitfully included in a survey of possible redirections. But what is needed is a method of focusing imagination and moral energies, an "experimentalism." We need social and moral thought that does not cling to the frozen aspirations of a century or two ago, but that adjusts to factual conditions at hand with the aid of our present intellectual materials. We need to reinterpret key terms like "welfare" and "individual" and to abandon fixed platonic conceptions that by definition are not grounded in present forces. A grasp of the historical relativity of ideals, of the need for continual reinterpretation of our central political concepts, as well as the realistic study of current facts are all required in order to bring into existence the institutions whose absence is implied by the popular imagery we have lately examined. Only through experimentations of this kind are we likely to transcend the static and blocked political and social relations these popular ideas force us to examine, and only through experimentation of this kind are we likely to overcome the strangeness (and even staleness) of much of our current ethical theory. As to the query, Why should we be moral? we can only remark that the realization of genuinely moral communities might teach us, through example but especially through our own participation, why we *want* to be moral and not merely why we "should" be moral as a matter of abstract obligation.

Chapter 4 / ECONOMIC JUSTICE IN HARD TIMES

ROBERT LEKACHMAN

As Alexis de Tocqueville long ago observed, an important clue to the comprehension of American society is the natives' ambiguous but powerful passion for equality. "The more I advanced in the study of American society," noted this aristocratic Frenchman,

> the more I observed that . . . equality of condition is the fundamental fact from which all others seemed to be derived, and the central point at which all my observations terminated.

Equality, not justice is the word that threads its way through American constitutional and statutory utterance. Section I of the Fourteenth Amendment, for example, prohibits states from so acting as to "deny any person within [their] jurisdiction the equal protection of the laws." In 1866, two years before the ratification of that amendment, an early civil rights act required that

ROBERT LEKACHMAN ● Department of Economics, Herbert H. Lehman College, City University of New York, Bronx, New York, 10468.

> All citizens of the Untied States shall have the same right,
> in every State and Territory, as is enjoyed by white cit-
> izens thereof to inherit, purchase, lease, sell, hold, and
> convey real and personal property.

After a disgracefully long period of political inertia, Congress renewed the thrust toward racial equality in the Civil
Rights Act of 1964. Title VII, which applies to employment,
extended promises of equality considerably beyond the black
community by declaring it to be

> an unlawful employment practice for an employer to fail
> or refuse to hire or to discharge any individual, or oth-
> erwise to discriminate against any individual with re-
> spect to his compensation, terms, conditions, or privi-
> leges of employment because of such individual's race,
> color, religion, sex, or national origin.

Within the political mainstream the pursuit of *some* version of equality is bipartisan, a passion equally of liberals and
conservatives, and in extreme form of such libertarians as
Robert Nozick. Thus Chief Justice Warren Burger, stigmatized
somewhat unfairly as deeply reactionary by Robert Wood-
ward and Scott Armstrong in their bestselling *The Brethren*,
nevertheless proved himself sensitive to the racial impact of
seemingly racially neutral testing and educational qualifications for employment. Piercing the veil of language, Burger
interpreted congressional intent as prohibiting "not only overt
discrimination but also practices that are fair in form, but
discriminatory in operation."

Affirmative action goals urged or administratively imposed upon corporations and universities justify themselves
by the intent to equalize competitive races for groups that
start out at very different points. Past discrimination handicaps living blacks, Hispanics, native Americans, and women.

Therefore, public policy must operate to minimize the impact of these handicaps on vocational and pecuniary outcomes.

Equality is as much in vogue among economists as among lawyers. Specialists in public finance justify progressive income taxes implicitly or explicitly with the aid of two strategic assumptions. First, human beings are more or less equally sensitive to the joys of spending and the pains of financial deprivation. Second, the pleasures to be derived from additional units of any specific good or service or even of that most generalized of commodities, money itself, diminish as the number of units within an individual's grasp increases. A fourth automobile adds less utility to the members of a three-car family than a first chariot conveys to a no-car family.

One might note parenthetically that from the libertarian standpoint these issues of tax equality conveniently vanish. If, as Nozick and the libertarian economist Murray Rothbard argue, taxation is unjust expropriation of the fruits of individual effort, their ideal ultraminimalist state will be no more than a conduit for the voluntary purchase of protective services.

From the Benthamite version of human psychology still in vogue among economists progressive taxation readily emerges as an objective equalization not of payments to the tax collector but of pains to the individual taxpayer. Hence poor, middling, and rich persons receive justice only by parting with *unequal* percentages of their taxable incomes, the larger the income the greater the share appropriately subtracted by the Internal Revenue Service.

Equality, in the sense of competition without legal or institutional constraint, is also popular among economists because free competition has long been held to promote efficiency in both the productive and the consumptive process, making it the supreme value of the profession. Milton Friedman and Gary Becker have repeatedly demonstrated to the gratification of any well-trained price theorist that for employers prejudice is an expensive luxury. Any employer who excludes Jews, blacks, women, Catholics, the short, the tall, the skinny, the corpulent, or any other disfavored group denies himself access to the full range of human talent in the labor pool as a whole. He will pay higher wages for less productive employees than he needs to or than his more intelligent rivals actually do pay.[1]

It is none too soon to attempt to sort out some of the diverse meanings lurking among the connotations of a word of such almost universally high repute as "equality." But first it will be helpful to say something about the libertarian conversion of equality into an individualism which Nozick construes in his influential *Anarchy, State and Utopia* to imply complete command by each person of his economic resources. Although the nearly complete absence of institutional specification in Nozick's book inhibits certainty on the point. Nozick appears to believe that existing distributions of income, wealth, and opportunity are either in some sense fair or, at worst, less unfair and restrictive of personal liberty than *any* rearrangement by the state. It is possible to infer further from Nozick's work that shrinkage of the state to an ideal ultraminimalist condition would allow the only desirable sort of redistribution of tangible and intangible resources, that which was the resultant of the free actions in pursuit of their own aims of unconstrained and untaxed individuals.

Friedman and his Chicago followers are minimalists, not ultraminimalists, but they travel a considerable distance in libertarian company. Although Henry Simon, one of the

---

[1]According to *Duns*, a business journal, most chief executive officers of large corporations are over six feet tall. Are boards of directors by artificially limiting their choice raising the price and lowering the average quality of business managers?

founding fathers of the free market tendency, was a believer in strong antitrust policy, contemporary free marketers at least of the Chicago variety seem convinced that almost any action by government is certain to worsen disarray elsewhere. And although Friedman considers legitimate such traditional functions of government as security and judicial enforcement of contract, his position otherwise is similar to that of the libertarians—the less government the better.

In a time of economic disorder, persistent inflation, flagging productivity, and declining family incomes, Friedman's position, as a new decade begins, has gained a great deal of public attention. His ten-part public television series, "Free to Choose," has attracted substantial audiences,[2] and the book of the same title that accompanies the series stood high on best-seller lists in the spring of 1980.

The fashion may be transient. Alternatively, what may be in progress is a genuine shift in popular attitudes in the direction of a minimalist state. At least the new mood must be borne in mind in the consideration which follows of the two competing interpretations of equality that have long held the semantic and political stage—equality of opportunity and equality of outcome or condition. Chief Justice Burger's animadversions against test and educational requirements unrelated to the jobs to which they were obstacles stemmed from his concern that blacks not be denied fair chances because for reasons beyond their control their schools and families prepared them poorly for formal tests.

In the funding of public education, equality of opportunity is again an animating principle. Is a youngster educated on a third of the resources expended on more fortunate chil-

---

[2]Goodyear Tire, among other large corporations, has been marching its employees in to see the program [on company time]. In the real world, it is not only government that curtails an individual's freedom to dispose of his time and attention.

dren in richer communities denied equal protection and handicapped forever in the contest for fame and fortune? Yes, concluded the Supreme Court of California (and several other state courts) in its influential *Serrano* v. *Priest* decision. No, held the Supreme Court of the United States in its even more influential ruling in the case of *Rodriguez* v. *San Antonio Independent School District.*

In its libertarian guise, equality of opportunity is consistent only with the ultraminimalist state. It is indeed a principle that, according to taste, can be made to justify a wide range of governmental interventions. In the wake of *Serrano* and similar decisions in other states, California, New Jersey, and New York are among the jurisdictions engaged in rearranging and equalizing school expenditures per pupil. Before Propositions 13 and 4 revolutionized California taxes and public spending, the state placed new and stronger emphasis on early childhood education. Once more equality of opportunity was at issue. It is as young children, notoriously, that middle-class boys and girls acquire advantages of motivation, vocabulary, personal confidence, and cultural experience that confer upon them *as unmerited gifts* permanent edges over less fortunate agemates. Early schooling just might partially compensate.

Equality of opportunity is susceptible to radical interpretation and to severe questioning of traditional structures of property. When income is unevenly distributed and wealth still more concentrated in the hands of a few, can genuine equality of opportunity be said to exist? Would Nelson Rockefeller have been four times governor of New York if his grandfather had been an oilfield roughneck instead of a petroleum billionaire? Would John F. Kennedy have become president in the absence of his father's financial backing? As a bitter primary opponent asked, would his youngest brother be in the United States Senate if his name was Edward Moore rather than Edward Moore Kennedy? It is possible but highly unlikely that on their merits Henry Ford II would have reached the top of the Ford Motor Company or that David Rockefeller would have become chairman of Chase Manhattan, also a family enterprise.

To phrase the matter gently, tension is inescapable between virtually unrestricted transmission of huge quantities of property from generation to generation and equal life chances for individuals of equivalent talent and determination. Seemly attention to historical evidence and the institutional consequences of full equality of opportunity at the least necessitates drastic taxation of property to interrupt its passage from the dead to the living.

Thus equality of opportunity is potentially an idea that is profoundly subversive of existing distributions of resources. For the most part, however, its contemporary partisans, however illogically, deploy the principle to prop up rather than change existing arrangements. In our time it is Tocqueville's equality of condition that arouses public passion. In lesser or greater degree, this aspiration has influenced groups that in the 1960s and 1970s have pushed the larger community a distance toward its realization.[3] Among other interest groups, black civil rights proponents, women's liberationists, partisans of the handicapped and elderly, Spanish-speaking organizations, and advocates of equality for homosexuals have typically begun by presenting claims for nondiscriminatory evaluation as potential employees, proceeded with equally logical demands for promotion, and sometimes ended by defining as the appropriate measure of equality the distribution

---

[3]The tentative shift in the new decade toward a minimalist state, alluded to above, has already halted and begun to reverse this movement.

of their members among excellent, average, and mediocre jobs in proportions that approximate those of the group to the population at large.

In three famous cases, the Supreme Court has interpreted (or dodged) resolution of the conflict between individualistic conceptions of equality of opportunity and group emphases upon equality of outcome. The earliest of the trio resolved the grievances of Marco deFunis, a Sephardic Jew who a generation ago might well have encountered discrimination because of his religion. In 1970 DeFunis applied to the University of Washington law school. The owner of an excellent undergraduate record and superior scores on the Law School Admission Test, he was nevertheless rejected and advised to renew his application the following year. While he was waiting, he enrolled in graduate school and collected 21 points of "A" credits while simultaneously working full-time for the Seattle Park Department. His last LSAT score, 668, located him in the top 7 percent nationally. All the same, the law school again turned him down. In contrast, it admitted 44 minority candidates (Philippine Americans, Chicanos, blacks, and native Americans), 36 of whom had lower predicted first-year averages than deFunis as calculated according to a formula that weighed equally LSAT scores and junior–senior grade point average.

As one of the state-court judges who heard deFunis's suit initially commented, among the minority admissions "were some whose college grades and aptitude scores were so low that, had they not been minority students, their applications would have been summarily denied." However, in upholding the university the Supreme Court of Washington reasoned that racial classifications were not necessarily unconstitutional unless they invidiously stigmatized a minority, and further held that the law school's effort to ensure "a reasonable representation" of minority students was indeed "color conscious" but in permissible pursuit of its attempt "to prevent the perpetuation of discrimination and to undo the effects of past segregation."

As the case crept with all deliberate sloth through the courts, deFunis was admitted to law school and by the time the Supreme Court acted he was a month or two away from graduation. Although this circumstance gave the Supreme Court a chance it eagerly grasped to declare the issue moot, Justice Douglas in a ringing and influential dissent attacked proportional representation based on race or ethnicity but accepted classifications premised upon wealth and poverty. In one sense, Douglas's criterion was more broadly egalitarian in thrust because it endorsed compensatory action on behalf of *all* persons handicapped by family poverty or inferior education. As a practical matter, however, adoption of the Douglas standard would militate against the interests of blacks, the group whose history of slavery and involuntary membership in American society constituted the strongest claim for compensatory action. Unless very large additional resources were devoted to such action, blacks would be offered fewer special opportunities.

In the *Bakke* case, the Supreme Court eventually grappled, though less than conclusively, with the central issue: Are the federal Constitution or relevant statutes breached by schemes such as that of the medical school at the Davis campus of the University of California that specifically prefer for admission minority applicants, even though by conventional standards they are not as highly qualified as some majority aspirants who are denied admission? Speaking with many voices at great length, the Court apparently decided in an opinion rendered by Justice Lewis Powell that explicit numerical goals (quotas?) were impermissible but that race, like other individual characteristics, could be taken into account by admissions committees.

For Jews with good memories, Powell's warm praise for Harvard's admissions procedures was ironic. His emphasis on balance in entering classes and reluctance to rely on strict meritocratic criteria—grades and tests—were precisely the tactics routinely pursued a generation ago by Ivy League institutions of utmost respectability to limit the entry of otherwise qualified Jews. Emphasis on the intangibles of personal quality and interviewer empathy may benefit disfavored groups. But it may also sanction revival of the preferences historically enjoyed by Anglo-Saxons, prep-school alumni, and the offspring of the wealthy and powerful.

In the third of these cases, the *Weber* case decided in 1978, the Supreme Court spoke somewhat more clearly. Under at least some circumstances, a corporation could on racial grounds prefer minority over majority applications for slots in apprenticeship programs. In sum, the Supreme Court first evaded, next muddled, and finally accepted, in private employment contexts but not in university admissions, formulation of numerical targets.

GROWTH AND EQUALITY

In our land, every controversy of consequence is conducted in the courts. The tension between justice as equality of opportunity and justice as parity of outcome with which a mediocre Supreme Court has thus far inconclusively grappled is no novelty of our national experience. It is more than an accident that in New York City Jews are overrepresented as teachers and still more as administrators in the public schools, whereas Irish officers are similarly prominent in the municipal fire and police service. Without fussy insistence on individual merit, ethnic groups have habitually cared for their own, very much as considerations of family have influenced apprenticeship chances in construction craft unions and executive opportunities in family-owned or -controlled enterprises.

At this time, the strain between the two opposing concepts of equality is especially acute. The society has experienced a contemporary revolution of entitlement, marked by upsurges of militancy on the part of blacks, women, Hispanics, the gay, the handicapped, and the elderly. These suddenly insistent claims for better treatment, compensation, or reparations are at the best and most prosperous of times difficult to cope with because they inevitably clash with the interests of traditionally dominant white males. It is scarcely necessary to say that these are not the best of times. Claims for the improvement of the condition of some collide with the enormous difficulties others confront in simply maintaining existing standards of consumption. For nearly a decade (I write in 1980) the American economy has been operating within the adverse climate of short-run economic crisis and longer-run sluggishness in productivity improvement and economic growth.

Three unsuccessful presidents—Nixon, Ford, and Carter—attest to the difficulties of governing a pluralist society during a time when claims upon national resources grow more rapidly than the resources to meet them. Inflation, the resource of weak governments, has been the American response.

Between 1945 and 1973 the rich capitalist countries —Western Europe, Japan, Australia, Canada, and the United States—grew at rates rapid enough to improve substantially general living standards without substantially altering existing distributions of income and wealth. Annual growth dividends, without disturbing inflationary side effects, financed steady expansion of welfare benefits and parallel enlargements of the real incomes of middle- and upper-middle-income families. Liberalism was a luxury of annual increments to the Gross National Product. Lyndon Johnson in 1964 and 1965 could simultaneously fight his "unconditional" war against poverty *and* sponsor sharp reductions in personal and corporate income taxes. For alert operators, centrist and even moderately liberal politics were a joy and a guarantee of reelection or promotion to higher office. Is there a happier challenge to a congressman than the opportunity to do a bit of good for most of his constituents? Economic growth facilitates the sort of welfare reorganization that theorists dream of: improvement in the positions of some without damage to the situations of others.

Manifestly those days of wine and roses have vanished. One need not swallow whole the earlier projections of the Club of Rome or Robert Heilbroner's eloquently gloomy speculations in his *An Inquiry into the Human Prospect* to recognize as a near certainty that energy, other raw materials, and foodstuffs will never again be as comparatively cheap as they were in the three decades after World War II. Even before OPEC's 1973 coup and the Iranian revolution, the terms of trade between advanced and developing nations had begun to shift against the former. The $90 to $100 billion, in excess of 1973 figures, which the United States was likely to transfer to OPEC in 1980, constitutes a major fraction of annual growth in the Gross National Product.

The post-OPEC world combines "real" and political evolution. OPEC's political clout would be negligible were it not for the fact that the United States is compelled, in the absence of alternative sources of energy or intensified conservation practices for which consensus thus far is inadequate, to import increasing percentages of the petroleum that heats homes, propels automobiles, fertilizes farms, converts into plastics and pharmaceuticals, and, in effect, powers an advanced in-

dustrial society. Political pressure from raw material producers in the Third World is also likely to become effective in
raising real prices, partly because the West competes with the
Soviet Union and China for influence but also because these
materials and minerals are already or potentially scarce.

In the 1970s and still more in the 1980s, Europeans, Japanese, and North Americans have been compelled to confront
in acute form the politics of distribution and redistribution
from which Americans believed themselves sheltered by the
reassurance of substantial growth increments only briefly in-
terrupted by recession.

It is growth alone, to reiterate an earlier point, that allows
adroit political leaders to gratify in adequate measure the aspirations of most constituents. When growth slows, government becomes more difficult because choices among claims of
competing groups are far more difficult to evade.

There are those who fear Hobbesian consequences. Here,
for example, is the British economist Rudolf Klein's fearful
sketch of events in a no-growth universe:

> Immediately the competition for resources becomes a
> zero-sum game. One man's prize is another man's loss.
> If the blacks want to improve their share of desirable
> goods, it can only be at the expense of the whites. If the
> over-65's are to be given higher pensions, it can only be
> at the expense of the working population or of the
> young.
>
> It would seem only too likely that the haves would man
> the barricades to defend their share of resources, against
> the have-nots. The politics of compromise would be re-
> placed by the politics of revolution, because the have-
> nots would be forced to challenge the whole basis of
> society, and its distribution of wealth and power.[4]

[4]Rudolf Klein, "The Trouble with a Zero-Growth World," *New York Times
Magazine*, 2 June, 1974, p.14.

ECONOMICS AND EQUALITY

Most disasters never occur, sometimes because those who luridly predict them stimulate the responses that avert calamity. Indeed, even within economics, ethical resources are available as alternatives to reversion to a state of nature. In the 1920s, for example, A. C. Pigou drew upon the Benthamite tradition in his classic *The Economics of Welfare* to justify a notion of justice as redistributive in an egalitarian direction. In Pigou's grave and judicious prose, radical policies sounded like sweet reason:

> . . . it is evident that any transference of income from a relatively rich man to a relatively poor man of similar temperament, since it enables more intense wants to be satisfied at the expense of less intense wants, must increase the aggregate sum of satisfaction. The old "law of diminishing utility" thus leads securely to the proposition: Any cause which increases the absolute share of real income in the hands of poor, provided that it does not lead to a contraction in the size of the national dividend, from any point of view will in general, increase economic welfare.[5]

The proviso about "the size of the national dividend" is important; and economic welfare is far less than the whole of human welfare. Nevertheless, Pigou's analysis at the very least, justified and continues to justify not only progressive income taxation but, even more conclusively, heavy levies upon inheritances which, by hypothesis, are unearned by their beneficiaries.

But when will the national dividend in fact be diminished by misguided egalitarian redistribution? Presumably the response is empirical and, as a result, variable in time and place.

[5]A. C. Pigou, *The Economics of Welfare* [London: Macmillan, 1920], p. 89.

Such a notably successful society as West Germany collects a larger share of its residents' incomes in taxes than does the less prosperous United States. Although Sweden has been enduring a spell of economic tribulation, its standard of living by most measures remains as high or possibly higher than the American. Yet Swedish taxes are heavier and more redistributive in their impact. Although Japanese taxes are lower than American, in good measure because Japan's defense budget is small, income is less unequally distributed there than in the United States.

The economist Lester Thurow has made an illuminating comparison between two American income distributions, among white males and among the population as a whole. Inequality among members of the first groups is substantially narrower than among the second. Since by standard earnings criteria white males are the most successful and productive portions of the labor force, it seems reasonable to infer, as does Thurow, that the extent of inequality in the whole population could be diminished at least to that of white males without coming against the Pigovian caveat.

In his widely discussed (and extensively controverted) *A Theory of Justice,* John Rawls has proposed an alternative to utilitarianism as justification for diminished inequality. Indeed, his reinterpretation of social contract doctrine generates dramatically redistributive consequences.

As a central metaphor, Rawls invites his readers to perform the mental experiment of asking themselves what a fair principle of income distribution would be if, under a veil of ignorance, they lacked information about the prosperity or poverty of their families and the comparative market value of their individual aptitudes, acquired skills, and attributes of mind, body, and personality. Rawls concludes that most individuals, afraid that they would be located at the low end of unequal distributions, would opt for equality.[6] Of course Rawls is completely aware that in the world of personal experience men and women are receptacles of opinions, information, and individual history which shape their choice of distributive principle. Nevertheless Rawls's psychological experiment, to the degree that his assumptions are intuitively corroborated by readers, is a powerful practical argument for public policies skewed in favor of economic reorganizations directed to diminished inequality.

However, like Pigou, Rawls inserts an important qualification. His difference principle advocates egalitarian policy in general but condones inequality if it conduces to the advantage of the community's least advantaged members, for

> The intuitive idea is that the social order is not to establish and secure the more attractive prospects of those better off unless doing so is to the advantage of those less fortunate.

Here again an abstract rule translates into an empirical problem of identifying the least advantaged and then determining the tendency of a given public action to improve, damage, or leave unaffected their condition. Although Rawls stresses the differences between utilitarian doctrine and his own alternative, differences that are indeed ethically important, the two doctrines in a range of plausible applications resemble each other more than they diverge. Both incorporate a bias in favor of less inequality and both complicate any automatic application of that bias with a major reservation.

---

[6]A criticism popular among economists concerns attitudes toward risk and speculation. Some people certainly and many people possibly might opt for an unequal distribution in the hope of securing a big prize even though they were aware that the odds were against them.

Benthamite concern for the preservation of property rights is allied to fear that abrupt deprivation of accumulated wealth would frighten investors and thus darken the economic prospects of proletarians as much or more than those of their capitalist employers. In our own environment, Rawls's difference principle might serve sophisticated conservatives as sanctioning tax benefits for the affluent, slashes in business taxes, and liberalized depreciation rules all in the name of stimulating investment, productivity, and per-capita income. There is even an argument on these premises for smaller welfare and unemployment benefits as stimulating incentives to work, earn, and improve individual income.

JUSTICE AND PHILOSOPHY

Rational discussion of economic policy in these difficult days appears to focus upon some variety of individualism, Benthamite utilitarianism, or Rawlsian egalitarianism. Despite their current popularity, ultraminimalist conceptions of the state are unlikely to command substantial popular support for very long. A society operated by large organizations intricately joined by private collusion and public regulation is highly unlikely to proceed very far toward dismantling essential services and protections. The 22 to 23 percent of national income that constitutes the federal tax share is dominated on the one hand by military expenditures and on the other by transfers to the elderly, disabled, unemployed, and ill. That popular scapegoat, welfare, represents a small fraction of income-maintenance programs. From Goldwater to Reagan, conservative politicians have discovered that the most conservative, antistatist of elderly voters rise indignantly to oppose any tampering with social security benefits.

If confidence in the good sense of fellow Americans allows exclusion from further discussion of the libertarian alternative, rational discussion will center on Bentham and Rawls. Hobbes's state of nature is not a chosen alternative. Rather it is the consequence of civic and political collapse. Nor is there much greater profit to be expected from that elegant intellectual curiosity, modern welfare theory. Following Vilfredo Pareto, some welfare theorists insist that since interpersonal comparisons of utility are impossible, the only public interventions or "welfare reorganizations" that are demonstrably beneficial are those that improve the welfare of one or more individuals without diminishing the welfare of any other. If Pareto is correct in the judgment that the very structure of contemporary industrial society determines its income distribution, Samuelson's inference is incontrovertible. "Essentially nothing can be done about inequality. The basic forces determining inequality are too strong and persistent to be affected by state intervention." Whatever the intellectual merits of such ruminations, democratic communities do not operate without making interpersonal and intergroup comparisons of utility, any more than their governing institutions refrain from attempts to reshape income distribution.

Let us descend to a lower level of abstraction and ask how all this applies to the American economy in the dreary spring of 1980. Since November 6, 1979 when the Federal Reserve Board, under the guidance of a new chairman Mr. Paul Volcker announced a new determination to restrict growth in the money supply, the Carter administration openly pinned its hopes of curbing inflation on the precipitation of a recession of uncertain duration and severity. In time, it was thought, high enough interest rates and sufficiently curtailed credit would dampen business investment and consumer spending, both highly dependent on borrowed funds.

Recessions inflict pain on a notably unequal basis. Factory workers and their white-collar colleagues are laid off. Merchants and communities dependent on their commodities suffer the miseries of reduced sales and profits. The collapse of real estate prices is perceived as a series of capital losses by homeowners who in time past consoled themselves over the inflated prices they had paid for their properties with the thought that they could be resold for even gaudier sums of money.

Unemployment itself is unfairly distributed. Blacks, women, and young workers, last hired, are generally first fired under seniority clauses written into union agreements and emulated by nonunion employers. In conflicts between affirmative action commitments by corporations and universities on the one hand and union seniority clauses on the other, it is the former that are almost invariably sacrificed.

These points are only to remind ourselves that in response to the conservative, apprehensive mood of their constituents, the masters of our economic fate appear to have stood the difference principle on its head by endorsing a series of interventions whose consequences improve the situation of the most advantaged at the expense of the least advantaged.

A defense could be made on Rawlsian grounds of tax reductions skewed to the affluent and other policies likely to aggravate existing inequalities of financial distribution. A Republican Rawlsian, if such an ideological anomaly walks the earth, would start naturally with Rawls's concession that it is proper to enrich further the already opulent if they are so led to act as to advance the welfare of the least advantaged.

Our hero of fancy if not fact would next group together several contemporary economic phenomena, among them stagnant or actually declining per-capita productivity, extraordinarily low savings rates, lagging innovation and productive investment, and persistent, escalating inflation. From here the argument flows smoothly. In our national history, disadvantaged groups have progressed not at the expense of the more fortunate but as participants in the rewards of wholesome economic growth. Quite typically, the ratio of black to white income improved during the 1960s when growth was fairly rapid, unemployment low, and prices (until the last two years of the decade) almost stable. And, just as predictably, black gains began to erode during the following decade, which was dominated by less growth and more unemployment and inflation.

Our virtuous Republican wishes to set the stage in the next decade for more rapid growth in the context of renewed price stability. There is no mystery about the sources of growth: they are located in individual productivity and reasonably complete employment of human and nonhuman resources. Productivity itself depends far less on individual effort than upon efficient organization and, above all, well-chosen capital investment.

There is the clue to national policy. Inflation must be reduced in the long-run interest *particularly* of the men and women who in the short run suffer the hardships of job and income loss. As inflation subsides, families will save more and funds for capital investment will become increasingly available at encouraging interest rates. Moreover, once the federal budget is at last brought into balance, the funds that finance existing deficits will be released for productive private use.

Egalitarians who cling to progressive income taxes, on this view, do the least advantaged no service when these levies discourage saving, investment, productivity, and eventual improvement in living standards. Those with an accurate vision of the future realize, paradoxical as it might seem, that facially "unfair" taxes like the Value Added Tax, which has won the support of such congressional grandees as Senate Finance Committee Chairman Russell Long and House Ways and Means Committee Chairman Al Ullman, will actually help the poor more than "fair" progressive imposts on income and profits.

On what grounds may a socialist Rawlsian proffer an alternative program that features credit rationing, wage and price controls, reduction of social security levies, and less draconian monetary policy? This Rawlsian, whose views coincidentally resemble mine, will avoid recession and unashamedly increase rather than diminish the extent of public intervention in the private economy.

CONCLUSION

It is time to flesh out the difference principle with a set of subsidiary rules. The first relates to the analytic process itself. Alfred Marshall was England's leading economic theorist for at least two generations. He nevertheless warned his colleagues against undue reliance on lengthy chains of reasoning. His strictures are well worth recalling:

> It is obvious that there is no room in economics for long trains of deductive reasoning: no economist, not even Ricardo, attempted them. It may indeed appear at first sight that the contrary is suggested by the frequent use of mathematical formulae in economic studies. But on investigation it will be found that this suggestion is illusory, except perhaps when a pure mathematician uses economic hypotheses for the purpose of mathematical diversions; for his concern is to show the potentialities

of mathematical methods on the supposition that material appropriate to their use had been supplied by economic study.[7]

It is precisely on this score that conservative Rawlsian prescriptions are most vulnerable. Their train of reasoning is long and fragile. Contemporary devotees of supply-side economics, the rubric that covers tax incentives to investors and savers and shifts from progressive to regressive tax arrangements, assume that (a) incentives will increase savings, (b) savings will be used for domestic rather than foreign investment, (c) the investments will increase per-capita output instead of feeding still larger quantities of speculative real estate development or other unproductive activities, (d) the rewards of such productive investment as actually does occur will filter down not only to managers and hourly employees but also to the least advantaged members of the community, and (e) no alternative set of economic policies will generate larger results for more poor people more quickly and more surely.

The next amplication of the difference principle is a corollary of the first. It is a preference for acting directly instead of indirectly. Thus improvement of the condition of the least advantaged is best achieved by directing resources directly to them. Two methods of doing precisely that are a negative income tax and comprehensive health protection. The first can readily be designed as an egalitarian, redistributive technique for welfare reform. All that need be done is to set benefit levels for families of four or more at $1,500 per person—$6,000 for parents and two children. Then reduce benefits by one dollar for every three of earned income. Up to earned incomes of

[7]Alfred Marshall, *Principles of Economics*, 8th ed. (London: Macmillan, 1920) p. 781. For contemporary economists Appendix D, "Uses of Abstract Reasoning in Economics" makes rewarding reading.

$18,000, the 1979 national median, families will receive some benefits. It must follow that the top half of the income distribution will suffer some losses.

But what about investment, productivity, growth? The hypothesized redistribution will stimulate consumer demand. Recipients of small and moderate incomes spend most or all of these incomes. As consumer demand grows, sellers and producers will be impelled to enlarge facilities and experiment with new products. At the same time as employment and incomes expand, Treasury receipts rise still more rapidly, one of the effects of a progressive income tax. The shrinking federal deficit will release funds for business investment and, as before, productivity and growth will accelerate.

Can I guarantee that events will meekly conform to this pattern? No, I cannot. But if I am wrong, at least those at the bottom of the income pyramid will have gained something along the way; for at worst their wedge of the national pie will be larger even if it turns out that the pie itself fails to get much larger. If, on the other hand, the partisans of the first approach are in error, it will be the affluent who gain and the poor who lose.

Still a third addition to the difference principle stems from human behavior in practical affairs. It is the caution to examine with extra care arguments made by those who directly benefit from the proposals to which their arguments lead. Sometimes, it is true, self-interest genuinely coincides with the general interest as Rawls defines it. Nonetheless it is rare and therefore unusually appealing to harken to a person who advocates policies from which he gains nothing or actually stands to lose something. In the wake of the Napoleonic wars, the great English economist David Ricardo may or may not have been well advised to urge capital levies to pay off his country's war debts. But the advocacy surely came with better grace from a substantial landowner like Ricardo than from a penniless handloom weaver or a displaced rural laborer. In our time, corporate spokespersons would sacrifice the interests of their employees more credibly if they complemented them by even more painful losses of their own.

I add as a final expansion of the difference principle a consideration related to the imperfections of current economic paradigms. Borrowing from Thomas Kuhn's useful *The Structure of Scientific Revolutions*, I am disposed to compare contemporary economics with the tag end of the mercantilist era or the exhaustion of the neoclassical model in the years that preceded the Great Depression of the 1930s. With the advantage of the keen vision of hindsight, we know now that in the eighteenth century everyone was waiting for Adam Smith and in the 1920s for John Maynard Keynes. We are currently waiting for a new analytic synthesis applicable to the 1980s and later.

In the meantime, economists, albeit with flagging conviction in their own devices, apply old models to data clogged by disquieting anomalies. Since economics is more and more an undependable guide to social action, all of us are still more justified in reliance upon ethical valuation and common-sense judgments that policies directed to the benefit of specific groups presumptively help those groups.

As an egalitarian, I naturally seek to narrow American disparities of income, wealth, power, and status. How far ought an egalitarian proceed before he risks seriously wounding economic incentives and achieving the equality of the poorhouse? The best answer addresses process rather than numerical targets. As the sociologist Herbert Gans acutely phrases the position, "I think of equality, not as an end-state, but as the direction or trend of a social process, that, as it leads to social change, creates costs as well as benefits."

I end as I began. The narrower limits of possible economic growth are likely to focus and sharpen the dispute between the powerful conceptions of equality that compete for primacy. Equality of opportunity will in the end carry the day only if reasonable numbers of prizes are available for the winning. If, as I believe almost inevitable, this condition is unlikely to be fulfilled, then increasing attention will be paid to the conditions of group equity, the politics of a conservative society will be transformed, a democratic left will emerge as an electoral force, and John Rawls will be a prophet in his own land.

Chapter 5 / RIGHTS VERSUS DUTIES

No Contest

ROBERT A. GOLDWIN

The question asked is why more cannot be done, why more is not done, to encourage a sense of citizen obligation in the United States, to accompany and balance the strong urge evidenced by all elements of the populace to demand their rights. Why cannot we Americans be more considerate of the rights of others and more willing to sacrifice for the good of the country, instead of concentrating, as we do, on the self-interested pursuit of personal and group advantage? This is the question posed to me. In responding, I propose to begin at the beginning.

RIGHTS AND DUTIES IN EVERYDAY LIFE

In our everyday lives, rights and duties are clearly linked. That every right has a reciprocal duty is the sort of thing "everybody knows." In family life, for example, the connec-

ROBERT A. GOLDWIN ● American Enterprise Institute for Public Policy Research, 1150 17th Street, Northwest, Washington D.C. 20036.

tion between rights and duties is so obvious that adults expect very young children to understand it. This has been true in all societies and at all times down through history, as far as one can judge from plays, stories, accounts of travelers, folk-tales, and even historical, sociological, and anthropological studies.

For example, in any society, including ours, where there is private family life, it is commonly understood that what might be called the right of a child to be fed a cooked meal by the mother entails some kind of corresponding duty—to help set the table or clear it, wash the dishes or put them away, or some other related task. If it is a rural family, then the chores that go with picking vegetables or collecting eggs or chopping wood are the commonly understood duties. (That a guest in one's home has no such obligation to help, although help may be volunteered, is a sign of special exemption, dis-tinguishing the unobliged guest from the obliged family mem-bers. The outsider, after all, has no right to be at the table, in the way that a son or daughter has, but only an invitation.)

A child may resist doing his duty; he may disobey; the parent may not require fulfillment of the child's duty. Yet the connection between the right and the duty is so obvious that all adults expect any child to be able to understand, with little or no explanation, that the benefit has a price, that the privilege is but half of a balanced relationship essential to a decent and viable familial society, that rights and duties are inextricable.

The same is true in relationships among friends, neigh-bors, associates, colleagues, and even strangers who must deal with each other. It is true that many people have the habit of taking advantage of others, of acting on the maxim that "what is yours is mine and what is mine is mine," but that is considered a bad habit and people who develop it are criticized, complained about, and scorned for it. Whatever we may do when we are looking out for ourselves at the expense of others (and probably all of us do so at one time or another), almost none of us disputes that the general rule is and ought to be that one is obliged to reciprocate, and that duties and rights, privileges and obligations extend equally.

One may claim rights without acknowledging duties, just as one may take goods from a store without paying, by stealth or fraud or force, but there is no great difficulty, in common sense and in moral theory, in recognizing the wrongness of doing it and the evil of trying to justify it. Theft is theft, whether of goods or rights. There is honor among thieves, as the saying goes; even they know that taking without reciprocal giving cannot be the basis of amicable human association.

I have used these simple arguments and homely examples because at the level of personal and family relationships the issues are truly simple—which is usually not the same as saying they are easy to grasp. (Elements are harder to detect and fathom than are combinations of them. Scholars and others who are at their best in studying complexities often make their most profound errors at the elementary level.) But if I am right in saying that rights and obligations have an obvious and universal and, one might say, natural connection, what, then, is the problem? Why should anyone raise a question about the connection between political rights and the obligations of citizens?

My answer is that political rights are different from the rights I have been speaking of. The political situation is very different from the familial and social ones. With regard to rights and duties in the political context, all is not as it seems, not as one would expect, not as any child can understand. My argument is that in political society it is essential to liberty that rights and duties *not* be directly linked in the law.

In the rest of this essay, I will try to explain the hidden trap in the question about the connection between rights and duties of citizens. My advice to anyone who cares seriously about protecting the rights of the people, when asked what duties are owed to society in exchange for the rights enjoyed, is a clear imperative: "Don't answer that question!" Exercise your right to remain silent until the question is reformulated. There is a good answer, as I will try to show, but not to that question.

RIGHTS AND DUTIES IN POLITICAL SOCIETIES

It may be too much to ask of citizens that their political credo be "one for all and all for one," but surely the *esprit* of any political society that hopes to persist must be somewhat closer to that than to "every man for himself." A society of any kind—from the Three Musketeers to a mass of hundreds of millions—can achieve the cohesion that makes individuals into a society only if there is a widely shared concern regarding what is good or harmful for the group or community as a whole. And since any human society is made up of individuals who can think for themselves—as distinguished from, say, social insects such as ants, bees, or termites—there is a fundamental problem.

Individuals who have the ability and inclination to calculate what is good for themselves as individuals, or for themselves as part of a smaller grouping (family, religious sect, ethnic group, special trade or business) within the larger community (neighborhood, city, nation, international alliance), unavoidably generate a tension between the personal or partial or partisan interest and the interest of the society as a whole.

The conflict between private interests and the public interest is inevitable in any political society, no matter what its character or form of government; societies differ, however, sometimes strikingly, in the methods they use to cope with or forestall or eliminate this conflict.

Many political societies have tried to prevent or minimize the conflict of private interests and the public good by education or indoctrination. Some have used myths, such as that the original founders of the community all sprang from the native soil and, therefore, all of its citizens have an indissoluble bond of responsibility to each other as brothers; or that the ruler presides by some ancient act of divine designation and right and that obedience is, therefore, owed, as if to the gods. Others use a combination of force and organization along military lines to turn the whole society into a disciplined group resembling an army, so that the safety of each seems linked to the strength of the whole. Ancient Sparta, we learn from Plutarch, was made into such a society by a sudden and drastic land reform that eliminated inequalities of wealth; a currency reform, making lead the only legal tender, that made commerce and foreign trade impossible; and by a decree that everyone had to eat in military-style dining clubs, which ended the softening influences of mother, family, home, and kitchen. On this constitutional foundation, it was possible to make all Spartans think of themselves as soldiers who put the good of the city ahead of personal concerns. That Spartan regime overcame many enemies and lasted for more than 600 years.

Other societies have attempted to achieve a sense of public duty through indoctrination, patriotism, inculcating love of the fatherland through a teaching of the national or racial or religious superiority of the tribe or sect or city or nation. We are all familiar with the practice in our personal experience, both the advantages and the dangers, through related phenomena known as school spirit or team spirit or, in military units, *esprit de corps*. It almost invariably has two aspects: (1) a cohesion developed by a sense of common aspiration or a common danger or shared superiority or *something* to set this group off from all others as distinctive and exclusive; and (2) strong disapproval of concern for individual benefit at the expense of others in the group, and strong approval of group loyalty and personal sacrifice for the sake of the group.

And of course there are numerous examples of force and terror to bring about behavior that serves the group at the expense of personal comfort and safety, although, even in the most horrifying cases, force is usually combined with other efforts. In Nazi Germany, for example, assertion of personal rights at the expense of the national purpose was physically dangerous if not suicidal; but terror and force were not relied on alone. Relentless propaganda and indoctrination were frighteningly successful. Allegiance to the Nazi cause and to Hitler's leadership was not only strong, but fanatically so. The standard of citizen obligation was extraordinarily high, bestial though it was.

In a very different regime with different principles and aims, we have seen on television disciplined troops of Iranian men flagellating themselves with heavy chains to display their devotion on a special holy day to a leader and to a cause above self. In watching them and appraising the sight, one must keep in mind that to do what these groups were doing in such precise rhythmic unison surely took months of repetitive rehearsal, as is common in our military drill teams and high school cheerleading squads. In short, they must devote a significant part of their lives training to beat themselves with chains, not just one day a year. Such denial of self for a common cause is as impressive as it is frightening.

A willingness to subordinate private to public ends must be inculcated, one way or another, in any society. The results are often amazing. The self-denial of some peoples, their self-discipline or disciplined obedience to others, their selflessness, their devotion to a cause, their readiness to sacrifice their means and even their lives impress us and often win our admiration. And yet, keeping the preceding examples in mind, we must have doubts about the methods used and the purposes served. Those examples remind us that regimes frequently use abhorrent methods to overcome the disruptive force of selfish assertion of rights. We also see that regimes seek to form the character of their citizens to suit the way they want the society to be constituted, and that not all of the regimes are admirable or consistent with political freedom, to say the least.

Every society seeks to make good citizens. Good citizens are attentive to the good of the society as a whole; that is, they do their public duty. But as Aristotle pointed out long ago, good citizens are not necessarily good men. A good man will not be a good citizen in an evil regime. The most admirable human beings in Hitler's Germany and Brezhnev's Soviet Union are recognized as bad citizens and are treated accordingly by imprisonment, exile, or execution. Solzhenitsyn loved his homeland, but he was not a good Soviet citizen.

A good man has less trouble being a good citizen in a good regime, but as even the best of actual political societies will have flaws and make demands that require conformity, and will often be foolish and sometimes wicked, the better the man, the more reluctant and qualified his devotion must be to some of the demands of citizenship. And that observation brings us to the special difficulty that a *free* society has in dealing with the conflict of private rights and public duty.

It seems easier for a military regime to deal with this conflict or a fascist dictatorship or a dictatorship of the proletariat or a theocracy or a monarchy based on divine right. Each in its own way compels a certain behavior. But how can a free society proceed, especially one that is based on the *primacy* of the rights of the individual? Selfishness must be restrained or overcome in one way or another. Because the tendency to serve self-interest is strong, all regimes must find a way to cope with it; but other regimes do not have the problem faced by a liberal democracy because only the latter elevates the right to pursue self-interest to a fundamental principle of government.

Not all regimes go to the lengths of Mao's China or Khomeini's Iran in discouraging the pursuit of self-interest, but few also go out of their way to encourage that pursuit. Where the personal rights of life, liberty, property, and the pursuit of happiness are the starting point for all political thought and action, there is obviously a special problem of reconciling private rights and public duty.

SELF-PRESERVATION: THE FOUNDATION OF RIGHTS

What are natural rights and how do we know we have them? The doctrine of natural rights is based on a view of human nature and a theory of the origin of political society, and as political theories go it is a quite modern teaching. Ancient writers such as Plato and Aristotle did not speak about rights, although they thought and wrote about political matters in an extraordinarily comprehensive way. To the best of my knowledge the Bible does not speak of rights; as we would expect, biblical teachings, old and new, are concerned with our duties to God, not rights that we might claim.

The natural rights teachings of authors like Thomas

Hobbes, John Locke, and Jean-Jacques Rousseau start with a description of men as being naturally free, independent of each other, equal, and without government. In their book, man is not a citizen by nature, not a part of a *polis* or any political community by nature. Instead, the natural state of man is to be without government. Aristotle had said that it is not possible to be human outside of a *polis*; one would be a brute or a god, but not a man. That is the meaning of his assertion that man is a political animal. Political community, in that view, is a necessary condition for the full development of human qualities; without political community we are unfinished, less than human, unnaturally stunted, short of the natural human completion.

Hobbes, Locke, and Rousseau took man as being in his natural state outside civil society. Locke, for example, considering what the human condition would be in that state of nature, argued that men have certain natural rights that are theirs and cannot be taken away: life, principally; the liberty necessary to defend that life; and the property or means to sustain it. Life, liberty, and property are the basic natural rights. (It was Jefferson's innovation to add "the pursuit of happiness" to the list, although that phrase, too, was Locke's.) What makes these rights basic is that they all stem from the desire for self-preservation.

The desire for self-preservation is the most powerful human desire, according to Locke. You cannot be persuaded that you are doing wrong, no matter how far you go, if you are protecting yourself against unprovoked, violent, deadly attack. And if it is impossible to persuade you that it is wrong, you know you are right, you know you have the right to defend yourself even if you must kill an aggressor. The desire for self-preservation, private and basic, is the not-very-lofty source of human rights.

The consequences of this teaching, basic to the American

Constitution and to our advocacy of human rights, are manifold. The individual human being is naturally free and independent and only artificially a citizen. The natural state of man is to be free of any control to which he has not freely given his consent. All men are equal in their rights (because they are all equally desirous of self-preservation). Political society and government are legitimate only if the governed have consented to the limits imposed on individual freedom by law. And, finally, the powers of government are limited to those necessary to protect life, liberty, property, and the pursuit of happiness—and that means that there are many powers that are not truly *political* powers, that cannot legitimately be exercised unless it can be shown that doing so serves to secure the rights of the people.

These are the grounds for talking about natural rights, or human rights, or unalienable rights, or rights of any name. Societies based on notions of man as a citizen by nature—that is, the *polis* as the natural state of man—or by divine decree—that is, a theocracy that makes duty to God the principal source of law and society's institutions—may be superior to ours. They may nurture finer human qualities and more dutiful and more virtuous citizens, but in such societies it makes no sense to speak of the natural rights of the people. In such societies, a citizen is granted permission to act as necessary to perform his duties to state or church. What would be in a free society the right to read anything becomes in a *polis* or a theocracy a duty to read everything necessary to fulfill one's obligations to society and to read nothing that would interfere with those obligations.

A government or church that controls the reading material of citizens or church members of every rank may forbid most to read the very writings they require a few others to study with great care, so that all can think and do what is best for the well-being of the society as a whole, whether it be prosperity on earth or the salvation of eternal souls. The presumption against censorship does not exist in all societies, but only in those whose principle is the primacy of the individual and his basic rights. It may not be the loftiest platform for asserting the right of free speech, but it is a solid one, to argue that a man can rightly assume that rulers who want to silence him may be doing so because they have in mind to deprive him of his liberty and perhaps even of his life. The right to speak about issues that affect one's life, liberty, property, or happiness can also be traced back to the strongest desire—that of self-preservation.

PITTING RIGHTS AGAINST RIGHTS

The United States was the first nation explicitly founded on the principle of the primacy and equality of natural human rights, and the founders were aware that such a nation has a special problem in promoting the kind of dutiful citizenship necessary for justice, good order, and prosperity. The method they devised, through the Constitution, to encourage good citizenship was an innovation, a practical if not a theoretical one.

The theoretical problem is difficult in itself and intimidating. Simply stated, it comes down to this: if the rights of citizens are derived from the single most powerful human desire, then rights are natural and powerful. No one needs to be exhorted to exercise these basic natural rights. But looking at the other side of it, if political society is artificial, a man-made entity, and man is not a citizen by nature, then our sense of duty to that society is not natural and will not be powerful enough to stand in opposition to natural rights.

When it comes to pitting private rights versus public obligations, the outcome must be, inevitably, no contest in a society whose citizens are educated in the doctrines of natural rights and whose institutions reinforce these doctrines.

How can the undue exercise of private rights be restrained in a society based on the primacy of private rights? The "new science of politics," proclaimed by the authors of the Constitution in *The Federalist*, is forthright and direct: pit private rights against private rights, let "ambition counteract ambition." Only the desire to exercise one's rights is strong enough, in the free society they envisaged, to oppose and restrain the free—but socially dangerous—exercise of the rights of others. It is in this way, they said, that "the private interest of every individual may be a sentinel over the public rights."[1]

The American solution to the age-old conflict of private rights and public duties was not to speak of obligations, but to develop a certain character and behavior of citizens by designing a regime with institutions that encourage the pursuit of private advantage through public activity. The founders had in mind town councils, state legislatures, jury duty, voting for officials at local, state, and federal levels, lobbying, organizing of interest groups—all those activities that often make private-sector and public-sector activities almost indistinguishable and certainly inseparable. Experience in the exercise of political rights would habituate the self-seeking in-

---

[1]Alexander Hamilton, James Madison, and John Jay, *The Federalist*, ed. Clinton Rossiter (New York: New American Library, 1961), no. 51, p. 322. According to Locke, once a civil society is established it may be said to acquire a life of its own, and then, "acting according to its own nature," it acts for "the preservation of the community" (*Two Treatises of Government*, Book II, Section 149). In this way, the "public rights" Madison speaks of also have self-preservation as their rock-bottom starting point.

dividual in behavior that was moderate, considerate of others, conciliatory, civil, and compromising, very much like that of a truly public-spirited citizen. A man who firmly believes that "honesty is the best policy" and is honest in his dealings for the sake of policy rather than for the sake of honesty will be, in his visible actions and habits, indistinguishable from the man who is honest for the sake of honesty.

The American constitutional scheme, as described by Madison and others, does not seek to balance rights and duties, nor does it encourage talk about rights *versus* duties. Rights are too likely to win out in every such contest. Only rights have a sufficient natural power to counter rights successfully. The discourse of the founders is full of talk about the rights and interests of the people and of the community as a whole but nearly silent about duties, although most of them, admirably and honorably, some even gloriously, devoted themselves to public service at very considerable personal sacrifice and risk of time, money, health,and life itself. They made clear what they were risking when they pledged to each other, at the end of the Declaration of Independence, "our lives, our fortunes, and our sacred honor."

HOW ARE RIGHTS SECURED IN AMERICA?

If my argument is correct, the protection of rights has a double importance in this country and in any other similarly constituted: the exercise of our rights is essential not only to personal liberty but also to the common good. The power of individuals and groups to act freely in their own interest is a safeguard, perhaps the chief safeguard, ultimately, of the public interest.

How are rights best protected? The answer an American is most likely to give is, "by the Bill of Rights," or for many other countries, "by the power of world public opinion." I will examine both of these answers, but first it is important to observe that the question—what truly serves to protect our rights?—is rarely asked today. For some reason it is not considered to require serious thought. In contrast, it was considered a question of paramount importance by Madison, and some of his best writing was devoted to it. Much of the superficiality of human rights doctrine today and much of the futility of human rights activism are related, I think, to the failure to ask and to ponder seriously this question.

The *Federalist* papers were written in 1787–1788 as part of the effort to assure ratification of the new Constitution in the state of New York. They are a detailed commentary on the Constitution with one persistent theme: that the chief purpose of the government to be established under the Constitution is to secure the rights of the people. But we must remind ourselves that at the time these papers were being written the Constitution did not contain the Bill of Rights; it was added, as everyone knows, in 1791, as the first ten amendments to the Constitution. Madison, therefore, in writing on this subject in *The Federalist* (Number 51) could not have given the answer we would now tend to give—that the Bill of Rights is what secures the rights of the people. How was the argument made that the Constitution without the Bill of Rights secures the rights of the people?

In fact, in the body of the Constitution the word "right" occurs only once, in the provision known as the copyright and patent clause, and there it is clear that "the exclusive right" of authors and inventors to benefit from "their writings and discoveries" is not a natural right. In other words, the document that Madison claimed was designed to protect the rights of the citizens did not even mention such rights, let alone guarantee their free exercise.

Madison's answer to the question—what truly protects rights?—follows from the principles of a free society: that rights are primary, that only rights are strong enough to restrain and control rights, and that the public good is best served by the habits developed by citizens exercising their rights in opposition to other citizens doing the same. "In a free government," Madison says,

> the security for civil rights must be the same as that for religious rights. It consists in the one case in the multiplicity of interests, and in the other in the multiplicity of sects. The degree of security in both cases will depend on the number of interests and sects.[2]

Madison later became the chief author of the First Amendment and would now no doubt agree with us that it is a powerful force in protecting our civil and religious rights; yet I doubt that he would modify his argument that the more interest groups we have and the more religious sects we have, the more security there is for civil and religious liberty. He might contend that the First Amendment continues to be effective in protecting rights, though similar provisions are ineffective in other countries, in large part because of the multiplicity of American interest groups and religious sects. He might even argue that one of the most important consequences of the First Amendment has been the encouragement it affords to the increase in the number of interest groups and religious sects. And he might add that even with the First Amendment religious freedom would be in great jeopardy in this country, as in many others, if at some time *any* religious sect became dominant.

[2]*The Federalist,* no. 51, p.324.

Much of the design of the institutions established under the Constitution has as its aim multiplying the interests and allowing them to assert themselves. The scheme of representation, for example, gives voice to a tremendous diversity of interests, giving them every chance to compete and yet making it difficult, if not impossible, for one to dominate as a persisting majority.

There is little that is morally satisfying in this formulation. Madison had no illusions, for instance, about disinterested congressmen with nothing in their minds but the common interest. We all know that it is wrong for any man to judge in his own cause, but, Madison asked, "what are the different classes of legislators but advocates and parties to the causes which they determine?"[3] There may be forces of moral excellence or religious restraint seeking to protect our rights, but we cannot rely on them. There is, in fact, the opposite assumption: that Americans are human beings and not angels, and when given the chance they are very likely to take advantage of others and violate their rights.

Even with our doctrine of the primacy of rights, the Constitution, the Bill of Rights, the separation of powers and federalism, the multiplicity of interests and sects, the whole history of American legislation and litigation—federal, state, and local—is nevertheless one long procession of groups and individuals struggling to deprive other groups and individuals of their rights. The best we can say for ourselves, and it is indeed a lot to say, is that our principles, laws, and institutions are almost all arrayed on the side of securing rights and against the efforts to violate them. In that struggle what we have been habituated to rely on is not a disinterested self-restraint but the energetic pursuit of self-interest by oth-

[3]*The Federalist*, no. 10, p. 79.

ers, if they are equally free, and the clash of interests and ambitions where there are enough competitors and none with an overwhelming and persisting concentration of power.

The expectation is that the clash of interests and ambitions will be guided, constrained, and ultimately transformed by the regular procedural channels that have been established by the Constitution for passing, executing, and interpreting the laws of the land. Those procedural pathways force some sort of mutual accommodation among the crudest forms of interest and ambition, and over time such accommodation, compromise, and mutual consideration become habitual. The result is behavior distinguishable from but very similar to that of restrained, considerate, public-spirited citizens.

The adequacy of such a citizenry to meet every test is doubtful. Patriotism, obviously, can be relied on only when the public danger is great enough to affect all or most private concerns, as when the nation is attacked by powerful enemies. But the response to a peacetime draft will be doubtful, that is, to demands for personal sacrifice when the national danger is neither clear nor present. And in matters less immediate than military danger, such as the energy shortage, it seems clear that for Americans there is no moral equivalent of war; energy conservation is the result of economic causation, not moral exhortation.

No lover of liberty should be willing to repeal the First Amendment, but we should be clear that by itself it cannot protect our rights of religion, speech, press, assembly, and petition. The Soviet Constitution, to give only one example of scores of constitutions that could be cited, has a list of rights that includes all those in the Bill of Rights and many, many more, and in addition *guarantees* those rights in a way that our Constitution does not attempt; yet we know that the exercise of the rights of religion, speech, press, petition, and assembly in the Soviet Union is very insecure if not non-existent.

Words on paper cannot secure rights unless they are buttressed by a certain ordering of the institutions, the society, and the economy of the nation. The written Constitution must correspond to the way the nation is truly constituted. If it does not, its protections of rights are a mere "parchment barrier," easily shredded by malevolent (or even by benevolent) forces. In any nation where there is a tremendous concentration of economic and political power and no diversity of interests and religious sects, the most that can be hoped for in human rights is a few minor concessions in individual cases when, for one reason or another of policy, it suits the advantage of those in power to make those concessions. But there can be no internal basis for security of rights—and exhortation or moral fervor will be ineffective. Madison put the point this way: "We well know that neither moral nor religious motives can be relied on as an adequate control."[4] He urged instead the "policy of supplying by opposite and rival interests, the defect of better motives."[5]

THE DANGER OF LINKING RIGHTS AND DUTIES

A free political society based on the primacy of rights cannot be fully satisfying to those whose hopes are for a nation founded on the loftiest principles and devoted to the development of the finest qualities of human nature. But even those who feel these lacks most keenly have no choice but to reconcile themselves to the sad fact that it is not just the United

[4]*The Federalist*, no. 10, p. 81.
[5]*The Federalist*, no. 51, p. 322.

States, not just the western liberal democracies, but modernity in its full flowering, with its roots in the Renaissance, that puts us in the position I have described.

We do not have a choice between our natural-rights doctrine and some other kinds of government based on ancient teachings of virtue, justice, and nobility characteristic of political philosophy before Machiavelli. The choice is limited either to what we and other liberal democracies have—a great degree of political liberty for most citizens, along with material prosperity (despite present ups and downs) unprecedented in the history of the world—or the alternatives that we see about us in a hostile and hateful world—Marxist dictatorships, military dictatorships, racist regimes, underdeveloped economies suffering in unspeakable ignorance and penury, theocratic tyrannies, and so on in a long catalog of political, economic, and social horrors.

At some point in the course of our long list of complaints about the undoubted defects of our political, economic, social, and moral institutions and principles we must eventually face up to the vulgar but sobering question: Compared to what? On the very question of this essay—the linking of citizen duties to private rights as a means of restraining and civilizing the ceaseless clashing, struggling, striving to outdo each other, the din, clamor and turmoil—could we not try *something* to strengthen our sense of duty, of obligation to our fellow citizens and to society as a whole? Why can't we at least try to imagine a constitution that would do that?

For instance, to return to the homely example I began with, is it really out of the question that in our Constitution, or somewhere, we could not say that it is the policy of this people that "children are obliged to show concern for their parents and to help them"? And to deal with the suffering of people who cannot find a place to live, guarantee them the right to housing, and at the same time to deal with one of the abuses that is so evident in all of our cities, provide that "citizens must take good care of the housing allocated to them?" And since there are, similarly, two major problems having to do with employment, on the one hand so many who cannot find a job and on the other hand so many who do not conscientiously look for a job, why not proclaim that "citizens have the right to labor—that is, to receive guaranteed work and remuneration" and tie it to the duty of working in "socially useful activity"?

To assure basic freedoms and at the same time try to restrain irresponsible excesses of the mass media, we could consider, although it might be going too far, linking "guaranteed freedom of speech, of the press, of assembly" and so on to the duty of using those rights only "in accordance with the people's interests and for the purpose of strengthening and developing" the system of government. But instead, perhaps we could devise a briefer and more comprehensive provision and not go into so many details—something like, "The exercise of rights and liberties is inseparable from the performance by citizens of their duties."

If those are all things we believe in, why not put them down in law and see if that does not have the same constructive and formative effect in making the citizenry duties-conscious that our centuries-long emphasis on rights has so obviously had in making us rights-conscious?

At this point, any attentive reader should suspect that some sort of trick is being offered and ought to remind himself of the advice given in the beginning of this essay that questions about linking rights and duties should not be answered, certainly not hastily. Yes, all of the suggested provisions for an "imagined" constitution explicitly linking duties and rights are quoted directly from the new Soviet Constitution of 1977.[6] For several reasons, it would be unreasonable to reject them simply because they come from an unsavory source. Many good ideas and principles are incorporated in bad contexts and do not change their nature when removed from that context, but their virtues become more visible. A diamond lying in a heap of dung is not garbage even while it lies in the village dump; but it is more likely to be seen to be just what it is, a precious gem, when it is removed.

The Constitution of the United States enumerates very few rights, and they are in the amendments. The Soviet Constitution enumerates all of the most familiar rights—of press, speech, assembly, religion—and many more: the rights to labor, rest, health care, material security in old age, housing, education, the use of cultural achievements, participation in public affairs, and to criticize state agencies. Not only are these rights enumerated, they are guaranteed. For example:

> USSR citizens have the right to labor—that is, to receive guaranteed work and remuneration for labor in accordance with its quantity and quality and not below the minimum amount established by the state. . . . This right is ensured by the socialist economic system, [and] the steady growth of productive forces.[7]

Implicit in a guarantee of a job to every citizen, if it is at all meaningful, is the necessity for the state to control the labor market, both the supply of jobs and the supply of workers for every kind of job. No president of the United States can honestly "guarantee" a job to every citizen (although such wording is increasingly found in our legislation and regulations), because he does not have enough control over the economy and the labor force and hiring and firing by millions

---

[6]*The New Soviet Constitution of 1977: Analysis and Text,* analysis by Robert Sharlet (Brunswick, Ohio: King's Court Communications, 1978), pp. 89–96.
[7]Ibid., p. 89.

of different employers. Behind the guarantee of a job to every citizen in the Soviet Union is the fact that there is really only one employer and that is the state. In the United States and in other similar nations there is a multiplicity of interests, industries, and employers all making independent decisions about hiring and firing on the basis of self-interest—that is, trying to earn a return on investment rather than on the basis of a government's judgment of what constitutes "socially useful activity."

This is a very great difference. When Alger Hiss was released from prison he was not a popular figure with the government or with the general public, but he found a job as an executive in a small company producing women's hair ornaments. Of the more than fifteen million independent enterprises in the United States, there is likely to be at least one with whom even a convicted perjurer can find employment. But in the Soviet Union, where there is only one employer, if a citizen has a falling out with that boss his plight is hopeless.

But let us keep our logic straight: the fact that there is but one employer in the Soviet Union is not the result of a guarantee of a job in the Soviet Constitution. It is the other way around: the fact that there is only one employer, the state, makes it honest and possible to guarantee a job to every citizen. Add to this that there is only one schoolmaster (guaranteed education for every citizen), only one landlord (guaranteed housing for every citizen), only one owner of travel agencies, resorts, and sports facilities (guaranteed rest and recreation for every citizen), and one begins to sense the sinister implications of a long list of constitutionally guaranteed rights of citizens. If a citizen somehow offends the only boss, the only landlord, the only schoolmaster, where will he work, where will he live, where will he be able to study?

If the list is long enough and the guarantees strong
enough, the result is a tremendous accretion of power in the
hands of the state, the source of these guaranteed rights. We
in the United States are in the habit of speaking of the First
Amendment as guaranteeing our rights of religion, speech,
press, and so on, but as a matter of fact that is inaccurate,
and dangerously so. The wording is strikingly different from
a guarantee of rights: "Congress shall make no law . . . prohibiting the free exercise" of religion or "abridging the freedom of speech." The negative formulation is a careful denial
of powers to the Congress, not a grant of powers. Furthermore, the list of rights that Congress cannot prohibit, abridge,
or infringe is very short, and all are basic. The concern was,
obviously, just as Madison argued in *The Federalist*:

> In framing a government which is to be administered by
> men over men, the great difficulty lies in this: you must
> first enable the government to control the governed; and
> in the next place oblige it to control itself.[8]

If great concentrations of power are placed in the hands of
the government, enough effectively to guarantee every citizen
housing, a job, education of every sort, and many other guarantees as well, nothing will be powerful enough to "oblige"
the government "to control itself"—and *that* is the obligation
about which we should be most concerned if we care about
liberty.

Linking duties to rights by law goes along well with long
lists of rights and guarantees of them. The rights enumerated
in the Soviet Constitution are clearly seen as gifts bestowed
on the citizens by the state. The Constitution is generous in
giving rights to the citizens, and so it seems appropriate that
there be a just price to pay for each beneficence. For the guar-

[8]*The Federalist*, no.51, p. 322.

anteed right to a job, the duty to do useful work; for the guaranteed right to "well-appointed housing" and "low apartment rents," the duty to take good care of the housing; for the guaranteed right to freedoms of speech and press, the duty to use them "in accordance with the people's interests and for the purpose of strengthening and developing the socialist system."

But rights as we Americans understand them, natural rights, are not given to us by the state. We have them, as we have life, independent of any gift from the state. We consent to be governed on the understanding that we have entrusted no power to the state to abridge those rights. We owe nothing to the state for those rights because we did not get them from the state. The gratitude and sense of duty we may feel to the society as a whole is not so much related to our rights as to all of the other sources of patriotic sentiments, which are many and powerful. But to the extent that they are related to rights, it is not for giving us the rights, but instead for helping to protect them.

The connecting of duties to rights has the following implications: that rights are bestowed by the state, which is wrong; that enjoyment of rights can be made conditional on the performance of duties and still be rights (mine *by right*, not by someone's concession), which is wrong; and that if duties are not performed, the rights can be withdrawn and still be spoken of as rights, which is wrong.

In short, connecting duties to rights under law is charging a price for something the state never owned, a form of selling stolen goods. As citizens we have many duties—to obey the laws, to pay our taxes, to defend the country—but however we regard these duties and however we encourage their performance, it is a grave mistake to link them to the enjoyment of our rights. When duties are linked to rights by law, the rights are not just weakened, they cease to be rights as our constitutional system understands them and as we have always advocated them.

CONCLUSION

We Americans are concerned, and rightly so, about the growth of the seemingly endless and insatiable claims of rights that all parts of the citizenry want to have satisfied. At the same time, a sense of service, of duty, of concern for the rights of others, of willingness to make even small sacrifices now for the sake of the general good later—all these seem to be weak and atrophying. But in our longing for a better balance, for an improvement in *esprit* and devotion to the American cause, we must be wary of false remedies that will only make the malady, such as it is, worse.

The American scheme that has served us well, when we have understood and used it well, is fundamentally moderate and antiutopian. We are not angels and we do not live in heaven. It is a special kind of present-day heresy to act as if our proper goal and expectation is to make a heaven on earth. Those who think so, consciously or not, run terrible risks—no less terrible for being unaware—of committing foul crimes against mankind at the worst, and of losing our liberties for us at the least.

We have the liberties we now enjoy and have enjoyed for almost 200 years because the founders knew the dangers of seeking guarantees for things—beautiful, highly desirable things—that cannot be guaranteed by "a government administered by men over men," that is, not by angels over angels. The effort to guarantee the full, total, complete, unblemished fulfillment of freedom, prosperity, and dutifulness will lead not to that success, but to the great concentrations of power in the hands of tyrants that *we see* in every country where the effort has been made.

The vice of greed is not limited to material things. There is also what might be called "moral greed,"[9] and its effects can be deadly, fatal to liberty, decency, restraint, and moderation. The alternative to the greedy pursuit of an unearthly perfection of protection of every right for every person, and assurance of a strong sense of dutifulness in all of us, is a willingness to accept imperfection—because this earth is imperfect, and we human beings are imperfect, and imperfection and incompleteness and partial success/partial failure are our proper lot until we shuffle off.

Moral greed is one vice our Founding Fathers did not suffer from, or suffer in others. Their whole founding effort was a rejection of that vice and a search, instead, for principles and institutions that would benefit, as much as possible, from human frailties that they did not much admire, but that they thought were so prevalent that one might better try to turn them to the benefit of mankind rather than try to eradicate them. For they knew from careful study and reflection on the political history of mankind up to their own time that human vice, weakness, and ugliness can be totally eradicated only by eradicating great masses of unoffending people.

Instead of seeking to establish a heaven on earth, they sought to make life freer, more decent, more comfortable, safer, and, for most people, happier. We trifle with those goals only at incredible peril. We already have a credo very well suited to "hard times," and we should not abandon it.

[9]I first heard the phrase "moral greed" from Lady Jacqueline Wheldon, the English novelist and playwright.

Chapter 6 / LAW AND THE LEGISLATION OF MORALITY

A. D. WOOZLEY

THE MYTH OF "MERE MORAL WRONGS"

There is an old saying that subjecting us to law cannot make us good, but can prevent us from behaving badly. Like many epigrams, that one is too clever by half—indeed, I think, by each half; for each of the two assertions that it makes is, I suspect, false. It assumes a ready distinction between what we are and what we do, and it implies that it cannot be among the tasks of the law to make us morally better people, because it *cannot* make us morally better; all it can do by its requirements, prescribing some conduct and prohibiting others, is to make our actions conform to its rules. And this assumption leads naturally to the view that it is the function of our law, as enforced and applied by police and courts, to criticize and chastise us, not for our moral failings, but for our conduct

A. D. WOOZLEY ● University Professor of Philosophy and Law, 521 Cabell Hall, University of Virginia, Charlottesville, Virginia 22903.

which is, or risks being, in one way or another a danger to society. This view forms one of the themes of a recent book, in which the author argues that crimes are not punished as moral wrongs, for (as an example) burglary is rightly punished as a serious crime, although it is only a minor moral wrong, and "mere moral wrongs are regarded by the criminal law as none of its business."[1] It is a view that may seem naturally to go along with legal positivism, the theory that laws are valid if and only if they have been made by whatever is the correct procedure, legislative and/or judicial, for the society whose laws they are; and it seems to be correspondingly opposed to the theory of natural law, according to which the validity of law is extralegal, deriving its authority from God or from the dictates of reason or from the nature of man.

Here I support the position of legal positivism, but not also the separation of law and morals, for that is not a consequence of the theory. It is logically possible for a society to have a legal system that does not in any way protect or promote what is morally valuable, or even the society's own moral values, but for that to be the case the society would have to be either under the tyranny of a stern dictatorship or in a state of chaos. In a representative democracy of any degree of civilization, law and morality cannot be unrelated; at the very least, if we accept the authority of law and are not merely subservient to it, the idea of morality is involved. The idea that the failings for which the law punishes us, and against which it legislates, are not moral failings rests on an unreflective prejudice about the nature of morality; some moral wrongs may be better not made the subject of legislation and adjudication, but nothing could be a *mere* moral wrong. The

[1]Hyman Gross, *A Theory of Criminal Justice* (New York: Oxford University Press, 1979), pp. 16–17.

trouble stems from the way we are brought up as children, and are subsequently conditioned as adults, which is to accept that questions of morals are limited by the field and scope of something called morality, instead of seeing that it must be the other way around, that the field and scope of morality are determined by the questions of morals. It is striking for how many of us "morality" refers to sexual morality; and the question whether and how far the law should concern itself with morality is often taken to be a question asking what the law should do about prostitution, homosexuality, and pornography, with possibly a look at the civil law on marital infidelity and divorce. That is an absurdly narrow and obsessive view of morality, and yet it tells us something, namely, that morality has for its principal concern relationships between people, which can be general or special. General relationships are those that we have to others as members of a class, as citizens, colleagues, users of the highway, consumers of limited resources, and so on. Special relationships are those that we have to others as individuals, as one's mother, wife, son, business partner. And sexual relationships are those special relationships where the nerve endings are most exposed, so that it is natural to think of sexual morality when we hear the question whether the law should concern itself with, and legislate for, morality. It is natural but wrong, because the good treatment and the bad treatment that people can give out to each other is far wider than that. Furthermore, people are not the only beings that people treat badly. What people should be allowed to do to animals in farming (especially as farming turns into agribusiness) and in scientific and medical experimentation is nothing if not a moral question; and it is something of a disgrace to our society that the law has so far bothered itself with that so little. Refusing to see it as a question is reflected in the branding as sentimentalists of those who do raise it. I am not suggesting that the treatment of animals is the most important area of morality, only that it is one, and therefore one in respect of which we should not be leaving our conscience in the hands of professional experts. I have made this reference to nonhuman animals not in order to stir up a hornets' nest, nor in order to air some bees, but because I believe questions of morals are far too much thought of (especially in this country) as questions of *rights*, and not nearly enough as questions of duty or, better still, of sensitivity. If we thought more in terms of How can we (or, if it is more comfortable, How can they) treat people like that? and, How can the law let them do it?, human and nonhuman animals might not appear as so widely separated concerns of morality.

The simple answer to the question whether the law should legislate morality is, *Why not?* but as simple answers have a way of being misunderstood, it must be made more complex. What it will come to is that, if the legislators are doing their job responsibly at all, they cannot avoid legislating morality. There is a widely held view that the law should not concern itself with morality, or, we can more clearly say here, immorality, unless what is immoral is also something else—something else that probably *is* the business of the law, such as the preservation of public order or safety, or the protection of individuals from harm. And a very clear example of this view is to be found in what is generally known in this country, as in England, as the Wolfenden Report, the English Report of the Committee on Homosexual Offences and Prostitution, 1957.[2] The following quotations from the report bear this out:

> In this field, the criminal law's function, as we see it, is
> to preserve public order and decency, to protect the cit-

[2]London, HMSO, Cmd. 247.

izen from what is offensive or injurious, and to provide sufficient safeguards against exploitation and corruption of others. . . . It is not, in our view, the function of the law to intervene in the private lives of citizens, or to seek to enforce any particular pattern of behaviour, further than is necessary to carry out the purposes we have outlined. (paras. 13–14)

. . . the argument which we believe to be decisive, namely the importance which society and the law ought to give to individual freedom of choice in matters of private morality. (para. 61)

It is not the duty of the law to concern itself with immorality as such. . . . It should confine itself to those activities which offend against public order and decency or expose the ordinary citizen to what is offensive or injurious. (para. 257)

It is unfortunate that Lord Devlin, in very properly attacking the confusions of thought about law and morality that ran through the committee's recommendations, contributed so many more confusions of his own that subsequent discussion has been distracted by them from what might better have been its main target.[3] The committee got itself into a muddle by stressing private morality, and then using two quite different notions of it: (1) conduct that, being neither injurious nor offensive to others, should be none of the law's business, and (2) conduct that is performed in private. And this separation made it easier for the committee to suppose that there was something that it was referring to in phrases such as "immorality as such." Running through the report is the pre-

---

[3]Patrick Devlin, "The Enforcement of Morals," in *Proceedings of the British Academy*, vol. xlv, reprinted with other lectures in *The Enforcement of Morals* (London: Oxford University Press, 1965, paperback 1968). Cf. Richard Wollheim, "Crime, Sin and Mr. Justice Devlin," *Encounter*, November 1959; H. L. A. Hart, *Law, Liberty and Morality* (London: Oxford University Press, 1963, paperback 1968); Ronald Dworkin, *Taking Rights Seriously*, rev. ed. (Cambridge: Harvard University Press, 1978) Ch. 10.

supposition that what is immoral can be recognized and identified as immoral independently of its being recognized or judged to have any other characteristics. From there the argument proceeds: conduct that is immoral may or may not have the further characteristic of being harmful to others; if it does, it becomes the legitimate concern of the law; if it does not, it does not become the legitimate concern of the law.

Now surely the belief that what is immoral can be simply identified as immoral is an instance of erroneous abstraction. What is immoral is what is morally wrong, and what is morally wrong is what is wrong, or not to be done, in a way that is not the proper way to treat the objects (or subjects) of our concern. Moral wrong is to be contrasted both with other coordinate wrongs, such as prudential wrong, legal wrong, economic wrong, and so on, and with the superordinate premoral wrong. On a road that is in a 25-mph zone it is legally wrong to drive at 35 mph, and it is prudentially wrong too, if there is a police patrol there with a radar detector: that is not the way to drive there, if you care about avoiding trouble with the police. If you are trying to make an omelette, using a low heat is the wrong way of doing it—you will, at best, end up with scrambled eggs. The Wrong Way signs posted at the exit of a one-way street, for example, at the bottom of an exit ramp from an interstate highway, are posted there to tell us that that is not the direction to drive in in that street or onto that interstate. In all those cases, and in the many and various other cases that could be added, we are being given reasons for not doing the thing called wrong; at the least we are being told that there is a reason, and we may also be being told what the reason is. If we are told that the government's monetary policy is economically wrong, we may not be being told what the reason is for criticizing it, but we are being told that there is a reason, probably having to do with lack of accordance between economic tactics and economic aim. In every case something is presupposed as wanted or aimed at. Moral wrongs are often thought of as different from all others, and in a special class by themselves, on the ground that they do not depend on wants or aims: they just are wrong in themselves. Such a view has the authority of Kant behind it, but is none the better for that. What is morally wrong depends on what is premorally chosen, accepted, or presupposed as positively or negatively valuable. If we see rational beings (as Kant did) as ends in themselves, we provide a premoral presupposition for our moral judgments of what we ought or ought not to do to creatures who are rational beings. If we find that too narrow a base for morality, because it excludes not only all (or almost all) nonhuman animals, but also among humans the infantile, the senile, the mentally sick, and the mentally retarded—each of whom fails in one way or another as much as, if not more than, a working dog to be a rational animal, but all of whom we think of as proper objects of our moral concern—then we are giving our morality a presupposition of wider scope.

That our premoral presupposition is at least wide enough to range over all human beings is, I think, undisputed; and for the purpose of the present discussion I need not make it wider. It has not always been so and is not everywhere so now. There is not a single, universal attitude toward the plight of the Vietnamese boat people. Although their reasons are quite different, the Arab governments of the Middle East and the Israeli government share an unconcern for the lives of the Palestinian refugees. And in this country we are able to accept the servitude of the itinerant fruit pickers by, like the Germans and the death camps, "not knowing" that they are there. But, in general, it can be said that in this society, despite our human frailty in ignoring what does not stare us in the face, we do believe that people matter; it comes out in our obsessive preoccupation with our own rights, when we think they are under challenge; it comes out, rather more creditably, in our reaction to the plight of an elderly couple facing the demand of a real estate broker for $10,000 if they are to recover the house that they lost to him for the nonpayment of a $3 tax.

Conduct is morally wrong when it is inimical to the interests, or rather the legitimate interests, of human beings and the institutions devised for the better living of their lives; whether an interest is a legitimate interest is determined by the culture of the society concerned. And conduct is morally wrong, not just *when* it is so inimical, but *as being* so inimical. That is why we can never properly speak of something as being "a *mere* moral wrong," as though something could be a moral wrong, but not also something else in virtue of which it was a moral wrong. A visitor from Mars with 20/20 vision, high intelligence, and keen powers of observation, but no knowledge at all of our society's traditions and patterns of human relations—as members of our family, as colleagues, teachers, pupils, customers, clients, neighbors, friends, and so on indefinitely—could not begin to see the moral qualities that we see in the conduct he observed. We cannot see abortion as a moral problem at all if we do not see that there is a question whether aborting a fetus is in some sense putting an end to a human life. Cross-town school busing, reverse discrimination, and so on are moral problems only because of what they do to (a) people who come out well and (b) people who come out badly by the use of them. We have to have opinions about the nonmoral facts of a situation—and it is better that we have knowledge, where possible, than that we have opinions—if we are to make moral judgments about them.

If the scope of morality is (at least) the range of what is helpful or harmful to the legitimate interests of human beings, then for any society that we can seriously consider—and it is best to consider our own, as the one we know best—it is impossible that law should not concern itself with morality. For, whatever our theory of law may be, we can hardly disagree that a prime function, if not indeed *the* function, of law is to regulate life in society by prescribing what is helpful and proscribing what is harmful to the interests of the society's members and their institutions.

Space does not allow me to give the notion of being harmful the elucidation that a full treatment would demand, but I wish to be understood to be using "harmful" in a wide way, to cover not only what does harm, not only also what risks or is likely to do harm, but in addition what is intended to do harm. It is important to keep this last in mind when discussing law, because (a) all criminal offenses, with the exception of a fortunately limited range of strict liability offenses, require intent, either general or specific; and (b) a person can be, and very properly so, guilty of an offense even though his conduct did no harm to any person or thing, even though there was, in the circumstances of his action, no likelihood, or even possibility, of its doing harm. It should not be forgotten that it is not only in our extralegal, so-called moral judgments that people are criticized for acting with intent to do harm, irrespective of whether through incompetence, bad judgment, interference, or sheer bad luck they do not succeed, and maybe could not have succeeded, in doing it.

If there could be a society in which there was absolutely no criminal prohibition of homicide, it would not be one in which any of us would choose to live. A society that made lawful the killing of anybody over the age of eighty might not seem morally attractive to us, but we can see how there could be a reason for it. But a society in which there are no limitations at all on the killing of anybody is one that we could

not accept. And in this country, in which the legal limitations
on killing are extensive and numerous, the shortcoming that
the police have the generous license to kill that they do have
is surely a moral shortcoming. Our grounds for wanting killing, injuring, raping, burning, robbing, swindling, and so on
proscribed by criminal law are moral grounds, namely, that
not to have the proscriptions, or not to have them enforced
and applied with a reasonable degree of efficacy, is to reduce
the quality of life for some, most, or all members of society.
It is no more the moral failing of a society that it tolerates the
open display of pornography and all the gimmickry of the sex
trade than that it tolerates the bullying and robbing of the
feeble elderly the moment that they have cashed their social
security checks. If our criminal laws cannot be justified on
moral grounds, then ultimately there can be no grounds on
which they can be justified at all.

THE MORAL AIM OF LAW

It might be objected that a legal system does not need to have
moral aims, for it is easy enough to imagine a society the aims
of which were those of strict mutual self-interest, and the
laws of which were designed, enforced, and applied solely
on a basis of enlightened prudence. Indeed such a society is
imaginable, although whether it could last long enough to
have a history is questionable; Plato made that point long ago
(*Republic* 351 d–e), the point caught in the maxim about the
need for honor among thieves. Again, if we turn from an
imaginable to an actual and observable society, that is, our
own, we find a striking illustration of the moral aim of law. A
society whose laws were designed solely to protect and promote the interests of, as it were, the existing members, even

if it could not avoid, as Plato thought it could not, acknowledging moral claims between members, clearly could avoid acknowledging moral claims of nonmembers against members; if foreigners were legally permitted to enter and reside in such a society, it could be the case that they were permitted to live there only on the basis of their usefulness to the citizens; they would have no rights, and whatever protection the laws gave them, which could be considerable, would be what contributed to the welfare of the citizens. In the same classification with foreigners would fall indigenous noncitizens (such as the American Indian here) and nonfree noncitizens. Plato's own Athens is an example of a society comprised of just such a range of elements; fortunately for us, who are its legatees, it is not also an example of a society dedicated entirely to the principle of self-help. A purely self-help society *might* have no conception of a morality at all, but, if Plato is right, it would have a restricted one, what we might call a citizen morality; what it would not have would be a human morality, which is what I have been meaning, and will continue to mean, by the unqualified word "morality."

The contrast between that society and our own is illuminating. When the American colonists broke away from England and set themselves up as an independent political society, the aim of enlightened self-interest and of self-help was understandably conspicuous. What is also conspicuous is the moral basis for the evolution of American law provided by the terms of the Constitution. In the first ten amendments, comprising the original Bill of Rights, *citizens* are not mentioned at all; the rights conferred by the amendments are conferred as constitutional rights on everybody, citizens and noncitizens alike. It is "the people" who have the right "peacefully to assemble," "to keep and bear arms," "to be secure . . . against unreasonable searches and seizures," and so on. The trial rights enumerated in the Fifth and Sixth Amendments are everybody's; "no person shall be held to answer . . ."; "in all criminal prosecutions the accused shall enjoy the right to a speedy and public trial . . ." In later amendments "citizen" does occasionally occur, but only (1) in the definition of citizenship, and (2) in amendments concerning electoral law. For my present topic the most interesting items are the due process and equal protection clauses of the Fourteenth Amendment. Immediately juxtaposed to a prohibition about American citizens, "no State shall make or enforce any law which shall abridge the privileges or immunities of citizens of the United States," stands "nor shall any State deprive any person of life, liberty or property without due process of law; nor deny to any person within its jurisdiction the equal protection of the laws." What this clause does is not only to give to the individual state rights corresponding to the federal rights of the Fifth and Sixth Amendments, but also to make it quite explicit that the individuals are not just those who are members of the club, citizens of the United States, but are anybody at all within the jurisdiction of the legal system concerned. A society whose legal system is required by its constitution to treat noncitizens in the same way as citizens is a society that officially acknowledges that laws are to be justified on moral grounds, on what they do for and to everybody subject to the authority and power of the society's government—or, in this case, plurality of governments.

If the function (or a principal function) of law is to protect the lives, liberties, and quality of life of those within the jurisdiction, and if it is to do so by regulating, to the extent that it is necessary, and subject to the constraints of the practically and reasonably possible, the conduct of those subject to it, then there is nothing in the whole range of human conduct that we can say a priori is not the law's business. There is plenty that we can argue should not be allowed to be the law's business, because it can more efficiently or less interferingly be dealt with otherwise, but there is nothing from which the law can properly be excluded on the ground that it is a purely moral matter. The fallacy that there can be something that is a moral matter but not also a possibly legitimate concern of the law is a fallacy underlying the thinking in the Wolfenden Report. In a paragraph from which I have already quoted (257), the committee agrees that "from the moral point of view there may be little or nothing to choose between the prostitute and her customer," and that, if it were right for the law to punish prostitution on the ground that it is immoral conduct, "then it would be right that it should provide for the punishment of the man as well as the woman." But in the opinion of the committee the antecedent clause in that hypothetical proposition is not fulfilled, for

> it is not the duty of the law to concern itself with immorality as such. . . . It should confine itself to those activities which offend against public order and decency or expose the ordinary citizen to what is offensive or injurious.

Such a passage could only be written by, or subscribed to by, one who has succumbed to argument by clichés. If by "immorality as such" is meant what can be objected to, with no reasons to be given, then there can be no immorality as such. If that is not meant, then what is immoral as such is what is immoral as being in some way harmful to some human being(s), or to the life of or relationships between human beings; and anything that is that is at least a candidate for the law's interest. If it is right that the law should not punish prostitution as such, it must be so either because there is no harm in prostitution as such (or not enough harm to go beyond the maxim *de minimis non curat lex*), or because on a cost–benefit calculation the costs of punishing it outweigh the benefits. If it is right that the law should punish the street-walking and soliciting activities of prostitutes, it must be so only because the harm to public order and so on is sufficient to justify the law's intervention; it is so only because the streetwalking and solicitation are sufficiently immoral. If the immorality of prostitution is *not* thought to be a good enough reason for making it criminal, then the question might be thought to arise whether public soliciting by prostitution should not be as much protected by the principle of free speech as supposedly is the public soliciting by Hare Krishna people who make themselves a nuisance to us in our airports.

There are many who would object to that line of argument, on the ground that to agree that the law does have moral aims as its concern is to concede to it a right to what could easily become a terrifying power of interference in our lives. Professor H. L. A. Hart has written warningly of what he sees as a revival of legal moralism in England.[4] Hart wrote in response to the use in a notorious case in 1961[5] of Lord Mansfield's dictum of 1774 that the Court of the King's Bench was the guardian of "public manners" and had the power, indeed the duty, of restraining and punishing "whatever is *contra bonos mores et decorum*."[6] The reaffirmation that there still was a common-law offense of corrupting public morals, with a corresponding one of conspiring to corrupt public morals,

---

[4]Hart, pp. 6–12.
[5]*Shaw* v. *D.P.P.* 1962 2 All E.R. 446.
[6]*Jones* v. *Randall* 98 Eng. Rep. 706, 707 (1774).

understandably produced shudders in many others besides Professor Hart. But what was objectionable about that decision, and the avenues that it opened for future courts, was not that it allowed the law (or confirmed that the law still was allowed) to concern itself with morality, but that the offense of corrupting public morals was so ill defined (as indeed it is) that on the one hand it deprived the subject of the ability to determine with reasonable certainty whether or not conduct that he was contemplating was criminal, and on the other hand it virtually licensed a jury to determine ex post facto any conduct at all to be corrupting of public morals if it saw fit to do so. However, a proposition is not shown to be false by pointing out the alarming consequences that may, or even probably will, follow from its being accepted as true. That the decision in *Shaw* was a bad one, for the reasons that Professor Hart and others have given, does not show that the view of the law's function on which it was based was incorrect. What it does show is that the relation between law and morality needs to be much better understood than it is, and in particular that when the charge is that of corrupting public morals, it should not be regarded as an open hunting license for juries to go after any quarries to which their moral hunches lead them. Wherever corrupting is an essential element in an offense, there is that danger, because the notion of corrupting is so unclear. Things are somewhat better when the offense is made statutory, because constraints of one sort or another can be built by the legislators into their legislation. The current law on obscenity in England is not the brightest jewel in the law's crown, but it is at least better since the acts of 1959 and 1964 than it was before, when obscene publication was a common-law offense and courts could do pretty well what they liked in deciding whether the material complained of had "the tendency to deprave and corrupt those whose minds are open to such immoral influences, and into whose hands a publication of this sort may fall."[7]

It might be argued against me that, even if my general thesis is acceptable, namely, that (1) a question of morality is a question about there being a harm, or risk of harm, or intended harm, to somebody which is produced by or manifested in conduct of such and such a kind, and that (2) there is no harmful conduct from which the law should a priori be excluded, yet there still will be some conduct that raises a question of morality but that should be left alone by the law. Would there not, for example, be something wrong with a law proscribing masturbation? Indeed there would, but we need to be clear in our minds why there would. In using masturbation as an example I am assuming it to be an activity that produces no harm to anybody else. If it does do harm to the agent himself, it does no physical harm; none of the alarming things with which grown-ups used to frighten young boys—you'll go blind, your hair will fall out, it will fall off—is going to happen. The harm that a person may do to himself by masturbating will be that of demeaning himself by the performance; and if he does not mind doing that, what possible business can it be of the law's? The general principle behind that line of arguing is that legal paternalism is wrong, that if a man chooses to engage in an activity that will harm nobody but himself, then there can be no justification for intervention by the law. Now although I have little sympathy with the practice of legal paternalism—because it gives the power of deciding over a man's interests to others who are liable to be at least as ignorant and prejudiced as he is himself—yet it has to be pointed out that, as a principle, an ab-

[7]R. v. *Hicklin* (1868) L.R. 3 Q.B. 360, 371.

solute prohibition of paternalism is untenable. We cannot seriously maintain that in all circumstances, no matter what they are, the value of a person's choosing for himself is more important than the value of his not being harmed by what he chooses. If we really did believe that, we would have to object *inter alia* to the laws that prohibit us from obtaining a vast range of medicine and drugs, except when prescribed by properly qualified and registered physicians and dispensed by licensed pharmacists. Either masturbation does no harm at all to the individual, or it does do some, however specified. If it does none, then there is no need for a law against it. If it does do some, then the question whether there is need for a law against it does arise. It is easy to answer: from the very nature and privacy of the activity, such a law would have negligible efficacy, except by giving the police powers of snooping that would be either alarmingly sinister or ludicrous in their scope. How ludicrous they could be is illustrated by a case (in this instance sodomy not masturbation is at issue) that the Supreme Court was asked to accept for decision a few years ago: whether, in the name of Fourteenth Amendment privacy, Virginia state troopers should be disallowed from peering down into closed toilet stalls in public rest rooms from hiding places in the ceilings above. Surely Virginia state troopers must have something better that they could be doing with their time.

The question what limits should be placed on the law's interference in what by our unreflective set of thought we have come to see as matters of morality is not one to which there can be a ready-made and all-purpose answer. I have tried to show that to characterize the matter in question as one of morality does not foreclose the question whether the law should intervene. It can do that only if we use "morality" in such a way that either something could be a matter of morality even although it produced or threatened no harm of any kind to anybody, or to say that something was purely a moral matter, or a matter of morality as such, would be to say that the harm that is done or threatens is not of a kind or degree to warrant legal intervention. Of those two alternatives, the first, as I have tried to bring out, gives us a contradiction, and the second gives us a tautology; its tautologous nature is concealed from those who use it by their failure to distinguish between indicating that there is a reason for something and indicating what the reason is.

In general, the question whether there should be legislation, or the implementation of existing law, for example, extension of its current use by judicial interpretation to cover some at present uncovered area of morality, is the question whether it is worth it. Legislation is not worth it if a law is not needed; it is not needed if we already have law enough to handle the problem, or if the problem in terms of harm to individuals or institutions is not serious enough or extensive enough, or if there are other acceptable extralegal ways of dealing with it. Legislation is not worth it if a law would be useless; it would be useless if it would not be enforced or applied (much current legislation is useless in this way, e.g., legislation to protect the lives and health of those working in dangerous industries), or if it could not be enforced and applied—either because of difficulties inherent in any effort to police it (e.g., the virtual impossibility of policing a ban on masturbation), or because such large numbers of the population against whom the law is directed will ignore it that the legal processes of arrest, indictment, and trial will be unable to digest them. The story of Prohibition is an extreme example of that. A less extreme example, but one that crops up occasionally, is a strike by federal employees (e.g., postal workers) whose strike, because they are federal employees, is illegal, but whose numbers are so great that the courts could not handle them; in the eventual resolution of the dispute the illegality of the strike is quietly forgotten.

INFLUENCE OF LAW ON ATTITUDES

I now want to make a major qualification to that last point, because it seems that much legislation can be useful even though it is little enforced and little enforceable. It will be useful if it affects our attitudes; and affecting attitudes is a way, an important way, of legislating morality. The theory of legislation, in a society that is politically organized as a representative democracy, is that laws are made in pursuit and promotion of policies that are believed (whether correctly or not) to be for the good of the society. That there is legislation that manifestly is not aimed at the promotion of society's good but at the good of specialized and powerful interests, including the interests of legislators in getting onto a gravy train or into a pork barrel, can be a distasteful fact of life and a basis of criticism of the society's condition. But, as long as there is enough legislation, and enough implementation of existing law, which is not thus tainted, the principle of the theory of legislation is unaffected. Now laws, if they are to work, must provide those who are to be expected to comply with them with reasons for complying. And those reasons are often thought to be found in the penalties for noncompliance. The penalties often, but not always, take the form of criminal punishments imposed by a court after conviction in a trial. But there is another form that they take with increasing frequency, as the government enlarges its range of funding enterprises that need money, and as the adjudication, and even the making, of law is done by the government's own administrative agencies. The power of HEW to cut off the flow of funds to educational institutions that do not toe its line over achieving racial integration is a clear example of providing a penalty that is not a criminal punishment as a reason for complying with the law. This may be called the direct reason; it can apply to each of us as the immediate and straightforward reason for conforming with whatever law concerns us in our situation of the moment. But that is not all. If it were all, then the law would be directed solely at our conduct and would not care what our reasons and attitudes were as long as our conduct was correct; and, just to make sure (as nearly as it can) that our conduct was correct, it would always give us the one telling reason of self-interest, or the wish not to be caught breaking the law, or to incur embarrassing and possibly costly consequences of being caught.

Now that is indeed a commonly held view of the relationship between the law and us, the subjects. I do not deny that it is an important part of the story, but I suggest that it is either overcynical or imperceptive to regard it as the whole. It is a mark of a society being in some degree civilized that the law's efficacy is achieved not only by an anxiety in people not to be caught breaking it, but also by an acceptance, which may be unreflective and inarticulate, of the law as setting a standard. In fact, it sets two standards: a minimum standard below which our conduct is not to fall, and a higher-than-minimum standard for our attitudes to reach up to. To the extent that that is true, law will affect not only our conduct but also, and more importantly, our attitudes—more importantly, because our attitudes are reflected in subsequent conduct; and we are better people if we do what we should, ungoaded by the incentive of avoiding the personally disagreeable consequences of being caught not doing it. It seems to me (although I suspect that many would not agree) that this assertion is true, and that an important feature of law and lawmaking in a society such as ours is what it can do (I am not claiming that it always does it) to our attitudes. Let me take as a first example a minor and very familiar one—the speed limit of 55 mph. It is an instance of a law that is very little enforced and very little enforceable; there are far too many cars and trucks on the highway, and far too few police cars equipped with radar detectors for there to be more than token enforcement. The risks of being caught can be much higher in some areas than in others, but over the country as a whole they are few, and especially on the interstate highways, where the speeds at which the trucks and the long-distance buses are traveling are a good indication of what, with their good intelligence service, they are expecting. So, generally speaking, almost nobody who was guided solely by rational considerations about the risk of being caught, and of the legal consequences of being caught, would bother. But it is a matter of observation that a large number do; I am regularly surprised at the number of cars that I overtake when I am not greatly exceeding the speed limit myself. Granted that there are other self-interested reasons for driving considerably slower than the safety limits of the car and the driver, the traffic and the road conditions: for example, the desire to economize on gas. But it seems to me clear, not only from the way that people drive but also from the way that they talk about the way they drive, that a very large number of American drivers, at least a sizable minority, accept the 55-mph limit as setting them a reasonable standard—something which, say, a typical German driver would find quite incomprehensible.

Now for a second and more serious example. The year

1979 was the twenty-fifth anniversary of the United States Supreme Court's decision in *Brown* v. *School Board of Topeka*,[8] in which the court ruled that "in the field of public education the doctrine of 'separate but equal' has no place." Because "separate educational facilities are inherently unequal," segregated schooling denies the equal protection of the laws to those who are the losers, and thereby violates the Fourteenth Amendment right which the Constitution guarantees them. Nobody will pretend that the implementation of the decision has turned the field of public education into a paradise of racial equality, but there is no doubt that it has made things far better than they were, even when we take into account the social costs of forced busing; and we should not forget that many of those costs were already there but unacknowledged because they were borne by the voiceless victims of segregation. But what I want to call attention to is less the changes in the structure of public school education that the law has brought about than the change in public outlook that it has achieved. And I want to illustrate that change by a story of the one state that I can be said to know at all, Virginia, and of the one town in it that I know, Charlottesville, a small town with a population of about 28,500 then and about 45,000 now, blacks being about 17 percent of the population then and about 13 percent now. As a southern state, the capital of which had been the Confederacy's capital, Virginia was not to be expected to be in the forefront of the move to integrate education. And it was not. The governor indeed did immediately declare that Virginia would comply with the Court's decision in *Brown,* and that state and local leaders would participate in planning for the ending of segregated schooling. But he was not strong enough to stand up to the

[8]347 U.S. 483 (1954).

power of the Byrd machine, and of the public opinion that backed it. Within a month he reversed himself, and the policy of massive resistance prevailed under the aegis of states' rights. The state board of education declared that it would continue the policy of segregation, and in 1956 the General Assembly enacted a bill empowering the governor to withhold state funds from and, if necessary, close down schools that enrolled both blacks and whites. In Charlottesville, petitions and then suits by black parents led to a federal court requiring the admission of blacks to the previously whites-only schools for the beginning of the school year in September 1956. But appeals against the order as far as the United States Supreme Court, although eventually unsuccessful there, brought delays while white voters continued to oppose integration, harassment continued, and crosses were burned. In May 1958 a new federal court order required the city school board to provide integrated schooling for the year 1958–1959. This directive was thwarted by a decision that all the black children who had applied for admission had failed to meet the requirements—which included, as well as test scores, residence sufficiently close to the schools and suitable family background. In September, the city's two white public schools were closed by the governor to prevent their desegregation. In January 1959 the Virginia Supreme Court ruled that the state's massive resistance laws were unconstitutional, private tutoring was provided for blacks at the two schools, and the board agreed that in September 1959 the schools would admit the twelve blacks whom the federal court had ordered admitted a year earlier. Apart from rearguard action, the legal battle was now over, and on September 8, 1959 the first black children entered the two city schools. They met with some insults, but no violence; indeed there had been very little violence at any stage. Simultaneously, two new private schools were opened in the city for the children of parents who wanted them given a whites-only education. Today, twenty years later, the schools still exist but are no longer segregated.[9] The NAACP's long campaign against the entrenched forces of the state and local authorities and against public opinion has been successful because of the law. The courts required a change of conduct, and finally, when the state's supreme court came out to support the federal courts, they got it. Conduct is all that the law can actually require of us, but it does not have to be all that it gets from us. Sometimes it is, but more often it is not; our attitudes are shaped by living with and coming to accept the law's requirements. The story of the change of heart toward association with blacks in many parts of Virginia is a vivid illustration of this point. I can believe that there are still holdouts in Charlottesville who will declare that it was wrong to mix blacks and whites together in school, but I have never met one. Without wishing to exaggerate the success of the decision in *Brown* (for plenty still remains to be done), I regard it as undeniable that (1) although officially, as always, the court was adjudicating, in fact, as indeed often, it was legislating; and that (2) through directly legislating conduct it indirectly legislated morality.

There is, of course, an obvious objection to that thesis, which is that we are not justified in saying that the law brought about the change in outlook toward educating together children of different races, because by now the outlook would have changed anyway, even without the intervention of the law. The objection is, indeed, obvious, but equally obviously it is fallacious—not because what it asserts is false, but be-

---

[9]The narrative in this paragraph is based on three retrospective reports in the *Charlottesville Daily Progress* of September 8 and 9, 1979. September 8 was the twentieth anniversary of the day on which the first black children entered the city's elementary and high schools.

cause even if what it asserts is true, that does not prove what it claims. It may be true that, even without *Brown* and its legal consequences, community attitudes toward schooling would have changed over the last twenty-five years and have become much what they are now. I have my doubts: if we look at the strength of the resistance to the change, and remember that the authorities were fighting in support of then prevailing white opinion with *legal* arguments, in particular the argument that the United States Supreme Court had itself got the Constitution wrong, and if we remember that Virginia changed sides only when their own *state* supreme court said that the United States Supreme Court had *not* got the Constitution wrong, it is not hard to believe that the change would not yet have reached so far as it has. But let us assume that it would have. That does not show that it is false that the law, by requiring conformity of conduct with what it judged to be a demand of the Constitution, indirectly internalized that requirement. The objection, in fact, rests on a simple fallacy: that it cannot be true that *a* caused *b* if it is also true that in the absence of *a* something else would have caused *b* instead. Anybody who can look that fallacy in the face and believe it can believe anything; unfortunately, there are such people.

I think that it has to be acknowledged that there is in many of us a deeply ingrained attitude toward the law to this effect: that although it is proper for the law to require conduct of us where the opposite conduct would be harmful to the legitimate interests of others (e.g., to require us to refrain from murdering, wounding, raping, or swindling each other), it is not proper for the law to require conduct of us where that conduct will be for the good of others. The law does indeed impose requirements of the latter kind, but does so in an indirect, impersonal way, mainly by levying taxes and by the appropriate governmental authority itself using the revenue to do something for the good of others. The raising by taxes on real estate of the funds needed to finance public education, the redistribution of wealth via social security contributions, and the provision of relief aid for the victims of disaster on the other side of the world are all instances. On the other hand, to be required by law to contribute to a charitable agency, such as United Way, is something that very many people would strongly object to. I suspect that even now a great many object to the coercion, or quasicoercion, to contribute that is exerted on them by employers and others, but that their objections are stifled by considerations of self-interest. That the law should require us actually and directly to do something *for* somebody else, something which, if only we are decent enough people we shall do anyway—that the law should require *that* of us is something many decent enough people find themselves unable to stomach. Why?

There is one law of this kind, which exists in some countries and has at least a toehold here, the so-called Good Samaritan law, requiring or encouraging us in certain circumstances to render aid to others. The only state, to my knowledge, to have the law in the strong form is Vermont, which has created a statutory duty to render such aid, for example to come to the assistance of somebody who is in serious physical danger, where the agent has no other competing and more important duties; the duty is coupled with immunity to criminal or civil liability, provided that the person trying to give help acts reasonably in what he does. Other states have a weaker version of the law, sometimes called the altruistic version, which, although not imposing a duty (with sanctions for nonperformance) to render aid, encourages it by removing the chief disincentive, namely, the risks of criminal or civil liability—the same kind of immunity as in Vermont.

A law of the Vermont kind is aimed at those people—and the story of Kitty Genovese's death suggests that many of us are among them—who seek to avoid giving help, because they do not want to become involved or because somebody else is sure to be along in a minute. And this attitude is rationalized into the objection that to require people by law actually to help others is to adulterate the moral purity of help, which should be given out of sympathy or other altruistic motive. The objection, which is invariably raised by somebody when Good Samaritan law is discussed, is, of course, entirely fallacious, because the law neither forces us to act from one motive nor prevents us from acting from another. The law on larceny, for example, does nothing to prevent us from displaying the virtue of honesty; if we see the woman in front of us in the checkout lane at the grocery drop a twenty-dollar bill on the floor as she takes money out of her purse, most of us will pick it up and give it back to her, and few of us will do that *because* the law makes it an offense for us to take the money for ourselves. Having a law requiring us to behave as would morally decent people does nothing to prevent us from behaving as morally decent people. And even if it did, it would be a creepy moral theory that would have the law, by inaction, require some people to suffer for the purpose of providing other people with the opportunity of exercising a moral virtue. The case for having a law imposing on us a duty to behave in a given area of life as would morally decent people is that without it, other people are suffering because not enough of us are behaving as morally decent people. If it were true that there should be no laws requiring conduct of a kind that a morally decent person could be expected to practice, and want to practice anyway, then there should be no laws against homicide, rape, violence, robbery, and so on. It may be argued against a Good Samar-

itan law that the costs, economic and social, of trying to operate it would so greatly outweigh the benefits that the law
would not be worth having: for example, that the evidentiary
difficulties would be in too many cases too great, that the identification of those who could have rendered aid but did not
would be in too many cases too difficult, that the number of
cases to which such a law would apply would be too small,
etc. Such objections are objections that would have to be
weighed. But how can it be an objection that the law would
require all to behave in the way in which any morally decent
person would behave? That objection can stem only from a
belief that the law should not concern itself with having us
behave well, only with not having us behave badly. But even
if that were true, it would not affect the claim that the law is
concerned with morality: that we not behave badly toward
each other *is* a matter of morality. There are no areas of conduct about which the question "Should people do that?" is
an improper question, although in many cases it may be a
pointless question because the reasons in favor of a resounding yes (or a resounding no) are overwhelming. Similarly,
there are no areas of conduct about which the question
"Should people be allowed to do that?" is an improper question, although in many cases and for the same reason it may
be a pointless question. It would be better for each of us to
legislate for himself instead of having others legislate for
us—if only it could be certain that each would legislate with
wisdom, with care for the interests of others, and harmoni-
ously with the legislation of every other. But as that, in fact,
represents an impossible ideal, as too many of us simply
would not legislate as we would need to even to approximate
the ideal, we have to submit ourselves to the rule of law. The
law should, therefore, set (at least) a minimum moral standard
below which our conduct should not be allowed to fall; and,

when opportunity provides, the standard should be raised, for example, as it has been from time to time in our society in the direction of preferring social justice to private prosperity. There can be no single, all-purpose rule for deciding what are to be the current limits for legislating morality other than the negative rule that legislation is not justified either when it is needless or when it would be useless. For the most part most of us manage our domestic and near-domestic relationships well enough not to need the law watching us; it is enough for it to provide the means of escape or rescue when things go seriously wrong, as in child abuse or spouse battering. And a law is useless if it is so far away from people's attitudes that they will not respond to it, and will submit to it only if they cannot avoid it. Submission to the prohibitions of the Eighteenth Amendment was easy enough to avoid, as is now submission to most of the marijuana laws, whereas submission to the requirements of most customs law is not; the latter is one of the not very common cases of law that is reasonably effective although not internalized. And there is the other side of the coin, that people tend to regard conduct as morally permissible as long as the law permits it. One of the hardest judgments that rulers have to make is whether to go ahead with reforming legislation that they believe to be desirable, in the hope that if it goes through it will in the long run change attitudes as well as conduct, or to hold off for fear that it will not.

CONCLUSION

By way of summary, let me try to emphasize what I have been trying to do and, equally important, what I have not been trying to do.

1. I have not asserted, indeed I have denied, that the law should concern itself with every detail of conduct. The less it can concern itself with, and the more it can leave for us to manage for ourselves as human beings and as members of our society, the better. Unfortunately, as we are what we are, there is much that we cannot be left to manage for ourselves without legal regulation.

2. For those areas of our lives where we can justifiably say that the law should keep out we can justifiably say it for one or other or both of two reasons: a law would be useless here, or a law is needless here; it is useless when it cannot achieve its purpose, and it is needless when its purpose can as well, or better, be achieved without it.

3. The claim about some matter of conduct that it is a purely moral matter is never a good reason for the law to keep out. Either the claim is that it is a matter that is moral and nothing else—and that is self-contradictory, for nothing can be moral except as being also something else; or the claim that something is a purely moral matter is a way of saying that it is one in which the law should not intervene—and in that case the claim that it is a purely moral matter from which the law should be excluded is tautologous. About every action on which it is appropriate to make moral judgment it is appropriate to ask whether there should be a law concerning it and actions of its kind. We can be thankful that the correct answer is so often no, but the question cannot be foreclosed by the claim that here we have purely a matter of morals.

4. I have not asserted that the law should legislate morality in the sense of its being its duty either to make us better people or to change (or maintain) our attitudes. Its prime concern is with conduct, and even there there are limitations, particularly in a democracy: there has to be some degree of accord between what a government legislates and what the

subjects will take. It is fortunate for government that subjects are usually lazy and acquiescent, and have a short span of attention; so, for example, proposed legislation requiring us to wear seat belts in our cars would provoke a storm of protest, but actual legislation could be enacted, and thereafter operated, with as little trouble as it is in countries that already have it.

5. I am not claiming that the law *ought* to try to inculcate moral attitudes in the subjects, let alone a single uniform moral outlook throughout the society. What I am saying is that it is characteristic of law, in a society such as ours, that it does inculcate moral attitudes. In a society where law does not sit easily on the shoulders of the subjects that will not be so; they will adopt a general attitude toward the law of conforming their conduct to it when they unavoidably must or cannot afford not to. For them, laws are collections of external rules, more or less irksome, which they have to live with as best they can and outwit whenever they can. For us, that is, for a substantial number of us, some laws are like that; for example, the customs laws which I mentioned earlier, and probably almost any tax law, where we even get official support for seeking and practicing every avoidance that we can, stopping short only of evasion. But that is not true of us and our law in general. It is part of our living under the rule of law that, for the most part, we do what has been called "internalizing" the law; we come to accept it as a standard, at least as a minimum standard, of conduct and of criticism of conduct. This is not an unalloyed good thing: as laws can change our attitudes for the better, they can also change them for the worse; and the law is readily taken to legitimize what it does not forbid.

6. To repeat my main point for emphasis: morality is legislated, not by the mere enactment and implementation of

a law, but by the way we live under it and absorb it into our moral bloodstream. Let me use as a final illustration a law which has not yet been passed, the prospects for which do not look particularly good, but which, if it were passed, could gradually make a difference that would be worth making. What can only be called the idiocy of the gun lobby stems from its inability to face more than one fact at a time. Of course, however severe the limitations on ownership of handguns were made, anybody who really wanted to would be able to get one. But that the same is already true of plenty of other things, for example, burglary tools and fuzzbusters, is not seen as a sufficient reason for not banning them. And the really important thing that is overlooked is that, if the law prohibited, or even only restricted, possession of handguns, many more people would not even think of buying them. The argument of this paper was reflected in the comment by a journalist after the attempt on President Reagan's life: "America will not begin to cope with its violence until it begins to change a habit of mind by changing its laws."[10]

[10]Henry Fairlie, 'What Is This Myth About America's Being Politically Violent?', *Washington Post*, 5 April 1981.

Chapter 7 / ANALYTIC METHODS AND THE ETHICS OF POLICY

THOMAS C. SCHELLING

Policy judgments are easier to come by the farther we are from our goals. If there are only two directions and we know which is forward, and there are limits to how fast we can go, no fine discrimination is needed. If aid to the poor is far too little, highway traffic far too fast, building codes far too lax, teachers' salaries far too low, or the rights of defendants far too little observed, we know what we need to know to get moving. We can worry about how much is enough when we get close, if we ever do. Meanwhile we can push on.

Knowing what to do is also easy if our capabilities are growing and our horizons receding, and yesterday's goals will be outgrown tomorrow. Like a family on a rising income, we need not worry about overshooting: if we buy too big a house today, we shall afford it tomorrow.

THOMAS C. SCHELLING • John F. Kennedy School of Government, 79 Bolyston Street, Harvard University, Cambridge, Massachusetts 02138.

I have often been glad that I was not in charge. It is gratifying to see plainly that there is too much inequality, and to help to reduce it, knowing that despite all efforts too much will remain. (Or illiteracy or ill health or injustice.) But if it were up to me to decide how much inequality is not too much, or how much injustice, or how much disregard for the elderly or for future generations, I would need more than a sense of direction. Discomfort also arises when, intent on speeding toward an ever-receding goal, when the goal suddenly stops receding, we threaten to overshoot.

There appears to be a widespread belief that overshoot is what we have done.

Worse, there is retrospective disenchantment with the mood that motivated the effort and set the goals in the first place. There is chagrin at having been too enthusiastic about what could be accomplished. There is disaffection toward those whose demands are insatiable and whose gratitude is inconspicuous.

Whatever the reason, there is a reexamination of policy, especially policy that reflects social obligation. There is retrenchment in the air and on the ballot, and second thoughts about what we can afford for ourselves and what we owe others.

It is not all sour grapes. Our projection of the possible has shrunk. Our economy is not behaving. Growing income no longer promises to make light of our burdens in another decade or two. We do not know what has been depressing our productivity and cannot be sure that, whatever it is, we shall recover soon. Inflation has a mind of its own. The demographics of the labor force are against us for the next couple of generations and at the same time the rules of the game allow endless numbers of people from faraway places, once over the line, to touch base and be safe. And there is angry reaction to the behavior of fuel prices.

So it is not surprising that commitments are being reassessed, "tradeoffs" discussed, costs weighed anew against benefits, and even constitutional initiatives promoted to enforce a policy of containment. The techniques of policy analysis that recently were despised as mean-spirited and stingy by people who preferred to base policy on vision and generosity are being superseded by what used to be called meat axes and straitjackets.

These are not "hard times" in the old sense. In this country life is still good and getting better for most people. But it is not measuring up to expectations. They might better be called "difficult times": it is the problems, not the times, that are hard. And among the hard issues are some ethical ones. They may not be the hardest or the most important, but they are important and they are hard.

I have been asked to address the uses of analytic methods in the ethics of policy. How can they help and how do they hinder in facing, or solving, or avoiding the ethical components of policy? Do the methods themselves represent a particular ethics; or, if not the methods, the people who use them?

THE ETHICS OF POLICY

What I shall mean by the *ethics of policy* I can explain with the income tax. Almost anybody can cheat, and many are tempted. If nearly everybody cheats a little, is it all right for me to do the normal amount? If I object to some things taxes are spent on, may I strike and refuse to pay? If an expense was legitimate but I have lost the receipt, may I forge documentation to support the claim? These choices are personal: *I* make them, and they affect *me.*

I deduct the *New York Times.* If the *Times* had comics or I could not get baseball scores from my local newspaper, I might feel that ethics was involved in treating a newspaper as a professional expense. I can discuss disinterestedly whether a doctor should deduct medical journals, but as a subscriber to the *Times* I have a personal interest in whether my profession is allowed to count it as required reading, just as I have never been quite neutral on whether college tuition should be deductible.

I am not personally affected by how to value inventory or the tax treatment of foster children. My personal interest is limited to the difference it makes to the taxes I pay if others take deductions that are inapplicable to my return.

I am trying to close in on what we should mean by the ethics of *policy.* I want to say that it is the relevant ethics when we think about rent control, minimum wages, Medicaid, food stamps, safety regulations, the financing of social security, cigarette taxes, or the financing of abortions, but not those policies in which we have a *personal* stake (to which a *personal* ethics is relevant). Farmers have an interest in price supports, laundry operators in minimum wage laws, doctors in the financing of Medicare, and electric utilities in clean air regulation, and until my youngest child is safely overage, I have a personal interest in the draft. I want to define the ethics of policy as what we try to bring to bear on *those issues in which we do not have a personal stake.* When people take sides on a leash law in a suburban town we do not expect them to argue it the way they might discuss space exploration.

It is hard, though, to find policies that are completely clean of personal interest. On abortion and capital punishment our personal ethics may dominate. Food stamps and highway programs affect us because they cost money. Someone meticulously interested in his own welfare could find at least a minuscule personal interest in a United Nations program for alphabet reform in a primitive society.

Still, most of us, on many important issues, *want* to think and to talk as though we were not interested parties. We want to discuss welfare and national defense and school construction and unemployment benefits and automobile mileage standards and the financing of Medicare as though we were not personally involved. There will typically be an unmistakable element of social obligation; nobody can discuss the rate structure of the income tax or the benefit levels for welfare without a participatory awareness that the poor and the unfortunate and the disadvantaged and the otherwise deserving have some legitimate claims on those among us who can afford to help. But although few issues are without financial impact somewhere, and most big issues involve important amounts of money, we can often confine our personal stake to an aggregate and nonspecific social obligation. Our position in the income scale affects our conditioning as well as our reasoning, but beyond that we can try to be neutral, removed, vicarious, and impartially judicious.

Incidentally, I dare to say these things only because I expect books like this one to be read by a special set of people. Most people probably devote most of their policy interest to things that concern themselves, and do it with a clear conscience. They do not need to get drawn into ethical abstractions. They may have strong ethical views on a limited number of subjects that do not flow from their stake in the outcome, but on matters called "bread-and-butter" they accept the ethic that in politics it is fair to look out for your own interest, expecting others to look out for theirs. Many of us in academic environments, especially students, try to take distributive issues seriously but not personally. Professors concerned for their *own* salaries are thought not to be playing the ethical game, but the tobacco farmer concerned with his own family's welfare is excused from scholarly disinterest. (Even students rebelling against higher tuition are reluctant to say that they do not want to spend their money. They join the picket line in behalf of somebody poorer.)

ANALYTIC METHODS AND WHAT THEY MAY DO

Up to this point I have tried only to identify the ethics of *policy*. I will now add a few words about *analytic methods*. By analytic methods I mean the theories and abstractions and models that come from economics, decision theory, game theory, systems analysis, and the like. I include the accounting and programming frameworks that have been devised to add neatness, orderliness, and comprehensiveness to decision making. Some of these techniques have names— "cost–benefit analysis," "program budgeting," "risk–benefit analysis." Some of them mainly help to keep track of what we are doing as we apply elementary judgment to the components of a problem; but some of them take the problem out of our hands altogether and, perhaps with the help of a high-speed computer, give back the answer to the question that we think we asked.

Economics began to move toward the mathematical about the time that wartime operations research was emerging as a discipline; decision theory and management science have progressed along with techniques of simulation and computer graphics. People who want to know where to build a dam or to locate rescue equipment, how to invest in energy and clean air or how to evaluate remedial teaching are more or less helped, and more or less intimidated, by the increasing availability of experts or expertise, not being the one and not having the other.

I have an opinion on what the attitude of a policy maker, or of someone who sits in judgment on policy or pays for it, should be toward these techniques that require formal instruction or the assistance of specialists. At the risk of appearing not to change my mind often enough I shall repeat what I said a dozen years ago in discussing for a Senate committee the relation of PPBS (Planning-Programming-Budgeting Systems) to foreign policy. PPBS was a system of quantitative evaluation that had been developed in the Department of Defense; it was ordered by President Johnson to be utilized by agencies concerned with housing and transport, health and education, and even foreign policy. I had spent some months looking into the subject and becoming sensitive to widespread expectations about what the new techniques could accomplish. I said:

> PPBS, backed up by a competent analytical staff, can hardly fail to be helpful to a decision maker who insists on making his own decisions and on understanding how he makes them; it can be a seductive comfort, and in the end an embarrassment, to a lazy executive who wants his decisions to come out of a process in which his own intellect does not participate. PPBS can be a splendid tool to help top management make decisions; but there has to be a top management that wants to make decisions.
>
> Let me use an analogy, if I may. A courtroom adversary proceeding has been evolved as a comparatively good way to provide the judge in the dispute with the arguments and evidence on which to base a decision; but the crucial element in the proceedings is the judge himself. Systems analysis and other modern techniques

of evaluation require a consumer, some responsible person or body that wants an orderly technique for bringing judgment to bear on a decision. PPBS works best for an aggressive master; and where there is no master, or where the master wants the machinery to produce his decisions without his own participation, the value of PPBS is likely to be modest and, depending on the people, may even be negative.[1]

I still believe that. I believe it for health, education, transportation, welfare, criminal justice, and most fields in which the scale of complexity of program decisions demands explicit and efficient ways of arriving at policy choices. I admit that in electronic communications, space exploration, and the deployment of fire and rescue equipment in a crisis the policy maker may often have to have trust in the results of an analytic process that is beyond his intellectual reach altogether, the results of which cannot even be rationalized for him in comprehensive terms. Sometimes this will be because our elementary processes of understanding and recognition take time and there is not enough time. In other instances the analytic process cannot be decomposed into digestible components even after one has the solution and is merely working backward to see why it fits the problem. (Those are likely, incidentally, to be the cases in which the ethical content of the issue has become comfortingly invisible.) But usually the results that come out of advanced analytic methods, even when the process is elegant and complex, can be rationalized and reformulated *afterward* to give the decision maker a feel for why the answer or the recommendation comes out the way it does, and whether it is an answer to the right question.

The expert is often good at seeing a helpful way to for-

---

[1]Thomas C. Schelling, "PPBS and Foreign Affairs," *The Public Interest*, Spring 1968, p. 27.

mulate an issue. But once he has perceived the way to for-
mulate it, the elementary test is simply whether his formulation is, in fact, helpful. The expert may be good at finding
a way to do something or a better way than the one already
in hand, and only he may be able to find it; but once he has
found it, the elementary test is whether it is indeed any good
or better than what we already had. Sometimes, as in finding
the key to a code, the correctness or incorrectness of the key
will be as transparent to the client as to the cryptographer.

I say this not to disparage these methods but in their
behalf. The methods, and sometimes those who are skilled
at the methods, can help in formulating an issue, concep-
tualizing what a resolution would be, finding and comparing
solutions, and evaluating their adequacy. The extent of ab-
dication or delegation of responsibility can often be quite
minimal. That depends, of course, on the expert's taking pride
in how helpful he or she can be in facilitating the decision,
not in how independently the decision can be made from the
person who is ultimately responsible.

This fact is particularly important where ethical considerations are concerned. Delegating decisions with an important ethical component is rarely satisfactory. Not every analyst
can be trusted to represent the values of the decision makers,
and some will feel morally obligated to substitute their own
ethical principles. Even when trying to be honest, the analyst
may not be fully up to the job of incorporating somebody
else's ethical principles. And if we are the ones responsible
for policy, many of us feel that we are able to weigh ethical
values in an implicit or intuitive manner better than we can
articulate them and quantify them for somebody else.

Finally, most decisions are made, socially or collectively,
by committees and boards and teams, or by persons who
want to talk their way through the problem, not just think

their way through it, or by judges who must articulate a justification for the decision reached. And although there are ways to put alternative ethical values into an analytic process, to see what different outcomes they lead to and how sensitive the outcome is with respect to what went in, usually the formal analytic help works best if it provides a disciplined framework for discussing the problem, rather than burying the reasoning in the machinery.

THE ETHICS OF THE MARKETPLACE

Students in my experience always like gasoline rationing. They base their belief in it on ethical principles. (They say they do, and they sound as if they do.) Evidently the principles lie deeper than rationing itself. The students must have some notion of what happens with rationing and without it, or with some specific alternative, and they must have a preference either for the outcome or for the process. Students are sensitive to distributive issues and know that there are gainers and losers; their ethics appear to relate to who gains, who loses, and how much.

I can talk most of my students out of it. It takes longer than fifty minutes, and I never try it if I have only a single class hour. They probably distrust my ethical principles and think I do not care about what they care about, or care as much. They very likely think my ethics are "process oriented" and the free market enchants me, whereas they are "consequences oriented" and do not like the results.

Time permitting, I approach their conversion in two stages. I warn them in advance that I am going to show them that if they like rationing there is something they should like better. I join them in believing the free market need not be let alone, but I do propose what is sometimes called "rationing by the purse." I suggest we let the price of gasoline rise until there is no shortage, and capture the price increase with a tax. Because that is hard on the poor my students do not like it.

The first step in subverting their ethical preference is to propose that under any system of rationing that they might devise—and I take a little while to show them that it is not easy to design a "fair" system of rations—people should be encouraged to buy and sell ration coupons. This proposal has little appeal. The rich will obviously burn more than their share of the gas, the poor being coerced by their very poverty into releasing coupons for the money they so desperately need. Eventually students begin to recognize that the poor, because they are poor, would like the privilege of turning their coupons into money. Where the gas coupons only provide them gas at a discount, transferable coupons can buy milk at a discount. If it is unfair that the poor cannot afford to drive as much as the rich, it is the poverty that is unfair, not the gasoline system.

That principle established, we observe that coupons are worth cash, whether you buy them, sell them, or merely turn in your own at the local service station. If gas at the pump is $1.50 and coupons are going for 50 cents, the net price of gasoline is $2.00 and anyone who gets ten gallons' worth of coupons from the Department of Energy is getting a slightly clumsy equivalent of $5 cash. The service station that sells ten gallons receives $15.00 in money and $5 in coupons that could have been traded for cash. What we have is a 50-cent tax at the pump payable in special money, and a cash disbursement to motorists paid in this special money. We could just as well do it all without the coupons. There is more to it than that, but the "more" usually does not involve much ethics.

It is not that we resolved an ethical issue or disposed of one. We merely lifted the veil of money and discovered that the ethical issue we thought was there was not. Or, perhaps better, the ethical issue that we associated with rationing was tangential to that procedure. Whatever the compensatory principle is that appeals to students' sense of fairness, there are many procedures that can achieve it, some better than others, rationing neither worst nor best; and once it is all converted to money it is easier to see what some of the alternatives are and whether they are ethically superior. Superficially it may seem wrong to give gas coupons to people who do not drive; but if the gasoline is taxed instead and the proceeds rebated to the public, one can judge the ethics of alternative distributions of the proceeds, not just those based on driver's licenses and car registrations.

It is a little harder to convince students about rent control, partly because they do not like landlords. We try to see whether there might be something better, even in principle; we try to see whether there are persons seeking apartments who are losers under rent control; whether some of the non-evictable tenants in rent-controlled apartments would like to cash in their precious property right and move, but are locked in because their claim is to a specific apartment. What I usually find is that by the time we have identified all the potentially interested parties and the likely magnitudes of their interests, and have considered a few alternative ways to accomplish some of the things their rent control is intended to accomplish, the liveliness of the policy issues is undiminished but the ethical loading has nearly evaporated.

I dislike "counting coup" over vanquished students in order to display, and to hope you are impressed with, one of the ways that economics can contribute to the clarification of ethical issues. But at least the claim for economics is modest: it often helps to diagnose misplaced identification of an ethical issue. And it does so solely by helping to identify what is happening, what the consequences are. It is not clarifying ethics, it is only clarifying economics.

Let me give a few more examples. Minimum wage laws are thought to have ethical content; but if their main effect, or their main purpose, is to keep the young and the old and the otherwise least valuable employees from working at all, the ethical issues may not be what the proponents thought they were. Making utilities pay the full cost of smoke abatement seems eminently fair unless the costs are borne by consumers of electricity and the clean air enjoyed by whoever lives downwind, in which case we may want to know who lives downwind and who buys the electricity, the utility company not having much interest in the matter. (Even if the electricity is procured mainly by business firms, we do not know yet who is paying until we know who buys the firm's products, or who will settle for lower wages when the other costs rise.) Even our feelings about people who evade the income tax by not declaring tips or fees or truck-garden sales will depend on whether the system merely lowers wages and prices in bars and restaurants and reduces the cost of getting dissertations typed.

The point of all this is not that I am smarter than my students or that you should let me handle rent control for you. It is that whatever I know as an economist that can help in the analysis of interacting behaviors in the market and in identifying where the ethical issues are, I can probably communicate it persuasively, if you have an hour or two. You need not just take my word on it and you need not think it is inaccessible.

THE CLASH BETWEEN EQUITY AND INCENTIVES

Policy issues are preponderantly concerned with helping, in compensatory fashion, the unfortunate and the disadvantaged. We have welfare for those who cannot work, unemployment benefits for people out of jobs, disability benefits for the disabled, hospital care for the injured and the ill, disaster relief for the victims of floods, income tax relief for the victims of accidental loss, and various emergency and rescue services for people who find themselves in difficulty or danger. Social security is based on the premise that people will arrive at postworking age with inadequate savings to live on.

An unsympathetic way to restate it is that a preponderance of government policies have the purpose of rewarding people who get into difficulty. People are paid handsomely for losing their jobs; if you smash your car the IRS will share the cost of a new one; and if your injury requires hospitalization you can stay in an air-conditioned room as long as the doctor certifies that you will recover better if you do not go home. By treating the absence of a "man in the house" as a special grievance for a woman with dependent children, families have even received a special bonus for a father's leaving home.

There is no getting away from it. Almost any compensatory program directed toward conditions or circumstances over which people have any kind of control, even remote and probabilistic control, provides some inducement to get into that condition, reduces the incentive to stay out of it, and detracts from the urgency of extricating oneself. It is a rare meliorative program that has no visible way, by its influence on behavior, to affect the likelihood, the duration, or the severity of the circumstances it is intended to ameliorate. And most commonly, not always but most commonly, the effect on behavior is undesired and unintended, or, at least, far more than is desired or intended, and in the wrong direction. The program aggravates the problem that it tries to relieve.

To keep the issue in perspective we can observe that private insurance, even the informal kind that allows us to ask for help when we run out of gas, can have the same adverse influence on behavior. People more willingly drive on slippery roads the more nearly complete their collision coverage; back doors are unlocked if the homeowner's policy is liberal in its provisions for burglary. I am more indulgent of my sore throat if my employer provides an ample quota of sick days.

There is no use denying it in defense of social programs. As is usually the case with important issues, principles conflict. We want, on one hand, to treat unemployment as a collective liability, sustaining the family at public expense when working members lose their livelihoods. On the other we want not to induce people to get conveniently unemployed or to feel no need when unemployed to seek work vigorously. What helps toward one objective hurts toward the other. Offering 90 percent of normal pay can make unemployment irresistible for some and even a net profit for those who can moonlight or work around the home. Providing only 40 percent over a protracted period makes living harsher than we want it to be. There is nothing to do but compromise. Worse, a compromise that makes unemployment a grave hardship for some makes it a pleasant respite for others, and we cannot even be comfortable with the compromise.

Decent welfare in a high-income state is bound to be at a higher level than in a low-income state. It induces migration. Even if we favor migration, the state that finds more and more migrants on its welfare roles did not intend to reduce the poverty of other states by helping any and all who could get up and move. But to provide an unattractive level of benefits would condemn the intended beneficiaries to a level of living below what their home state wanted to provide them. Again, two principles conflict.

There are exceptions to this tendency of benefits to induce the wrong behavior. Federal deposit insurance was designed in the 1930s to provide restitution to people whose bank deposits were lost; by generating confidence, the insurance reduced precisely the behavior that caused the problem. And a benefit strictly related to age can presumably have no effect on the speed with which people grow older. But the tendency is pervasive and accounts for a good part of the escalation of medical costs.

I do not know whether one of the principles, helping the disadvantaged, should be considered ethical and the other, not letting them get away with it, not. Much of the discussion about welfare rights, about not apportioning medical care to ability to pay, and about not producing a "work ethic" by threatening the unemployed with starvation is in an ethical mode. To a lesser extent ethical considerations are invoked over encouragement of malingering, rewarding those who beat the system, or inducing dependence on the state. Once it is recognized, however, that two principles conflict, that two desiderata point in opposite directions and neither is so overwhelming that the other can be ignored, that both objectives have merit and even that there is no ideal compromise because it is a diversified population at risk, the ethical contents of the principles begin to seem tangential to the inescapable problem of locating an acceptable compromise.

It is a universal problem. It will not go away. It cannot be neglected. It is not even unique to *public* policy. The word "compromise" has those two different meanings: compromising a principle does not sound good; but it is all right to compromise *between* principles.

VALUING THE PRICELESS

Among the poignant issues that policy has to face, explicitly or by default, are some that seem to pit finite cost against infinite value. What is it worth to save a life? How much to spend to assure fair trial to protect the innocent against false verdicts? What limits to put on the measures, some costly in money and some in anguish, to extend the lives of people who will die soon anyway or whose lives, in someone's judgment, are not worth preserving?

These issues are nearly ubiquitous. They are unavoidably involved in designing a national health program. They are directly involved in decisions for traffic lights, airport safety, medical research, fire and Coast Guard protection, and the safety of government employees. They are implicitly involved, because somebody has to pay the costs, in regulations for occupational safety or safe water supplies, in building codes and speed laws, even helmets for motorcyclists.

It is characteristic of policy makers, especially at the level of federal government in a nation of 200 million, that they are usually making decisions that affect others, not themselves. Hurricane and tornado warnings are for people who live where the hurricanes and tornadoes strike; mine safety is a responsibility of legislators and public officials in offices above ground, concerning the lives of people "out there" who work underground. Policies toward the senile, the comatose, the paralyzed, and the terminally ill are deliberated by people who are none of the above. Occasionally the legislator debating a 55 mph speed limit pauses to think whether the benefits in safety to his own family will be worth the added driving time, but if he or she is conscientious that personal calculation is likely to be surreptitious.

The situation must be different when a very small community considers a mobile cardiac unit or a new fire truck. The question then is not what we ought to spend to save someone else's life, but what we can afford to make *our* lives safer. Spending or stinting on the lives of others invites moral contemplation; budgeting my expenditures for my own benefit, alone or with neighbors for the school safety program, is less a moral judgment than a consumer choice, a weighing of some reduction in risk against the other things that money will buy.

There is a suggestion here. Maybe we can reduce the unmanageable moral content of that paternalistic decision at the national level by making it more genuinely vicarious. Instead of the question, What is society's obligation to *them*, we should ask, How would *they* want *us* to spend *their* money? When deciding how much to require people to spend on their own seat belts, smoke alarms, fire extinguishers, and lightning rods it is easier to be vicarious and it is legitimate to get our bearings by reflections on how much we might reasonably spend on our own safety. The question still may not be easy, but it is less morally intimidating.

Surely, if we were all similarly at risk and in like economic circumstances, that would be the way to look at it, whether for the town bandstand or the town ambulance. On a national scale it is less transparently so, but nevertheless so, that we should want our appropriations committees to think of themselves as spending our money in our behalf. We want them neither to skimp where it really counts nor to go overboard to prepare at great expense—our expense—for the remotest of dangers. We want them to be thinking not about what concern the government owes its citizens for their safety but how much of their own money those taxpayers want spent for their safety.

With that perspective it is remarkable how quickly the issue, now collectively *self-regarding* instead of *other-regarding*, drops its ethical content, or appears without the ethical content that was merely a construct of the initial formulation. We can still find ethical issues, but not the one that seemed so central.

We could call this approach the contractual approach to social obligation. In the absence of an understanding, I may owe you, in your extremity, unbounded attention and concern, comfort and livelihood, room and board, and the best medical attention in perpetuity, and feel guilty whenever I stop to wonder whether you are worth the burden you are putting on us. When it is my turn, of course, I will expect the same from you (or from whoever has the corresponding responsibility toward me that I had toward you), feeling perhaps a little guilty but not enough to relinquish my claim. But if we could sit down together at an early age in good health and legislate our relation to each other, specifying the entitlements we wished to obtain between us, recognizing equal likelihood of being beneficiaries or providers, we could elect to eschew any exorbitant claims and it would not strike us as a decision with ethical content.

The contractual approach can help with some of those other tantalizing dilemmas, such as which planeload of passengers to save, the big plane with many passengers or the little one with few, if both are at risk and one at most can be saved. What I should do in the control tower if that God-like decision were mine is an ethical dilemma that, for some thoughtful people, has no easy answer. But if I am merely an airline passenger answering a questionnaire for the FAA on what rule I want the control tower to follow in future emergencies, the issue is neither ethical nor a dilemma.

I cheated a little in supposing that we were all similarly situated with respect to some risk and alike in our ability to afford protective measures. We usually are not. But the value of this conceptual approach, of considering what the safety is worth to the people who are safer, may still be salvaged. If you are more at risk than I—let us say you are at risk and I am not at all—and the rule is that we share the cost of reducing the risk and we are purely self-regarding, I shall find the measures worth nothing whereas you find the measures twice as attractive as if you had to pay it all yourself. If you fly a plane and I do not, the new runway lights at the local airport will cost us each a thousand dollars and may be worth it to you but not to me. If they are worth more than $2,000 to you, they ought to be bought, at least if you will pay for them. (Whether I ought to pay half is a separable issue.) But suppose you would not pay more than $1,500 for the slight contribution the runway lights make to your safety. I propose that they should not be bought.

Even though we divide on the issue of whether, paying a thousand dollars apiece, we ought to buy the lights, the economist in me formulates the problem this way: If because your personal safety is involved, you are entitled to my contributing a thousand dollars to the purchase of runway lights, that is, to your personal safety, and I acknowledge your claim and put up my thousand dollars for your exclusive benefit, do you really want to buy the runway lights or would you rather take my thousand and keep it? I do not care. I may be annoyed that you are spending my thousand dollars along with yours on something that even you did not consider worth the cost. In fact we could both be better off if instead of purchasing the lights, I just gave you $750 in cash and we forgot the lights.

For some among us that may not settle the issue. But I propose that it is, nevertheless, a useful perspective, a relevant consideration, and although other considerations are relevant too, they may not be ethical ones, or if they are, they are not the ethical question of whether our little two-person society put too low a value on *your* life in deciding not to buy the runway lights. (*You* may have put too low a value on your life, but I do not know why I should feel guilty about that. You may need better lighting in your driveway even more.)

A little harder is the question of what to do if you are poor and I am rich and you use a cheap little airport and I use a better-equipped one, and better runway lights are now available and they are to be provided, if provided at all, out of a common fund for airport safety. If the lights will make as much difference to safety at your airport as at mine, and someone raises the question whether we should afford the same expensive lifesaving apparatus at your cheap airport as at my more lavish one, we really come up against the question of whether your life is worth as much as mine. (Let us leave aside the possibility that there are more of you to benefit from the lights, or fewer of you, compared with the traffic at my airport.)

Let us face the question. If you are poor and I am rich is your life worth less than mine? "Worth" refers here to how much might properly be spent to protect it from some specified risk. (Notice that "worth" is an arithmetical construct: If we are willing to spend $2,000 per capita, but not more than $2,000, to protect everybody from something that is fatal for 1 person in 500, we shall spend an average of one million dollars per life saved. In that respect and only in that respect have we "valued" each life at one million dollars.) And when we ask what your life is worth, or what my life is worth, and whether your life is worth less than my life, it may help in straightening out what we have in mind if we ask, *Worth to whom?*

I believe it likely, if you are substantially poorer than I, that in terms of money *your* life is worth less to *you* than *my* life is worth to *me*. In the same way your dinner or your comfort or your holiday is worth less to you than mine to me. Not necessarily—you may take your dining more seriously than I, or your comfort, or even your personal safety—but generally you can afford to pay less for anything, including personal safety, than I, precisely because you are poorer.

We expect the poor to invest less in home or auto safety than the well-to-do, because it is at the expense of more urgent necessities; we expect a poor town to spend less on fire protection than a well-to-do town, because the poor town can afford less taxes and needs schools and streets as well as fire engines. But does that mean that a government air-safety program might properly deny you those new runway lights whereas my airport gets them at government expense?

The economist in me wants to say yes. The policy adviser in me will go only as far as maybe. But the affirmative argument contains something worth knowing. It runs as follows.

If the users of each runway had to pay for all the facilities, including safety facilities, we might find that the folks at your airport did not consider the marginal addition to safety contributed by the new lights to be worth the money, whereas the well-to-do people at my airport considered the lights a good bargain. We may share your feelings about life and death but the expenditures we forgo to pay for our lights are less important to us than if we were as poor as you. So we should not be surprised to find that our airport gets the lights and yours does not.

If, now, a federal safety authority were to consider requiring those new lights, the lights still to be paid for by each airport's users, to require you to buy the lights they would have to believe that you had made a mistake. Assuming that you knew the cost of the lights, they would have to assume either that you did not know how much the lights would reduce the risks of landing and takeoff, or that you did not know how to weigh your own safety against your money. But notice that they would have to believe that you had made a mistake from your *own* point of view, and if they can ascertain that you did understand how much reduction in risk the lights would provide, they must now think that you undervalue your life or overvalue the other things you have to buy out of your income. Maybe you do, but you may not see why they should be expected to have a better idea than you do of what your money is worth to you. You might reasonably protest the requirement that you equip your airport with those expensive runway lights.

Now let the authorities dispose of funds with which to provide safety equipment, including those new lights. They offer them to your airport at public expense. You may refuse them, but they will be provided free, and although they are worth less to you than what they cost, they are better than the old lights. Is it proper that you be provided with those lights at public expense?

I try to teach my students that whenever asked a question like that they should ask in return: *What is the alternative?* If the alternative is tax reduction—your taxes—so that you are really paying for those lights indirectly, paying taxes while receiving the lights "free of charge," you might elect lower taxes, a smaller public air–safety budget, and the old lights.

But maybe, being poor, you pay less in taxes than we do who fly in and out of the other airport. If you decline the lights you will save us most of the cost; your share of the cost, in the taxes you pay, may be less than what the lights are worth to you. Now should you take the lights with a clear conscience?

There is one more alternative. If the air-safety authorities give you the price of the lights, and do not oblige you actually to spend it on lights—if they give you the lights and you can sell them to somebody else and keep the cash value—you will probably choose the money. Any maybe I do not care. Or maybe you will settle for less money than the lights would have cost and save a little in taxes.

I think that is a powerful argument in favor of the proposition that a government might properly spend less per capita to save the lives of poor people than to save the lives of people who are well-to-do. But it is not a decisive argument. In some context it may be of no weight, or no help in resolving the issue. If the money is available only for those lights, and you cannot take the money and run; if it is available only for air safety, and not for faster or more comfortable airplanes, better schools, or reduced airport noise; if we who pay more taxes than you do will respond to your appeal for comparable airport safety but will *not* give you other services or the equivalent value in tax reduction; then your alternative to more safety is only less safety. The above line of reasoning will not help you get something better than runway lights.

But these qualifications, important as they are and decisive as they will often be, are more like political constraints on programming for safety than the ethical issue that initially seemed to arise in the question: Should the lives of the poor as a matter of policy get less protection than the lives of the rich? Still, when a plane crashes at that airport with the obsolete lights we may find it hard to explain to our children why that little airport on the other side of the tracks was of less apparent concern to the safety authorities than our own airport. The authorities may have trouble explaining it to their children, too. Ethical issues still exist, if not quite the one we first perceived.

THE "SOMETHING BETTER" APPROACH

What the reader will have noticed both with gas rationing and with airport safety is a technique that economics commonly employs in addressing whether a particular condition or policy or program should be considered to have virtue. That technique is to explore whether, in respect of alternative outcomes or consequences, some alternative policy or condition or program technique is "better." And "better" has a particular definition: superior, as an outcome, for *everyone* involved or, somewhat less ambitiously, for all the identifiable interests. With gasoline rationing we explore whether there is something better, something that meets whatever objectives rationing was supposed to fulfill and does a little more besides, or meets some of them more amply, or achieves the same results at lower costs to someone concerned. To find something better does not necessarily mean that rationing is not among the better policies, only that it is still inferior to some identifiable alternative. Sometimes, but not always, it is possible to offer a measure or an estimate, a lower or upper bound, to the magnitude of the superiority. And sometimes, if an alternative is better for not quite everybody and disadvantageous to some, we can find a way to estimate the extent of disadvantage, or put an upper bound on it.

The example of runway lights illustrates precisely what this reasoning accomplishes and some of its limitations. It is concerned only with *outcomes*, not with appearances, not with processes. Most important, the reasoning does not demonstrate that the superior policy or program technique is achievable. In particular it may depend on institutions that do not exist or politics that are unacceptable or administrative determinations that are infeasible. I doubt whether many readers will be any more convinced than I am of the wisdom of publicly providing inferior airport safety at the airport utilized by lower-income passengers and crews, even though in principle a deal could be struck according to which they obtained something instead (money for example) worth more to them in their own judgment than the uneconomically modest improvement in runway safety.

To explore the example further, I conjecture that if airport safety were a municipal rather than a federal responsibility we would not expect the same investment in lifesaving facilities at municipal airports used mainly by low-income people as we would expect at airports frequented by business executives and wealthier tourists. We might not feel obliged to tax the passengers at the wealthier airports and transfer the proceeds to the less favored cities. We might even expect people in search of economy fares to fly in and out of the less well-protected airports, taking advantage of lower fares reflecting lower airport fees reflecting lower-cost ground equipment. And if it were then proposed that the federal budget should subsidize ground equipment at the poorer municipal airports, there would appear competing claimants to argue that more good could be done or more lives could be saved by programs for nutrition, pest control, toxic waste disposal, or police and medical care downtown instead of runway lights at the airport.

Let me close this part of the discussion by reiterating with emphasis two points. First, this line of reasoning attempts, when honestly done, to reshuffle the consequences by rearranging proposed programs and comparing alternatives, leaving intact the original weighting system by which the outcomes for different affected individuals, or different affected interests, were to be evaluated. In other words, it explores alternative consequences, assessing those consequences from the points of view of all the affected parties, to see whether, whatever the proposal is or the situation being evaluated, there is "something better." It is therefore of limited, if genuine, usefulness. And the second point is that there is no mystery involved, nothing that cannot be penetrated by a responsible policy maker who is willing to make an appreciable effort to discover whether, indeed, there is something better.

Unfortunately, economists use the term "efficiency" (or the more esoteric "pareto-optimality") to describe this process, and often distinguish between considerations of "equity" and "efficiency." The word "efficiency" sounds more like engineering than human satisfaction, and if I tell you that it is not "efficient" to put the best runway lights at the poorer airport you are likely to think you know exactly what I mean and not like it, perhaps also not liking me. If I tell you that "not efficient" merely means that I can think of something better—something potentially better from the points of view of all parties concerned—you can at least be excused for wondering why I use "efficient" in such an unaccustomed way. The only answer I can think of is that economists talk mainly to each other.

ISSUES IN INCOME DISTRIBUTION

Among the most divisive issues that policy deals with is the distribution of income, or, more inclusively, of income and wealth. Taxation and tariffs, welfare and food stamps, rent control, farm price supports, the regulation of natural gas, minimum wage laws, public housing, social security and its financing, electric-rate regulation, and laws about labor relations and collective bargaining are mainly about the *distribution of income*. At least, controversies over those policies and programs are controversies about the gains and costs to the farmers and the unemployed and the unskilled and the chronically ill and the healthy and the well-to-do. *Freedom* is an issue, but often what is fought over is freedom to pursue profit or livelihood. *Rights* are an issue, but the rights are often rights to welfare, rights to work, rights to life-preserving medical attention, rights to persist in a threatened occupation like fishing or farming, or rights to compete for jobs and markets.

Capital punishment, abortion, and preventive detention are issues that divide us and that are not primarily concerned with the distribution of income. But even these are loaded with distributional significance: recently it has been abortion at public expense, more than the right to procure an abortion, that has dominated policy; capital punishment and the rights of defendants involve procedures that may be suspect precisely because they discriminate by income.

Ethics aside, we expect controversy along lines of economic interest. The auto industry wants protection against foreign automobiles, the steel industry against foreign steel, and the meat industry against foreign beef, and we expect both business and labor to couch their self-serving arguments in the most captivating moral terms they can think of, and their political adversaries to do likewise. But for those among us who want to affect a disinterested stance and to judge right and wrong by reference to the public interest, with special concern for the ethical implications of particular policies or the overall distribution of income, what help can we get from economics, or from economics and those related analytic disciplines?

One part of the answer is, precious little on the relative virtues of different distributions of income or on how much money a poor person has to get in order to justify a policy that denies a dollar to somebody who is not poor. True to the somewhat ethically evasive character that I have been imputing to economics, economic reasoning is better at helping to choose ways to accomplish a distributional objective than at helping to choose objectives. It can help in minimizing the cost to the rich of doing something good for the poor. And in case that does not interest you, it can help to point out that it ought to, because there is more for the poor at any given cost to the rich, if you do it in the least wasteful way. And often the way economics does that is simply by looking at two things at a time.

Economics is often like a broker or mediator in a bargaining process, good at promoting "integrative bargaining." Integrative bargaining is searching for superior trades, finding ways to bring to the bargaining table those things that matter more to the beneficiary of a concession than to the party making the concession. If your coffee break costs me as much as an expanded medical program that you would rather have, trading coffee for medicine may make us both better off. But it requires bringing both topics to the table together.

Let me illustrate with another tantalizing proposition that I put to my students, who reject it, and to whom I then make it palatable by dealing with it in two dimensions rather than one.

We go back to the income tax. The income tax allows you to subtract, in going from gross income to taxable income, $1,000 per child. It allows it whether the child is an infant or a teenager, whether you have six or only one, and—what I want to focus on—whether your income is $20,000 or $120,000 per year. The question is, if at $20,000 per year $1,000 is allowed for each child, at $120,000 should the deduction still be $1,000? Let me propose, as I do to my students, that the figure ought to be much larger than $1,000 per child at the higher income.

One way to make the case is that high-income families spend much more on children and the "cost" of raising a child is much more. There are counterarguments. One is that the children of the rich are already so privileged that they do not need tax privileges, too, compared with poor children; it should not be official policy that rich children enjoy several thousand dollars of family income whereas poor children get along on $1,000. Another is that although the rich children indeed "cost" more than the poor children and there is no need to begrudge them their superior life and environment, there is also no reason why taxpayers should collectively support well-to-do families with many children. There are other worthy causes that deserve more tax relief. It can also be argued that some wealthy couples like nice automobiles and expensive living, some like pets, and some like children; and whether or not we approve of those who choose to spend their money on children, we need not share the cost with them, especially if we ourselves are less fortunate.

That is not an easy argument for my side to win. But to set the stage I point out an anomaly. The tax schedule that Congress legislates is in two parts. First there is a schedule of taxes for a married couple without children; then there is a formula to adjust for family size. It is this familysize formula that allows the invariant $1,000 per child. To increase that allowance for the well-to-do would lower the taxes for well-to-do families with children, and reduce the total taxes paid by the well-to-do. But Congress could just as well have legislated a tax schedule not for the childless couple but for the "typical" family, say a family with two children or three. Thus, the basic schedule would be the schedule for the family with children. Then there would be an adjustment, because families without children can afford to pay more income tax. A "childless premium" might be attached; that could be done either by canceling some other deductions and exemptions, say $1,000 worth for the family that had one child and $2,000 for the family with two children, or by adding "virtual income" to the basic income in arriving at taxable income. Question: In raising the taxable income of the childless couple, compared with the base-rate family with two or three children, do we *add* the same amount of taxable income to the family with only $20,000 as we add to the family with $120,000?

Evidently the family earning $20,000 can pay somewhat more taxes if it has no children than if it has two or three, but not much; the childless couple with $60,000 or $120,000 appears able to pay a good deal more. Just sending a child to college can cost $5,000 or $10,000 per year. If the object is to get all the taxes we can from the well-to-do families, once we have screwed the taxes as tightly as we can on families with three children there ought to be a lot more still to be squeezed out of that childless couple living on $60,000 or $120,000 a year. It looks as though the adjustment for childlessness should be much larger for the family that has three or six times $20,000.

But that is simply the mathematical contradiction of the principle we worked out a moment ago! We originally found it difficult to argue that the taxable-income difference should be larger for the rich family than for the poor; now we find that the taxable-income difference ought to be much larger for the rich family than for the poor. Since the same income tax can be formulated either as a base schedule for the childless couple with an adjustment for children, or as a base schedule for the family with children plus an adjustment for childlessness, it should not make any difference which way we do it. But by merely reformulating the same income tax we seem to have arrived at a diametrically opposite conclusion.

By themselves, the students work it out if I give them a little time, but my pedagogic interest is not in the tax treatment of children in different families but in the proposition that two dimensions give you more freedom than one. So I resolve the issue for them.

We have a two-dimensional tax schedule. One dimension is income, the other is family size. We can manipulate them independently. True, with any particular income schedule a larger *deduction* for children at high-income levels reduces the taxes paid by the rich. If *your* ways and means subcommittee first sets the basic schedule for childless families and *my* sub-committee gets only to determine the size of the deduction for children, there is no way that I can enlarge the child differential at high incomes without merely forgiving some wealthy families some taxes. But if my subcommittee goes first, and we determine larger differentials for high-income families with children, you can set as progressive a schedule as you please, making sure that the rich pay the same amount of taxes you would have wanted them to pay if my subcom-mittee had treated children quite differently. Together we can have as wide a child differential as we please at high-income levels without providing any average tax advantage to the rich, by designing the schedule so that the *childless rich* pay more than they would have if the child differential were small.

In two dimensions we can have it both ways. We adjust the child differentials to conform to our notions *at each income level* of what difference children ought to make to the taxes paid at that income. And we design the basic income tax schedule so that, compared with the poor, the well-to-do pay whatever we want them to pay. The income dimension and the familysize dimension allow us two degrees of freedom and we can meet both objectives.

The test of my success is not whether I have changed the minds of the students and they can go propose over lunch that the children of the rich should receive larger income tax deductions, and proceed to persuade their incredulous luncheon partners. The test is whether on the next issue that arises, such as energy pricing, they understand the principle well enough to see how it applies there.

And how is that? Well, *that* is that rising energy prices during a time when energy costs are going up and shortages are becoming common, do two things. They induce an "efficient" response to the rising cost of energy. And they impose an income loss on consumers, a loss that may be quite disproportionate in its distribution, perhaps especially affecting the poor or at least the poor who live in cold climates or depend on transportation.

By an "efficient" response I mean (a) that people will use less fuel because it costs more in the other things money will buy, (b) that those who have stronger needs for fuel will pay for more and burn it whereas those who have less urgent needs will save their money for other things, and (c) that the supply of fuels will be enhanced from sources that were not economical at lower prices, or through new technologies that are economical now that fuel savings are worth more. (Whether the term "efficient" is being used in the same or a different way is a little intricate, and we need not resolve the matter here.)

If the decision is whether to let the price of fuel go up or instead to impose price control, to subsidize imports, or to reduce demand by denying specific uses, we have a dilemma. We have what in the jargon is sometimes called a "tradeoff." We can hurt the poor (and many others in all kinds of special categories that are especially dependent on fuel) by making them spend more for the fuel they need with less left over for other necessities, or we can spare them that hardship while pricing fuel in a way that encourages waste and discourages conservation and new supplies. Here we are again weighing "equity" against "efficiency." An inescapable dilemma? Nothing to do but compromise, with strongly divided interests in compromising toward the energy-efficient end of the scale and toward the hardship-minimizing end?

To the rescue we bring the two-dimensional approach. We have two problems. We can call them the energy problem and the poverty problem. They may turn out to be an efficiency problem and an equity problem, but our object is to avoid that. Like a Supreme Court that shies away from constitutional questions if it can settle a case on other merits, we try to resolve the competing claims of poverty and energy without choosing sides between equity and efficiency. The way we do so is to recognize that although we have two objectives or criteria or competing claims, we also have two sets of instruments for coping. We have an energy problem and a poverty problem; we have an energy program and a poverty program. With two programs to work with, and two objectives to meet, we may be able to evade the ethical dilemma.

All we need technically is a way to identify the poor (and the otherwise deserving) who would suffer severely with higher fuel prices, estimate what they would lose in the higher prices, and give them an income subsidy. Not easy, but not likely to be terribly difficult. No program is perfect in targeting help to *all* of those and *only* those who are intended to receive it; but compared with holding down the price of natural gas—while fending off all the customers who want cheap gas but cannot be accommodated, and discouraging exploration for new supply, letting rich and poor alike enjoy the cheap gas as long as they are among those lucky enough to be old customers, the rich getting proportionately more benefit because, being rich, they can buy more of everything including gas—a combination of higher gas prices and a separate compensatory program targeted on the not-rich, or on the poor, or on the very poor, can easily be a superior policy.

It will be opposed, of course, by those who benefit from cheap fuel who could not put forward a legitimate claim under a poverty program. It will also be opposed by the poor or their representatives if they have learned by experience that the principle of splitting the problem into two parts is sometimes an excuse for relieving the one part from responsibility for what happens to the poor while proceeding to neglect the second part that was supposed to take care of them. (Indeed, having separate congressional committees deal with energy and with programs that compensate the poor makes it appear that if the energy committee does not protect the poor, there is no assurance that another committee will.)

But again we may have transformed an ethical problem into a political problem.

We may also have run up against another ethical problem, one that did not reveal itself in the original formulation. If we have funds with which to compensate the poor, why compensate only the poor who are made worse off by the rising prices of fuel? Specifically, suppose we put a 50-cent tax on gasoline and dedicate a fraction of the proceeds to offsetting the cost increases to families whose income is below the bottom quartile. As a way to buy off the poor's opposition to the tax, concentrating assistance on those, and only those, whose poverty will be aggravated by the tax can be shrewd politics. But once we have the tax and a source of revenue to help the poor in proportions determined by their dependence on fuel, somebody will propose that there are people in the bottom 10 percent who were *already* poorer, before the tax, than a lot of low-income people after the tax. The family with $12,000 that has burned eight gallons of gasoline per week stands to lose $200 a year from the 50-cent tax and fall to $11,800, whereas the elderly couple that has no car and lives on $6,000 qualifies for no gasoline bonus. The poor family that paints its modest home and finds the cost of paint up $200 might prefer that the gas-tax revenue help all the disadvantaged, not only those who burn gasoline.

This issue looks like an ethical one, and not the one we started with. It reflects our political system. Our system recognizes that there are some poor and otherwise disadvantaged and deserving people who should receive help. But instead of dealing with their needs in a unified way, deciding how much we want to help, we tend to help the poor a little in each of many different and uncoordinated things we do. We help with food stamps and medical care and housing and tax relief and reduced subway fares, and we invoke hardship in programs to keep farm prices up and rents down. This piecemeal approach does not necessarily do a bad job, but it does repeatedly create that ethical dilemma that arose out of our compensatory programs for gasoline and heating fuel.

If a family loses its rent-controlled apartment because rent controls are eliminated or because the apartment is eliminated, and if taxes are raised on all rental apartments and some of the proceeds set aside to help the disadvantaged, do we help only those disadvantaged by loss of rent-controlled apartments or all who are disadvantaged by race, handicap, or low income?

THE MARKET ETHIC

Nothing distinguishes economists from other people as much as a belief in the market system, or what some call the free market. A perennial difficulty in dealing with policy is the inability of people who are not economists (and some who are economists) to ascertain how much of the economists' interest in and confidence in the way markets work is faith and how much is analysis; or, how much is due to the economists' observation of the way markets work and their judgments about *outcomes* and how much is a belief that the *process* is right and just (or right, if occasionally unjust; or right and justice is indeterminate).

The problem is compounded because some economists do identify markets with freedom of choice, or construe markets as processes that yield returns to individuals that are commensurate with their deserts. A conclusion that arises in the analysis of a perfectly working competitive free market is that people who work for hire are paid amounts equivalent to their marginal contributions to the total product, "marginal" referring to the difference it makes "at the margin" if one's contribution is withdrawn while the rest of the system continues. An ethical question is whether one's marginal product constitutes an appropriate rate of remuneration. Critics of the theory, however, typically divert their energies toward the empirical issue, arguing that actual markets work differently. Nevertheless there are economists who have given considerable thought to the matter who find that a system that distributes the fruits of economic activity in accordance with marginal contributions, be they contributions in effort or ideas or property, is ethically attractive, and others who have given considerable thought to it and find that such a system has great practical merit but little ethical claim. Most of these others see a need for policies to readjust the results.

There is even an important socialist school of market economics, building on pioneering work by Abba Lerner and Oscar Lange in the 1930s, that asserts that pricing in a socialist economy should mimic the pricing of a perfectly competitive free market, that such an economy would be least wasteful of resources, and that extramarket income transfers should compensate for any results that one does not like.

And there is a large body of professional opinion among economists, perhaps more among older than among younger ones, to the effect that markets, left to themselves, may turn in a pretty poor performance, but not nearly as poor when left alone as when tinkered with, especially when the tinkering is simplistically done or done cleverly to disguise the size and distribution of the costs or losses associated with some "innocuous" favoritism.

Whether or not an economist shares the ethic or the ideology that values the working of the market system for its own sake (or that identifies it not only *with* personal freedom but *as* personal freedom), most professional economists accept certain principles that others, if not the economists themselves, would recognize to have ethical content.

An example is the role of incentives. Economists see economic incentives operating everywhere; they find nothing offensive or "coercive" about the responses of people to economic opportunities and sanctions; they have no interest in overcoming or opposing incentives for the sake of victory over an enemy; and they have a predilection toward tilting incentives, augmenting, dampening, restructuring incentives, and even inventing incentives to induce people to behave in ways that are collectively more rewarding or less frustrating. You can usually tell an economist from a noneconomist by asking whether at the peak season for tourism and camping there should be substantial entrance fees at the campgrounds of national parks.

A related touchstone of market economics is the idea that most people are better at spending their own money than somebody else is at spending it for them. Sometimes this idea is directly elevated into an ethical principle: the consumer's right to make his own mistakes. But usually it is simply that giving a poor family a shopping cart filled from the shelves of a supermarket is not as good as giving the family equivalent money and letting them do their own shopping. The idea is that *they* will get more for *your* money if *they* get to spend it. A given amount of your money will do more good for the family from the family's point of view if it is spent the way they want it spent.

Economists have a long checklist of exceptions to this principle, exceptions from the point of view of the family's welfare and from other points of view, but generally the economist thinks the burden of proof belongs on those who want to give food stamps or subway tokens or eyeglasses to the poor and the elderly. Proof may not be hard to come by; but the burden, for most economists, should be on those who do not trust the efficacy of money. It often sounds like an ethical principle. Maybe it is.

There have been proposals to compensate poor families in cash for the exact amount by which their heating bills, at deregulated prices, exceed what the same fuel would have cost at regulated prices. The question was raised whether they should not merely receive unconditionally an amount of money estimated in advance by that formula. The negative retort was that, being poor, they could not be trusted to spend the money on heating fuel. They might spend it on something else! This is the point at which most economists can only shake their heads slowly in speechless frustration.

Economists also tend to believe in a number of legal and institutional arrangements—certain property rights and contractual arrangements—and to oppose some regulations or impediments to market behavior in ways that appear to attach value, positive or negative, to the institutions and arrangements themselves. Often economists reasoned their way to these views so long ago that they remember *what* they favor better than *why*, and act as if value attached to the arrangements themselves. But usually what they have, or think they have, is an understanding of a complex system of multifarious interacting units of behavior—individuals, families, firms, municipalities, clubs, foundations—and their reasoning has led them to conclude that certain arrangements are justified in terms of the *results* they lead to, and other arrangements not.

What makes it difficult in communication is that the economist, like a physiologist or a physicist, or like a scientifically trained forest ranger presiding over the complex ecology of forest wildlife, has a big investment in some intellectual equipment that he or she can neither show nor share. With time, yes: a bright, motivated, captive college audience can get the idea after a hundred class hours augmented by appropriate reading, but even they do not have the experience to use that paraphernalia on live subjects outside the classroom.

How can I say this, having told you at the beginning of this essay that if he and she are worth their salt, the analysts can communicate at least the plausibility of their results in an hour or two or three if you are willing to participate intellectually?

The reconciliation is thus. If fluent in analysis, he or she should be able to cope with a particular problem *locally*. By "locally" I mean to deal with any particular proposal on its local merits, judging it as a particular addition or subtraction or intrusion or adjustment to what otherwise exists. It is like making or disposing of a particular proposal to improve the plumbing system of your house, or your body, by showing that whatever Proposal X was intended to do can be done better some other way, or by showing that whatever Proposal X was to accomplish it has side effects that you may wish to judge too high a price. The rangers may need all of their ecological science to perceive the value of culling a herd of deer or letting a fire continue burning; they may not need to share all of that science with you to show you that, with your values, and perceiving the things that they can make plausibly evident to you, you might prefer to cull the herd or let the fire burn.

If they *cannot* explain it in a way that lets you make the value judgments, forest rangers or economists, do not rely on them. If they *will* not explain it, insist.

Chapter 8 / THE AMERICAN PLURALIST CONCEPTION OF POLITICS

SHELDON S. WOLIN

PLURALISM AND POWER

During the past two decades, roughly from 1960 to 1980, the major political institutions of this country have exhibited increasing signs of disintegration, even of collapse. The presidency is unable to generate sustained leadership and, as a result, retreats fitfully to the more secure role of manager of the executive branch and, from that redoubt, issues tired pronouncements and promises about making government more efficient and less expensive. The Congress, which has always been plagued by fragmentation, is now almost completely reduced to a feudal system in which powerful (and usually senior) senators and congressmen play the role of

SHELDON S. WOLIN ● Department of Politics, 206 Corwin Hall, Princeton University, Princeton, New Jersey 08540.

liege lords, and surrounded by retainers and servants in the form of staff experts (who, of course, often exercise considerable influence over their masters), they develop relations of influence and favor with lesser congressional lords, with various strategically placed bureaucratic agencies, and with the emissaries of powerful economic and social groups. Congress is not so much a "branch" of government as a honeycomb in which the maze of power and influence produces circularity rather than direction or purpose, except to manufacture honey. In the eyes of the public—as virtually every opinion poll has demonstrated—this elected branch has little credibility and less respect, even though, in constitutional theory, it is supposed to stand closest to the people. The executive branch, or administration, has grown so cumbersome and distended that the marvel is that it functions at all. It governs the society on a daily basis, which has come to mean bureaucratic regulation and bureaucratic benefit.

The major political institution in the most critical condition is the system of political parties. Early on in the history of our republic, the political party was perceived to be a crucial institution if the rigidities of the Constitution, with its omnipresent possibility of stalemate between the main branches of government, were to be eased. Throughout most of our history parties served to give our politics the small focus it has had. They have organized our politics by nominating candidates, offering a vague political identity to voters, furthering compromises, blurring issues and so defusing them, coordinating (in a loose fashion) local, state, and national organizations, developing political elites, and providing a modest opposing check to whichever party happened to be in power. At the present time very little remains of these traditional functions, except to legitimate candidates by appearing to nominate them and to furnish a central banking service for the collection, disbursement, and laundering of funds.

Yet amid all this facade and rubble there is one fundamental principle of American politics, which was recognized to be operative even before the Constitution was ratified and is still regarded as exerting the most decisive influence over the actual practice of politics, as well as over the ideological expression of it. It is, further, the basic element in most attempts by political scientists to explain how the American political system works. This surviving principle is "pluralism." So powerful, persistent, and persuasive has been its hold over American political life and political consciousness that if there is such a thing as a "genius" or spirit at work in American politics, pluralism's claim to be that genius comes close to being undisputed. The defenders of pluralist politics have argued that it is the American alternative to a politics based on class struggle or to one based on sharply opposing ideologies.

The distinguishing feature of pluralist politics is that the main actors are not individual politicians but organized groups. Although there are numerous sorts of groups active in American politics, including cultural, patriotic, scholarly, and ethnic ones, the most publicized and the most powerful is the economic interest group. The interest group may be defined as the organization of economic activities, entities, and power for the purpose of securing favorable treatment from those in positions of political or public authority. The perceived characteristics of the interest group are suggested by other names that have been given to it, such as "lobby" and "pressure group." These are intended to evoke an image of political activity as carried on behind the scenes, rather than out in the open. Pressure groups, as such, do not seek to be elected and they take care to avoid public exposure and visibility unless they can make themselves appear as public benefactors. But the interest group or lobby, although the most powerful form of pluralism, is not the only form. Pluralism is also practiced as a mode of representation. Public bodies such as councils, boards, or commissions will include—as a result of either a statutory mandate, an informal decision, or a concession to pressure from organized interests —representation from some group(s).

Both forms of pluralism have important implications for the practice of politics, especially for a society that conceives itself to be, in some serious way, committed to democracy and to the egalitarianism associated with that political ideal. Some of these implications can be identified by means of two contemporary examples of pluralist representation.

On October 30, 1979 the long-awaited report of the President's Commission on the Accident at Three Mile Island was made public. The subject of that report was the most serious nuclear accident in history. In dealing with it, the commission had to consider some highly technical matters involving physics, engineering, information systems, and administrative management. Of the twelve members appointed to the commission, only six could be said to have strong scientific or engineering backgrounds. Of the remaining six members, one was described as "the mother of six children," another as the president of the United Steelworkers' Union, another as a professor of journalism, another as a professor of sociology, another as a governor, and still another as an exgovernor who was also president of the National Audubon Society and a chemist.

It is not easy to discern here a consistent principle that justified the selection of some representatives or the exclusion of others. Why, for example, was there a professor of journalism, but not of economics? Or a trade union president, but not a spokesman for the urban poor? Or, for that matter, for the urban rich? Who did the actual selecting? Was there an unpublicized network that furnished nominations to the president or to his advisors, and how was it established? Some of these questions could be answered by saying that some representatives were symbols of categories—for example, housewives—rather than of organized groups, and that their function was to legitimate rather than to represent. But our other questions point to the existence of a structure of power that enabled some groups to be represented and others not.

Representation of groups appears as the end result of a process of screening by which some groups are connected with authoritative structures of powers whereas other groups are denied that connection. Accordingly, we shall have to ask whether some groups are consistently more successful in acquiring that connection and systematically advantaged by it; and whether other groups fail to connect with the structure of power and influence and, as a consequence, are systematically disadvantaged. If the practice of pluralism works in this way, then what is the justification for a system that works unequally, favoring some over others? And is that justification actually made, or, instead, has an ideology been concocted that obscures the reality of inequality by the appearance of pluralism?

When we turn from the formal structure of pluralism to consider the content of the decisions that a pluralistically representative body is expected to deliver, we find considerable obscurity once more. It could not have been expected of the Three Mile Island commission that its mainly nontechnicial membership would produce an expert judgment concerning the events in question, much less one about the future design of nuclear reactors or the relative merits of nuclear energy as a source of power. Whatever authority might attach to the commission's findings and recommendations, it could not be the authoritativeness associated with scientific expertise.

Does that mean that the logic governing the choice of the commission's members recognized that the uniqueness of the circumstances of the accident, its unprecedented character, excluded the likelihood that there could be a definitive expert judgment? Or is it that, although in principle an expert judgment could have been made—that is, a judgment based on facts, scientific knowledge, and the intuitions of experienced administrators and scientists—such a judgment was not politically feasible, given the level of public anxiety and confusion?

If this latter consideration was uppermost in the minds of those who had actually determined the composition of the commission, then the pluralism of the commission appears in a different light. Its heterogeneity was intended primarily to soothe public anxiety and to blunt the effect of antinuclear criticism without seriously compromising the preexisting investments and projected commitments to the development of nuclear power. By this reading, pluralism and the toleration of diversity embodied in the composition of the commission are but the surface appearance of the reality of the power of the groups which, for a variety of reasons, were committed to the further development of nuclear power.

What was at stake was the legitimacy of a distinctively contemporary form of power, the power of government, corporations, and applied scientific knowledge. The politics surrounding and pervading the issue cannot be crudely analyzed as an attempt to "stack" a public body so that it would compose an apologia for nuclear power and private utilities. As a matter of fact the report was critical of the operators of the Three Mile Island facility and of the Nuclear Regulatory Commission. The report, however, has mostly been ignored by the president and Congress. This outcome is not unusual, and it points to an important lesson about the difference between groups with meager resources that must be husbanded and used very selectively, and for whom a well-publicized defeat is often disastrous and groups whose economic resources and political connections are such that they can afford to lose a few highly publicized and brief skirmishes because they are powerful enough to play pluralist politics for the long run. Indeed, to the extent that a group is very powerful it can practice a "rational" politics that accepts defeats because those defeats will actually help to legitimate the successes that, ultimately, cannot be denied to the most powerful groups. It is easier to sanction a victory when the victor is seen as having experienced defeats previously in the same "game." Although the invocation of the long run reminds us, perhaps morbidly, of Lord Keynes's remark that in the long run we are all dead, it should also remind us of the ancient legal maxim that corporations are immortal.

Perhaps another illustration will help. The National Institutes of Health has established a program to appraise medical practices and technologies that, on their face, have important consequences for the health and solvency of many Americans. The scope of the program is wide: any drug, device, or medical or surgical procedure may be reviewed. The reviewing process itself was designed to incorporate representation other than, and in addition to, the medical profession, sciences, or public health services. Its aim, in the words of the director, Dr. Seymour M. Perry, is "consensus development." Accordingly, consensus is "developed" by selecting consumers, lawyers, and—a recent innovation in the practice of pluralism—"ethicists" for appointment to review committees. As a result of discussions instituted under the program, several guidelines have been suggested (e.g., regarding mastectomies, the use of insect-bite kits, ear tubes, etc.) although the program is not accompanied by any power to enforce its recommendations.

Once more some of the same questions emerge as with the Three Mile Island commission. How pluralistic and representative can a process be when it is instituted and controlled by an organization that is not selected by those who are ultimately affected by its programs and that, historically, has stood far closer to the interests whose procedures and products are at issue? Is there a code of respectability to which critical or oppositionist groups must conform if they wish to be included in the procedures and processes of pluralism? Does the operation of pluralism, therefore, impose tacit but nonetheless effective constraints upon the extent to which a group can display a critical, militant, or radical viewpoint? Is the phenomenon of pluralism less the "spontaneous" expression of social and cultural diversity than of the requirements of bureaucracies, governmental, economic, and professional, and hence shaped by technobureaucratic needs which, in turn are grounded in the power structure of the political economy that has supplanted the old bifurcated system in which "government" and "economy" were, in some degree, distinguishable?

This question was implicit in the structure of the Three Mile Island commission and in the presuppositions of its report. In this instance as in the vast majority of instances of pluralist representation the bodies are presented with choices among the *consequences* rather than among the structure or devices that have produced the consequences. The mother of six, the journalism professor, or even the governors were not consulted regarding the initial decision to invest in nuclear energy, just as they, or their counterparts, were not consulted when mastectomies were introduced.

This point raises the possibility that the purpose of representation is not to elicit participation or to produce a policy statement reflecting diverse viewpoints, but to clothe power with authority. The power of certain groups had established the structure of the nuclear industry, public and private; but the Three Mile Island accident had provoked opposition that was threatening to that structure. The problem of the proponents of nuclear power was to restore legitimacy for their enterprise in the aftermath of the accident.

Legitimacy is a complex notion. Minimally, it means that one is legally authorized or entitled to perform some act. But in a political context legitimacy acquires an added element, a certain aura which earlier centuries sometimes called *dignitas* or *majestas*, but which in modern, more democratic times comes from the great value that is associated with law and from the belief that the authority of the law is derived from the supreme authority in a human society, the sovereign body of the people. Law stands for the highest form of standards in a system of standards to which all members of the society are obligated. In a society whose political identity is affirmed to be importantly linked with free and popular elections, the exalted status of law is usually attributed to the fact that legislation is primarily the creation of a legislature elected by the people. An undertaking that is legitimated is one that has been established or confirmed by public authority and hence, in a political sense, has been declared "right," that is, the power that the actor or agency will exercise is beneficial to the public good. Legitimacy is valuable because it reduces opposition or "friction" and enables power to proceed more efficiently, without having to ward off attacks directed against the basic structure—in this case, of the nuclear power industry.

Pluralism presents a problem for a theory of legitimacy

because its implicit presupposition is that no such collective entity or actor as "the people" exists. Society is composed of a variety of different interest groups and social classes. Pluralism is thus the dissolvent of the idea of the people and hence of any claim that "the people" can act or will. But if that is the case, we are the possessors of a form of politics that has no theory of legitimacy to accompany it and to clothe its results in "right."

EVOLUTION OF PLURALISM

How things appear may not be what they are. This ancient maxim is familiar enough in everyday life, as well as in the laboratory. It has a special force, however, when we are dealing with political or social phenomena. Such phenomena do not simply "appear" and they are no more random than so-called "natural phenomena." They, too, are the manifestation of structures and processes, but unlike their analog in the "natural world"—whatever that phrase might mean—social and political structures and processes are sometimes designed, but more frequently shaped, so as to produce certain types of appearance and to obscure or conceal certain realities.

Men and women of science are accustomed to think in terms of objects that are unaffected by history. There is no history of the cell, although there is a history of ideas, conceptions, and knowledge about it. Political phenomena are not like that. They *are* their history and that history is one in which the terms or concepts may remain constant, but the content and meaning do not. We shall find this to be the case with the complex of terms that make up the idea of pluralism.

It will be my premise that the reality represented by the interrelation of these terms can only be understood politically and theoretically if we attempt to understand it historically. Without a historical understanding, we stand a good chance of being misled by the appearances that the structure of pluralism intends to produce.

The main postulates of pluralism are these: (a) Society consists essentially of a variety of groups organized around what they conceive to be their particular "interests." (b) In order to promote and defend their interests, groups use their resources to influence public officials and politicians, hoping thereby to shape public laws, decisions, and policies. (c) Conflict and competition among groups is restrained by a tacit consensus among the groups that they will observe the "rules of the game" as embodied in the relevant constitutional and public laws. (d) If group politics is to be kept within socially desirable limits, public officials and group leaders must accept a "politics of negotiation" in which bargaining and compromise are the primary forms of political action and the substantive determinants of public policies.

Bargaining and compromise are not only familiar modes of action, but political values as well. They express the conviction that unless rival and conflicting groups recognize limits to their behavior and accept defeats as part of the "game," social peace and unity will constantly be endangered. Although the value of compromise seems the obvious and natural complement to the politics of pluralism, it seems obvious mainly when economic or material issues are at stake. But when pluralism takes the form of religious, ethnic, or cultural diversities, it seems less appropriate, even wrong, to install compromise as the primary value. Toleration is the value that seems more appropriate to these forms of pluralism.

Toleration is often treated like compromise, as the natural ethical complement to pluralism. The reasoning runs roughly in this way. It is a necessary condition of social peace in a society, which, in fact, is pluralistic, that all groups should be allowed the freedom to act as they see fit, provided they do not harm other groups, interfere with their freedom, or upset public order. Toleration further stipulates that public authority should be neutral toward the various groups. One major problem created by toleration concerns its implications for a condition in which groups differ not only in their values but in their power. There is something incongruous about invoking toleration for economic concentrations of power, for example. As we shall see, however, that has, in fact, been done.

Leaving this matter aside for the moment, neither toleration nor compromise provides much in the way of guidance for resolving public controversies. Toleration seems mainly a negative ethic; compromise suggests a counsel of prudence that advises against pushing one's power or claims to the extreme. Accordingly, there seems to be need for a political ethic that would serve in guiding action toward what is "right" in circumstances where claims, values, and powers are in conflict. Ethics, in this context, stands for the need to have public norms to which there can be appeal in order to reconcile the inevitable conflicts among diverse groups, or to judge among them, selecting the one that appears—by some standard—"right," even if it involves enforcing a policy against the wishes of some powerful groups.

Of these three terms, I shall first examine pluralism because it is the more fundamental one. As my earlier remarks suggested, the other terms—toleration and ethics—although important, are derivative.

Students of American government and politics have long considered pluralism to be the master principle of the American system, "the good society itself in operation."[1] It is at

---

[1]Seymour M. Lipset, *Political Man* (Garden City, N.Y.: Doubleday, 1960), p. 403.

once the explanation of why and how that system works, as well as why it is deserving of our admiration, gratitude, and loyalty. The postulates of pluralism are conveniently stated by one of its ablest expositors:

> Instead of a single center of sovereign power there must be multiple centers of power . . . no part of the people, such as a majority, ought to be absolutely sovereign.
>
> Because one center of power is set against another, power itself will be tamed, civilized, controlled, and limited to decent human purposes, while coercion, the most evil form of power, will be reduced to a minimum.
>
> Because even minorities are provided with opportunities to veto solutions they strongly object to, the consent of all will be won in the long run.
>
> Because constant negotiations among different centers of power are necessary in order to make decisions, citizens and leaders will perfect the precious art of dealing peacefully with their conflicts, and not merely to the benefit of one partisan but to the mutual benefit of all the parties to a conflict.[2]

As a theory of politics pluralism is regarded by its exponents as the mirror image of the "real world," and not as an arbitrary construct of the theoretical imagination. They see it as the expression of the unique nature of American history. Thus, the following quotation from a widely used textbook contends, America has been a pluralist society from the beginning:

> American society in its colonial and early national periods was fragmented by various religious, ethnic, regional, and economic differences. . . . During the 19th century, these trends were continued through new immigration and internal migration. . . . As the nation moved from agriculture to industry, our economic structure became more specialized, increasing the number of

[2]Robert A. Dahl, *Pluralist Democracy in the United States* (Chicago: Rand McNally, 1967), p. 24.

industries and the competition within industries and
giving rise to a heterogeneous labor force. These socioeconomic forces produced a diversified society, and in
such a society a broad range of interests sought expression in the political system.[3]

In contemporary political and social science, pluralism is
primarily associated with the organized activities of economic
interests. Descriptions like the above make it seem as though
the natural form of pluralism is the economic interest group.
Historically, however, this notion is an oversimplification that
conceals the important struggle that saw the interest conception of groups take over and dominate the idea of pluralism.
This shift represents a later stage in the historical development
of the idea of pluralism. Its modern beginnings, as distinct
from its medieval origins,[4] were expressed not in the experience of economic groups but in the struggles of religious
groups to survive in a world where religious uniformity was
regarded as the necessary condition of social stability and
political authority. Pluralism emerges in the modern controversy concerning the spiritual and political implications of the
principle of toleration; it was not inspired by conflicts involving
material interests in the strict sense. A brief discussion of the
historical controversy over religious toleration will be helpful
because later pluralism transformed what was originally a
political theory of religious groups into a justification of a form
of politics that legitimated the domination of society by powerful economic groups. Pluralism began as a plea for the state
to allow spiritual groups to exist; it became an ideology that
legitimated the great power of "private" groups and made

[3]Emmett S. Redford *et al.*, *Politics and Government in the United States*, 2nd ed.,
National edition (New York: Harcourt, Brace, & World, 1968), p. 114.
[4]Otto von Gierke, *Political Theories of the Middle Age*, trans. Frederick W.
Maitland (Cambridge: Cambridge University Press, 1900).

the political order into a means for advancing and protecting the interests of the greatest of these great private powers.

The principle of toleration was inspired by the European experience of the sixteenth and seventeenth centuries, when bloody and destructive civil and national wars were fought to decide which of the competing religions was "the" true one. The first sustained defense of toleration was not made by any of the major sects or by the Catholic church. Instead it was developed by a group of sixteenth century French writers, the *Politiques,* who became convinced that social peace and political order would never be established except on a principle that refused supremacy to any one faith and extended security to all or most sects. The next major battleground of religious struggle was England. During the revolutionary and civil wars of the seventeenth century there were several voices raised in defense of religious toleration, but it was not until late in the century, after the first restoration of the monarchy in 1660 and the later alteration of it by the Glorious Revolution of 1688, that a start was made in enacting legal guarantees of toleration.

A theoretical connection between toleration and pluralism was forged by a famous pamphlet published in 1689, *Letter on Toleration,* written by John Locke, one of the greatest of modern political theorists and an important influence on American political thought in the eighteenth century. Although the immediate effect of Locke's plea for a broad extension of toleration—Catholics and Jews excepted—was to benefit the cause of religious freedom, its long-run significance was rather different and more ironic, although not at all inconsistent with the proprietarian bias of Locke's ideas.

Locke's contemporaries immediately recognized that his interest in toleration sprang less from religious zeal than from material concerns, and that it had as much to do with the future of economic associations as with congregations of the faithful. As one of his earliest critics remarked, Locke's principles of toleration tended more "to the advancement of trade and commerce" than to "True Religion . . ."[5] This point could be stated in another way that brings out the general historical significance of his argument. For what Locke did was to break down the centuries-old distinction between religious concerns and socioeconomic interests, between the spiritual and the material, the sacred and the profane. He argued that the two realms, although not identical, were comparable in crucial respects. Although the ostensible purpose behind this strategy was to take the state out of the business of exploiting and policing religious doctrines, Locke's arguments were constructed in such a way that, as religious fervor gave way to secularism, as it did in the eighteenth century, they could be and were used to justify the form of behavior that was to distinguish liberal politics, especially in America, from the end of the eighteenth century down to the present, the form known as "the interest group."

Locke's case for pluralism rested on three fundamental principles: that government existed to protect individual interests, not to regulate them; that individuals were free to organize their individual interests into collective groupings; and that the freedom of individuals and the legal-political protection of individual interests also belonged by right to groups, if the groups were, like civil society itself, voluntary associations created by the consent of individuals.

The assumption behind Locke's first principle is so familiar a dogma of liberalism that its boldness is apt to be overlooked. Locke's claim, that the role of government depended for its

---

[5]Cited in Maurice Cranston, *John Locke* (London: Longmans, Green, 1957), p. 331.

definition on the primary value of individual interests, was nothing less than a reversal of the main arguments for toleration that had been made earlier in the century. Many politicians, despairing of any possibility of getting religious zealots to agree to a settlement of their differences, adopted an Erastian viewpoint that subordinated spiritual to political concerns. They believed that the terms of a religious settlement ought to be determined in the first instance by the needs of the political order. Toleration was needed because the strength of the state was being exhausted by interminable religious disputes. The needs of the state, not of the individual conscience, were proclaimed the decisive factor.

Locke, however, reversed the sequence and its priorities. His case began from the premise that individual interests were the primary value and that the state should be shaped by what those interests required for their well-being. This note was struck at the outset of the *Letter on Toleration* where Locke offered his definition of the "commonwealth":

> The commonwealth seems to me to be a society of men constituted only for the procuring, preserving, and advancing their own civil interests.
>
> Civil interests I call life, liberty, health, and indolency of body [i.e., leisure]; and the possession of outward things, such as money, lands, houses, furniture, and the like.[6]

Within this secular and, one might even say, materialistic context, Locke proceeded to argue that the "salvation of souls" was to be numbered among men's "civil interests."

The argument that Locke developed to accompany his defense of conscience was strikingly similar to the conception

[6]John Locke, *A Letter Concerning Toleration,* ed. John Gough (Oxford: Blackwell, 1948), p. 126.

of private property, which he was among the first to adumbrate and which, in the next two centuries and more, was to become highly influential. He conceived religion as he had private property, as a private matter, a thing appropriated by the individual and carrying the stamp of his activity. Religious beliefs were like objects acquired and owned by the individual conscience; they could not be imposed on the individual by the state—not because political magistrates might not try, but because it was the peculiar nature of beliefs that they could not be truly held unless the individual was freely convinced of their truth. "No religion," Locke asserted, "which I believe not to be true can be either true or profitable unto me."[7] "The care of every man's soul," he went on, "belongs unto himself, and is to be left unto himself."[8]

Although Locke supported these assertions in part by appealing to Scripture, he also drew heavily from everyday economic experience:

> In private domestic affairs, in the management of estates, in the conservation of bodily health, every man may consider what suits his own convenience, and follow what course he likes best. No man complains of the ill-management of his neighbour's affairs. . . . . Nobody corrects a spendthrift.[9]

But, Locke then asked rhetorically, "what if he neglect the care of his soul?" The answer was equally rhetorical:

> What if he neglect the care of his health or of his estate? . . . Will the magistrate provide by an express law that such a one shall not become poor or sick? . . . No man can be forced to be rich or healthful. . . . God himself will not save men against their wills.[10]

[7]Ibid., p. 141.
[8]Ibid., p. 137.
[9]Ibid., p. 136.
[10]Ibid., p. 137.

Locke's advocacy of toleration pointed in two seemingly unrelated directions. The first was the reduction of religion to essentially a matter of private life at the expense of public life. For the paradox of the Christian as well as the Judaic tradition was that whereas both religions exalted the sacred above the profane, both conceived religion to be a part of the public world and one of its main bulwarks. For the most part, neither religion regarded its concerns as a species of private interest. Religious truths were to be shared and used, not appropriated or, as Locke said of property, "fenced off."

The crucial consequence of the privatization of religion can be identified only when we appreciate that religion was the source of most moral and political notions. To make religion a private affair was to encourage the subjectivization of moral and political beliefs derived from, or justified by, private wishes, desires, or interests. Locke's argument prepared the way for a revolution in which moral and political positions were to be justified because they issued from private interests and highly personal convictions. Religion was to be an expression of freedom rather than community.

Locke not only depoliticalized religion by privatizing it, he also redefined the practice of it in ways that made it appear democratic in a radically individualistic sense. Every individual, he proclaimed, had a soul, a conscience over which he was the supreme authority: "Every man . . . has the supreme and absolute authority of judging for himself. And the reason is that nobody else is concerned in it"[11] Formulated in these radically individualistic terms, Locke's conception of conscience appears to have become so personalized as to be without political bearing. Locke did not, however, stop at this point but proceeded to extend the protections of conscience from the individual to the organized group of believers.

[11]Ibid., p. 152.

> A church . . . is a free and voluntary society of men,
> joining themselves together of their own accord in order
> to [sic] the public worshipping of God in such manner
> as they judge acceptable to him, and effectual to the
> salvation of their souls.[12]

Locke's conception of a church as a voluntary association, "absolutely free and spontaneous,"[13] might seem on its face to champion a harmless form of human grouping devoted to prayer, salvation, otherworldliness, and love. In reality, Locke's characterization of the voluntary nature of churches was immediately followed by a claim of a very different sort. He asked, "What is the power of this church?"[14] The question about power has to be raised, Locke explained, because no association "whether of philosophers for learning, of merchants for commerce, . . . no church or company" can "hold together" unless it has the power to regulate its internal affairs and exercise some discipline over its members.[15]

The genius of this move by Locke lay in assimilating churches to worldly associations, including "merchants for commerce," and vice versa: worldly associations gained status by being located on the same plane as spiritual bodies at the same time that they also gained immunity from the state. These consequences were implicit in Locke's starting point that a political society was an arrangement for protecting men's private goods; but the logical character of the consequences also served to disguise the fact that an argument for individual conscience had been shaped into a justification of the power, immunity, and legitimacy of "private" associations. Thus the appearance that Locke constructed was of a

[12]Ibid., p. 129. (I have slightly changed the order of Locke's comments.)
[13]Ibid., pp. 130, 133.
[14]Ibid., p. 129.
[15]Ibid., pp. 129–130, 131–132.

social universe of voluntary, private associations composed of free, uncoerced individuals; the reality was of power groups that, increasingly, were to exploit their immunity as private associations to escape public control while simultaneously employing their resources to influence, even to dictate, public policies.[16]

A final word on Locke's contribution to pluralism. His argument for toleration, as we have seen, appealed to a democratic principle of the equality of all individual consciences: each individual possessed a conscience and each was entitled as much as any other person to be free in the exercise of it. However, the political significance of freedom of conscience is that it did more for material interests than for spiritual concerns. Locke's argument that each conscience should be equally sacrosanct and protected seems perfectly in keeping with the spiritual character of religious belief and of religious associations. The individual conscience is presumed safe in the keeping of a spiritual association. The latter, Locke allowed, might teach, exhort, warn, and, in extremity, expel a member, but it could not deprive him or her of "civil rights and worldly goods."[17] Plainly, a church that could not impose penalties backed by material punishments would, perforce, be limited to the exercise of a truly "spiritual" power, to a form of suasion rather than coercion. Moreover, any individual who felt uncomfortable in one church had only to leave it for another, or found his or her own. Thus the nature of

[16]The utopian version of this inversion of reality and appearance was expressed a short time ago by the presidential nominee of the Libertarian Party. That party is ostensibly dedicated to eliminating government altogether, and so its standard-bearer could declare: "Ultimately we believe in the complete privatization of society and the transferral of public functions, such as roads, etc., to private hands" (*New York Times*, 21 January 1980). The candidate was, I should add, a company lawyer.

[17]Locke, p. 135.

the church in the Lockean scheme was a perfect mirror of Lockean notions of equality. Since the church had no effective power, it could not promote and enforce inequality among believers.

But when we turn to other associations brought under the protective umbrella of Locke's principles of toleration, the results are different. Some of those associations, notably those devoted to economic and scientific concerns, could be expected to produce inequalities in the normal pursuit of their objectives. Yet under Locke's conception of "civil interests," which lumped conscience and property under the same rubric, these associations would gain protection from the same democratic principle of equal rights that was protecting believers and churches. Thereby the democratic principle of equal rights would work to promote and defend inequality and, at the same time, to reduce democracy to a formal principle for most members of society.[18]

To summarize, Locke's contribution to the development of pluralism had been to expand the principle of toleration from a defense of individual conscience to a defense of group autonomy, and to enable economic groups to derive protection and legitimation from the principles that, ostensibly, were being fashioned to preserve sacred values. The next phase in the historical relationship between pluralism and toleration would be the creation of a form of politics shaped to the special needs of a pluralist society. Locke had labeled these needs as "civil interests" and he had defined their contents in strikingly materialistic terms. A pluralist society was thus acquiring a particular identity as the locus of man's in-

---

[18]This principle was recently endorsed by the chief justice of the United States Supreme Court when he opined that corporations should be entitled to freedom of speech in the same way that individuals are guaranteed it by the First Amendment.

terests, the domain where he was engaged in promoting, increasing, and defending his material goods and the social status and power they represented. Although Locke had sketched the political institutions that he thought would suit a society devoted to material interests—an elected, representative legislature, a system of impartial laws fairly interpreted by the courts and enforced by an executive of limited authority—he had not filled in the details concerning how the political authorities would come to decide matters of legislation, policy, and administration in a context of opposing social classes, conflicting forms of wealth, status, and power, and competing interests organized into groups.

The first sketch of a solution was provided, appropriately, by the founder of classical economics, Adam Smith. In his great work, *The Wealth of Nations,* he devoted close attention to what we would call public policy questions. One of the issues he raised was whether it was preferable, as a matter of policy, to tolerate numerous small religious sects or, instead, to favor a single national church. The question might seem out of place in a work that was destined to serve as the foundation of modern economics. However, Smith's answer revealed how the question could be formulated so as to accommodate it to the new needs of economic reasoning which he was helping to invent. If it were possible to show that spiritual matters could be translated into the "vocabulary" of the new science of economics and treated according to its prescriptions, then it might also be possible for the new science to supply the terms for understanding the distinctive politics emerging from the new form of society that Adam Smith saw himself as helping to bring into being. If this latter possibility were realized, the new science would fully merit its name, "political" economy.

Taking the same principle that he would make famous

as the foundation of free market behavior and adapting it to religion, Smith repeated the Lockean formula, saying that the social order was best served where each person was free "to chuse his own priest and his own religion as he thought proper." The effect of this principle, Smith acknowledged, would be to produce a multiplicity of sects and a variety of "truths," many of them doubtless fanatical or bizarre. Nonetheless, he argued, the evils of social confusion would be less than if one sect were supreme, or if two or three sects, "acting by concert," dominated the religious scene. Smith's reasoning was simply the application of his market principle that monopolies and trade conspiracies, where one or a few sellers controlled the market, were less desirable and beneficial than having numerous small producers and sellers offering their wares to a multitude of individual consumers, each of whom was free to choose according to his economic "conscience."

The political advantages to society of numerous organized but small-scale sellers of religious beliefs were similar to the economic advantages of a condition where a vast number of small-scale producers were competing on the market and had to adjust their behavior, tactics, and product to their rivals. Competition among numerous small religious sects would exert a moderating effect, Smith averred, on the more fanatical sects. Since none of the sects would be large enough "to disturb the public tranquillity," each would quickly realize that no advantage was to be gained by extremism. Consequently, religion would generally come to display "good temper and moderation."[19] Thus group competition would produce moderation without requiring either a law to enforce

---

[19]Adam Smith, *An Inquiry into the Nature and Causes of the Wealth of Nations*, vol. 2, ed. R. H. Campbell, A. S. Skinner, and W. B. Todd (Oxford: Oxford University Press, 1976), Book 5, Ch. 1, (g), pp. 792–794 (8–9).

it or a civic ethic to promote it. The unseen hand could be made to work for the cause of political order as well as for economic well-being.

It remained, however, for an American, James Madison, to draw out, extend, and complete this line of thought and to make it the fundamental principle of a new form of politics adapted to the new world and to its geography, economy, society, and political and religious traditions. From Locke and Smith he took the strand of thought that wove together religious freedom and economic interests and combined it with another strand that conceived politics as the consequence of the activity of economic interests organized to concert their power politically. Madison accepted a third strand from Smith, the principle of the salutary effects of group competition, but he modified it in order to make certain that the principle would not produce the wrong results. For there was one particular group that Madison feared above all—just as Smith had feared the monopolists and Locke the dominant established church—and that one group was the majority. So he surrounded the competition among economic interest groups with a complex set of constitutional devices to blunt what he called "the superior force of an . . . overbearing majority"[20] and he connected these devices with the regional diversity of America and the seemingly unlimited space of the continent so that the entire system, constitutional, and economic, and geographic, would work against democracy.

[20]Jacob Cooke, ed., *The Federalist* (Middletown, Conn.: Wesleyan University Press, 1961), no. 10, p. 57. At the Philadelphia Convention Madison had remarked that it had been the threats to "providing more effectually for the security of private rights, and the steady dispensation of justice [that] had perhaps more than anything else produced the convention." Max Farrand, ed., *The Records of the Federal Convention*, vol. 1 (New Haven: Yale University Press, 1911), p. 134.

Madison's achievement was to make pluralism the hedge against democracy. He did it by successfully redefining pluralism to stand for "minority rights" and democracy to stand for the tyranny of the majority.

Madisonian pluralism was a bold and innovative project for combining a new constitutional form with a new conception of politics. The form was to be republican yet unlike any previous instance or theoretical conception of that ancient type of polity. It was to be presidential at its apex, representative in its middle, popular at its base, and federal in structure.

In Madison's eyes the boldest quality of the new scheme was its challenge to the received wisdom that republics could flourish only if their geographic boundaries were limited. A vast republic was considered to be a contradiction in terms. Madison and the other framers of the Constitution set themselves against this restriction. Writing in *The Federalist*, Hamilton declared that Americans might make a signal contribution to the "science of politics" by demonstrating that the principle of federalism could be employed to "enlarge" greatly the "orbit" of the republican form.[21]

The group conception of politics envisaged for the new polity was equally novel, although it too had a lineage in the history of political thought. As we have noted, the conception drew partly from sixteenth- and seventeenth-century ideas about religious groups and partly from seventeenth- and eighteenth-century notions of politics as a competition for power. This conception of politics was given its clearest expression by Hobbes, Locke, and Adam Smith. In their view, the driving force of politics came mainly, although not exclu-

[21]*The Federalist*, no. 9, p. 52.

sively, from economic interests. Interest was the basic reality, the bedrock of politics. The pluralist conception of politics blended the elements of egoism and interest to create a new entity. It can best be understood with the help of an archaic verb. Pluralism "corporated" the two elements of egoism and interest, that is, conceived of a group as united and compact, or corporate, despite its embodiment of the element of egoism, which, traditionally, had been considered a byword for divisiveness and disunity.

When interest and egoism are translated into a conception of the nature of groups, the older, church-related notion virtually disappears and the group becomes an enlarged version of the egoistic individual. But the group is also a more powerful entity than the individual and also a more effective actor than the socioeconomic class. Unlike a social class, which will inevitably include disparate elements (e.g., small *and* large landowners, minor *and* grand aristocrats, merchants *and* manufacturers), a group can restrict itself to more homogeneous elements and thereby avoid internal divisions that inhibit effective action.

The composition of groups—egoistic, materialistic, and potentially powerful—posed an obvious and explicit threat to social peace and political order. The theoretical problem was to legitimate the inevitable while neutralizing the undesirable. Organized groups constituted a fact of political life, but not all organized groups represented a political/economic value, at least not for the Founding Fathers. This bias had been in evidence when the call for the Constitutional Convention had first gone out. As the framers of the Constitution were frank to acknowledge, the only reason why the early movement for a constitutional convention took hold was because it was supported by certain specific groups with a stake in controlling the issue of paper money, reducing the barriers to commerce, and preventing the poorer groups from writing more legislation in favor of debtors. So the problem was to legitimate groups in a way that protected the right groups and blocked the wrong ones. That meant devising a principle of legitimation that in appearance sanctioned all groups, but in reality favored some at the expense of others. This principle was derived not from a theory of natural law or moral philosophy, but was furnished by the new "science of politics," which Madison praised, and his mentor, David Hume, had practiced. The principle was based on the experience with religious sects. It held that rights (in this case, of religious freedom) were more secure when they were being exercised by several sects rather than by one or a few. Treating this principle as one that could be given more extended application, Madison argued that:

> In a free government the security for civil rights must be the same as that for religious rights. It consists in the one case in the multiplicity of interests and in the other in the multiplicity of sects.[22]

Having made a "multiplicity of interests" equivalent to a "multiplicity of sects," Madison could avail himself of the support of historical memories that associated religious persecution with policies that had been urged on political authorities by the established church whose membership was generally far larger than that of the dissenting congregations. Thus, historically, the religious sects of seventeenth-century England had most feared the established Anglican church. The usual formula employed by Anglicans was to speak of

[22]Ibid., no. 51, pp. 351–352.

their church as "one and indivisible," that is, presenting a unifed, compact presence against the welter of dissenting "minorities." The modern use of the word "minority" originates in the religious controversies of the sixteenth and seventeenth centuries. "Minority" came to stand for a "lesser number," a "part" of a larger whole (i.e., of Christendom). Many of the colonists had, of course, come to American to escape the "majority" or established church, that is, the Anglican church.

The historical memory of religious oppression of the minority by the majority was exploited by Madison for the purpose of warning against a new kind of majority, a majority of the people:

> If a majority be united by a common interest, the rights of the minority will be insecure.[23] . . . Either the existence of the same passion or interest in a majority, having such coexistent passion or interest, must be rendered, in their number and local situation, unable to concert and carry into effect schemes of oppression.[24]

At the same time, the majority–minority distinction, which appears naïvely as a contrast between a large number and a small number of persons, with the physical force of the one threatening to overwhelm the other, served to distract attention from the possibility, even likelihood, that numbers were not the only measure of power, that a tiny number of persons might, for example, own a majority of the wealth or property in a society.

The context that Madison set for his discussion of minorities was to be decisive in shaping the political consciousness of subsequent generations. It was that politics was the

[23]Ibid., p. 351.
[24]Ibid., no. 10, p. 6l.

competitive struggle among selfish groups—nothing more, nothing less. The task of a political structure or a constitution was to contain the struggle, to block, neutralize, and prevent the groups from gaining control over government. In other words, the aim of the structure was negative, to check politics.

This conception of politics as unclean and dangerous activity can best be described as a secular version of Calvinism. Human nature was painted in unrelievedly dark tones: mankind is selfish, deceitful, fickle, and above all, always grasping for power. "What is government itself," Madison asked, "but the greatest of all reflections on human nature?"[25] The specific political form that human depravity took was "faction." "This dangerous vice," as Madison called it, was to be so all-pervasive and ineradicable, so overpowering, that it became in the eyes of Madison and of subsequent generations the quintessence of politics. His definition of it warrants our attention because it appears on its face to be an evenhanded attack on all sorts of factions, when in truth it is a way of attacking the majority by reducing it to the same level as the most disreputable of minorities.

> By a faction I understand a number of citizens, whether amounting to a majority or a minority of the whole, who are united and activated by some common impulse of passion, or of interest, adverse to the rights of other citizens, or to the permanent and aggregate interests of the community.[26]

Madison discerned numerous types of factions, some organized around religious beliefs, others around political ideas or individual leaders; but he singled out one source of faction as the most important, "the various and unequal dis-

[25]Ibid., no. 51, p. 349.
[26]Ibid., no. 10, p. 57.

tribution of property." There were, he noted, those with property, and those without it. That, however, was only the crudest form of factions. "Distinct interests" were formed by creditors, debtors, a "landed interest, a moneyed interest, with many lesser interests." These were "different classes, actuated by different sentiments and vices."[27]

Since, by Madison's own definition, a minority was a faction and hence prone to advance its own interests at the expense of the public good, how was it possible to protect against the evils of faction without injuring or constricting those valuable interests that were "the permanent and aggregate interests of the community" and that were, so to speak, the natural breeding ground of factions? Patently one could not eliminate or even closely regulate all factions without harming vital economic activities such as agriculture, commerce, manufacturing, and finance that sustained the life of society. The problem for Madison was: How to control factions, while protecting interests? He resolved it in a way that was ingenious, antidemocratic, and strongly weighted in favor of the propertied classes.

Madison argued that it was impossible to eradicate factions without destroying liberty, just as it was "impracticable" to solve the problem by appealing to the "reason" of citizens and expecting them to come to the same conclusion about any question where their interests or passions were involved. Since, as Madison put it, "the latent causes of faction are . . . sown in the nature of man,"[28] the only realistic solution was to control the effects of faction, not to eliminate the causes. That could be done by devising an intricate system of institutional checks and balances as well as divided gov-

[27]Ibid., p. 59.
[28]Ibid., p. 58.

ernmental powers, which would render it extremely unlikely that any faction, and especially a majority faction, would secure control of all of the major institutions for an extended period of time. This ingenious arrangement was the constitutional solution to the problem of interest groups.

A second line of solution was to capitalize on the vast unoccupied space of the continent by encouraging expansionism and thereby multiplying and complicating the number of interests while at the same time diffusing them so widely that the possibilities of factious mischief were greatly reduced:

> Extend the sphere and you take in a greater variety of parties and interests; you make it less probable that a majority of the whole will have a common motive to invade the rights of other citizens; or if such a common motive exists, it will be more difficult for all who feel it to discover their own strength and to act in unison with each other.[29]

This was the geographic solution. It symbolized more than a policy of basing politics on the bounty of nature or even of creating a new form of imperialism to ward off the potentially dangerous buildup of internal pressures arising from the deliberate effort at scotching majority rule. Instead it based the entire scheme of interest-group politics on the assumption—which, in its own way, was quite utopian in the long run—of a constant increase in the supply of objects upon which interest-group activity was fixated. This assumption of ever-increasing abundance and availability of material goods and of psychic rewards as well was not simply an assumption about economic growth, although it was certainly that. It was in addition an urgent necessity given the explosive political potential that was clearly evident in Madison's conception of

[29]Ibid., p. 64.

the nature of interests. Interests were nothing less than the materialized expression of human inequality.

To appreciate the significance of this point, which was fundamental to Madison's conception of the kind of political and constitutional arrangements that interest-group politics required, we must return to his assertion that "the latent causes of faction are . . . sown in the nature of man." He meant by this assertion that men were by nature self-interested, but also that, by nature, men were led to express their self-interestedness in a variety of different and highly subjective ways. The proliferation of differences was welcomed by Madison because it contained the potential of a natural dissolvent. The greater the number of different interests, the less likelihood that a solidified majority could take shape and concert its power. He expressed this point in a way that openly revealed the hostility between pluralism and democracy: the political constitution of pluralism was designed to protect property against the majority, but the crucial political importance of property was that it stood for inequality; and hence, the constitutional protection of property meant the protection, perpetuation, and even encouragement of inequality. Here are Madison's words:

> The diversity in the faculties of men, from which the rights or property originate, is not less an insuperable obstacle to a uniformity of interests. The protection of these faculties is the first object of government. From the protection of different and unequal faculties of acquiring property, the possession of different degrees and kinds of property immediately results: and from the influence of these on the sentiments and views of the respective proprietors, ensues a division of society into different interests and parties.[30]

---

[30]Ibid., p. 58.

LIMITS OF PLURALISM

The protection of inequality becomes a hazardous business, as European societies were to discover from 1789 to 1848, if the condition of the unequal many is hopeless. But hope is a function of expectation and expectations are a function of opportunities. And that is where Madison's stratagem, of connecting interests with unoccupied space and hence unexploited opportunities, was so appealing. Inequality can be protected and promoted as long as opportunities encourage the unequal to hope.

At the present time, as we move toward the end of the twentieth century and pause on the way in order to celebrate the bicentennial of our Constitution, there is increasing evidence that the social and economic expectations of the unequal will have to be lowered. Thus, for example, no political leader or party today believes that full employment is a genuine possibility, although a quarter-century ago that opinion was not uncommon. Assuming that we are moving toward, if we are not already in, a period of diminishing expectations for the unequal, there are two major questions raised by that possibility that need to be directed at the theory of pluralist politics—questions that are urgent because pluralism is the practice of American politics, not just a theory about it.

The first question is: If politics is essentially the means by which organized economic interests pursue their interests, how is it possible for there to be public policies that are just and rational? Who stands for justice and rationality when power is exerted by highly organized and self-interested groups, such as the American Petroleum Institute, the Farm Bureau, the Business Roundtable, and the American Medical Association? Where are there to be found the political means for articulating share political ends when the structure of political security is composed primarily of self-interested groups?

The history of American political institutions is a chronicle of the failure of these institutions to perform that articulating function. The exceptions have occurred during moments of extreme crisis—war, domestic rebellion, and severe economic depression—when a general climate of fear has created the opportunity for a "strong" president to transcend the limits of pressure politics and to pursue common goals. But in less heroic times all branches of government tend to resume the two main political functions prescribed by pluralism—maintaining the rules of group politics and negotiating settlements among conflicting group interests. Because shared interests have no constituency, public authority has no source of power peculiarly its own. For existing sources of power are already organized by dominant economic groups, whereas the new forms of power, which are continuously being created by the dynamics of a scientific and technological economy, are appropriated by or incorporated into the structure of control developed by the dominant groups. There is no significant source of power that is peculiarly the "property" of public agents. Instead, public authority has only what might be called the residual constituencies that, for historical and economic reasons, have not been wholly absorbed into the dominant groups. These are ethnic and racial minorities, farm workers, unorganized industrial workers, and those who are almost totally dependent on the welfare state. In other words, public authority has the constituency of the powerless.

The most recent and in some ways the most spectacular confirmation of this point is the current and successful attempts of organized groups to deprive public agents of power, literally to strip them of power by sharply reducing the tax base and thereby the amount of public funds, most of which had previously been devoted to public purposes. In such a setting, what remains to public agents is not power, but the one element that interest groups cannot create—the element of legitimate authority. Now pluralist politics depicts legitimate authority as needing one indispensable quality, that of "disinterestedness." John Locke had referred to it as the principle of the "indifferent judge" or "neutral umpire." A self-interested authority, according to this view, is a contradiction in terms. By the same token, a disinterested economic interest group is a contradiction in terms.[31] So, by a process of exclusion, public "authority" survives as the only claimant to disinterestedness. The difficulty, however, is that authority is imperfectly convertible into power and vice versa. There may be more of one than of the other. Organized interest groups have power but no authority, whereas public officials have authority but no separate source of power other than that supplied by periodic elections. The result is that the actions and policies of public authority are to be understood not as embodiments of the public good, but as correcting the shortsighted tendencies in a politics of self-centered groups.

The reason for this weakness lies in the stipulation that authority is being authentically political when it is being disinterested. But such a passive view, in which the agents of the political are prohibited from cultivating a "public" interest, leads to a deficiency of public power.

Once again, this feature of our political condition can be better understood if we observe its historical genesis in the efforts of the founders to find the place of disinterestedness in the main political system. The crucial moment came when

[31]"I have never known much good done by those who affected to trade for the publick good. It is an affectation, indeed, not very common among merchants, and very few words need be employed in dissuading them from it" (Smith, vol. 2, book 4, ii, p. 456).

Madison confronted the one question that, throughout the entire history of western political thought and practice, has stood as the ultimate test of disinterestedness—the question of justice and its political realization.

"Justice," Madison proclaimed in the fifty-first *Federalist*, "is the end of government. It is the end of civil society."[32] But justice can hardly be promoted without exerting some control over social and economic interests, as Madison himself pointed out. "The regulation of these various and interfering interests forms the principal task of modern legislation."[33] The difficulty was, as Madison acknowledged, that a free society permits the pursuit of interests and even opens up its political institutions—by elections, representation, and petitioning (i.e., lobbying)—to the influence of interest groups. "The spirit of party and faction," Madison wrote, is involved "in the necessary and ordinary operations of the government." How can there be an appeal to justice when the interested groups "must be themselves the judges" and when "the most powerful must be expected to prevail?"[34]

Although Madison posed the question, his answer offered only the contradictory hope that perhaps the undemocratic system of representation would devolve power upon

> a small number of citizens . . . whose wisdom may best discern the true interest of their country, and whose patriotism and love of justice will be least likely to sacrifice it to temporary or partial considerations.[35]

Madison never attempted to square this faith in the appearance of a disinterested elite with his principle that mankind always acted from motives of power and self-interest.

---

[32]*The Federalist*, no. 51, p. 352.
[33]Ibid., no. 10, p. 59.
[34]Ibid., pp. 59, 60.
[35]Ibid., p. 62.

He returned to the problem of justice in a later paper in which he offered a different argument, one that was ingenious in explaining how justice might come into existence, but evasive in describing the content of justice: "Justice," he asserted, "is the end of government. It is the end of civil society." He associated justice with "security" for the rights of the citizen, and hence the problem of justice, as he conceived it, took the form of asking why "the more powerful factions or parties" would "submit to a government which may protect the weak as well themselves."[36] His answer was that the stronger faction would forgo tyrannizing over the weak because in submitting to government the strong put an end to their own insecurity.

Underlying these various notions—of the calculations by the strong and the equating of justice with security—was an important premise about the subordinate or instrumental nature of reason itself, a premise that ultimately went back to Hobbes and Locke and had recently been popularized by David Hume, a contemporary of Madison's and much admired by him. As Hume's aphorism had it, reason is an "inert" principle and "it is and ought to be the slave of the passions." Through this denial of an autonomous status to reason, public or political norms were left without any objective truth-status. They were instead the expression of self-interest, passion, or ambition. As the first great twentieth-century theorist of pluralism, A. E. Bentley put it, "the only reality" of ideas and ideals "is their reflection of the groups, only that and nothing more."[37] In other words, because there was no "public," only a welter of group interests, there could

[36]Ibid., no. 50, p. 352.
[37]Arthur F. Bentley, *The Process of Government* (Evanston, Ill.: Principia Press, 1908/1935), p. 206.

be no public basis for justice. The basis of justice has to be distilled from the rational self-interest of groups. Politically, there could be no rational basis of justice independent of group interest. There was only the hypothetical possibility that the interest defined by a coalition of groups might be sufficiently extensive in scope so that, for all practical purposes, it might pass as the interest of the whole or most of society.

Madison had foreseen this possibility as inherent in the carefully contrived difficulties under which the majority would be required to operate under the new system:

> In the extended republic of the United States, and among the great variety of interests, parties and sects which it embraces, a coalition of a majority of the whole society could seldom take place on any other principle than those of justice and the general good.[38]

This development was momentous. It involved nothing less than what might be called the "delegitimation of political reason," that is, the discreditation of a belief as old as the ancient Greeks that public laws, policies, decisions, and actions must be grounded in and justified by political reasoning. Political reason was not a synonym for logical consistency applied to political affairs. That would be the least interesting and least decisive criterion. Political reason concerned the way of thinking that is appropriate to public purposes. Public purposes are expressed through the acts of constituted authorities, most often in the form of statutes that seek to promote or protect the norms that, traditionally, were viewed as the distinctive concern of political collectivities: justice, right, equality, and security. For centuries it was believed that reason could discern these norms, establish their meaning, and bring them to bear upon concrete circumstances. According

[38]*The Federalist*, no. 51, p. 353.

to most political theorists, although all men might possess
the capacity to reason, its actual application was a skill that
had to be learned. In a political life, reason would be called
upon to form a judgment on the basis of competing considerations and to deliberate over conflicting values. Human
beings became political beings by acquiring the arts of rational
deliberation. It was not like learning how to seek one's self-
interest. That came naturally.

All of which brings us to the present condition of pluralism. I want only to draw attention to three problems, which
I think are among the most serious and which require a re-
consideration of some of the basic assumptions of pluralism.

The first problem can be called "the imperatives of technical rationality versus the principle of interest-group power
and/or representation." It is common knowledge that today's
governmental decisions are increasingly concerned with technical subjects. Such matters demand highly specialized types
of knowledge—scientific, mathematical, medical, and so on.
The political issue does not arise because suddenly a new
species of problem has materialized, the technical problem.
It is rather that virtually all areas of public policy have evolved,
or been resolved, into highly technical fields. This situation has
given rise to a widespread belief among scientists, techni-
cians, and administrators that the number of problems that
require technical solutions is increasing; that most problems,
at least in principle, admit of technical solutions; and that,
ideally, problems should be treated strictly on their technical
merits.

What, one might inquire, is meant by a technical solution? Three criteria may be singled out as characteristic. One
is that a solution should be dictated by "internal consideration," that is, a solution that, as far as possible, relies only
on scientific knowledge. A contemporary defender of pluralism

has tried to incorporate this principle into decision making by proposing "a criterion of Competence as an appropriate basis for authority." The principle would signify the ability of a few experts to act for the benefit of all in the area of their expertise.[39]

A second, widely recognized criterion for a technical solution is that such solutions are not wholly value-neutral. Accordingly, it relies upon the principle of efficiency and cost–benefit analysis of modern economics. The criterion states that the preferred solution is one that produces the maximum advantages with the least expenditure of energy and resources; or simply, that the advantages outweigh the disadvantages.

Third, a solution is technically sound if it can be administered. Technical solutions have to be shaped so that bureaucracy, the primary institution of advanced societies, can put them into operation. That means that technical solutions must, in principle, be compatible with modes of action that are hierarchical, rigid rather than flexible, and rule oriented in their mentality.

Now the evolution of pluralism has placed it on a collision course with technical rationality. The latter is problem oriented, that is, it believes that problems can importantly be reduced to objective factors that admit of scientific or quantitative analysis; and that from such analysis solutions should be created. Pluralism dictates that each interest is entitled to organize in order to influence any and all policies in ways that the interested group deems beneficial to itself. It takes its orientation not from the problem, but from the perceived implications of the problem for its own well-being.

[39]Robert A. Dahl, *After the Revolution? Authority in a Good Society* (New Haven: Yale University Press, 1970), p. 28.

But that is only the beginning of the difficulties. If the society as a whole faces a future of lessening expectation, scarcer resources, and painful decisions, it will be no easy task to persuade highly organized groups to accept the so-called "hard choices." But why should they, when for over 200 years they have been encouraged to practice a politics based on each group seeking its own advantage and, above all, to do so while mindful of the cynical knowledge that all hard choices are not equally hard for all groups or classes, that unequal power of some groups makes it inevitable that the choices will be framed to reflect that power?

It is not surprising that in recent years there has been a noticeable reaction to pluralism. Some have argued that the urgent need for policies based on objective considerations requires that the power of interest groups be restricted so that rational decisions and long-range planning—both of which are demanded by a world of scarce resources and nuclear proliferation—may be facilitated. One of the strongest reactions against pluralism has been registered by political scientists whose academic field of study was identified historically with the refinement of the theory of pluralism. In an effort to find a theoretical basis for an alternative to pluralism and its political divisiveness, some political scientists have revived the idea of a powerful state. We need, so the argument runs, an authority above the selfish squabbles of interest groups, one that can take the actions needed in these troubled times without first being blackmailed by powerful groups.[40]

---

[40]See, for example, Samuel Huntington, "The United States," in *The Crisis of Democracy* (New York: New York University Press, 1975), pp. 59–118; Stephen D. Krasner, *Defending the National Interest* (Princeton: Princeton University Press, 1978), Ch. 1.

The argument represents a historical regression in the sense that it attempts to revive the same institution, the sovereign state, that pluralism had originally attacked and tried to supplant. The difficulty is that three centuries cannot be rolled back so easily. During that long period of time the politics of pluralism has weakened the very elements that are needed if there is to be a revival of political life. Pluralism has undercut the practice of political citizenship by replacing the idea of a civic person who continuously shares and participates in the common concerns of society with the idea of the special-interest-group member who emerges from that small circle to vote every few years but is otherwise preoccupied with private interests. Pluralism has also discredited the idea that, except for national defense, there are no common values that, as a collectivity, we can develop and share. There are only common means we can use to further individual, group, organizational, and class ends.

The dangerous situation in which pluralism has deposited us is one where political values have been squandered for ends that are no longer possible and where economic pressures are building to a demand for "strong" and "positive leadership." But strong leadership erected on an exhausted political base raises the specter that the progenitors of pluralism feared most, arbitrary power.

Chapter 9 / MINIMALIST ETHICS

On the Pacification of Morality

DANIEL CALLAHAN

The attraction of morality in times of affluence is that not much of it seems needed. More choices are available and thus fewer harsh dilemmas arise. If they arise, money can be used to buy out of or evade the consequences of choice. The wages of sin are offset by the cheapness of therapy, drugs, liquor, economy flights, and a career change. If all else fails, public confessions can profitably be produced as a miniseries. Vice is rewarded because everything is rewarded, even virtue.

Matters are otherwise in hard times. Options are fewer, choices nastier. Where forgiveness and therapeutic labels could once be afforded, blaming and denunciation become more congenial. If life is going poorly, someone obviously must be at fault, if not the government, then my neighbor, wife, or child. The warm, expansive self, indulgent of the foibles of others, gives way to the harsh, competitive self; enemies abound, foreign and domestic. It is not so much that

DANIEL CALLAHAN ● Director, The Hastings Center, Institute of Society, Ethics, and the Life Sciences, 360 Broadway, Hastings-on-Hudson, New York 10706 the "least well-off" cease to count (though they do), but that all imagine they are now in that category. Nastiness becomes the standard of civility, exposé the goal of journalism, a lawsuit the way friends, families, and colleagues reconcile their differences.

Meanwhile, in hard times, every would-be Jeremiah has plentiful material with which to work, and the moral panaceas may be just the opposite of the economic ones. Ethical conservatives want a fatter moral budget: more prayer in more schools, more bombs in more missiles, and more virtue in more hearts to keep the family together. Liberals want a leaner moral budget: less personal moral judgment, less social coercion, and less dominance by the military-industrial-multinational-pharmaceutical-technological-expert-Political Action Committee complex.

What, then, is the problem to be diagnosed? Here is the question I want to ask, and attempt to address: As we move into what will most likely be chronically hard economic times, how can our society muster the moral resources necessary to endure as a viable human culture? Three assumptions underlie that question. The first is that economic strength and military power have no necessary ethical connection with the internal human and moral viability of a culture; they can only help assure its mere existence. The second is that the era of sustained economic growth is over, and with it the perennially optimistic psychology of affluence. The prospects are for at best a steady-state economy, one where the next generation can only hope that it will do as well as the previous generation; only that, and no more, and probably less.

My third assumption is that the kind of morality that was able to flourish during times of affluence will, if carried over unchanged into hard times, lead to moral chaos and maybe worse. What has been that morality? It has been one that stressed the transcendence of the individual over the community, the need to tolerate all moral viewpoints, the autonomy of the self as the highest human good, and the voluntary, informed consent contract as the model of human relationships. To be sure, in its "great society" phase, it was a morality sensitive to poverty and economic oppression, just as it more recently supported a quest for universal human rights. But its central agenda was always that of individual liberty, that of the self seeking a liberation from both economic and cultural restraints, free to find its own truth and its own way. What is that "truth" and what is the "way"? If you felt you had to ask yourself that question, you probably missed the whole point, failing to use your freedom creatively. If you went so far as to press that question with insistence upon others, you could be certain of some suspicion among those for whom the essential value of autonomy is its resistance to any universal content. Free choice is its own reward, and the philosophical road to hell, supposedly, is paved with teleological ends, ultimate purposes, and essentialist meanings.

Now all of that autonomy is doubtless fine, and lofty, and lovely. But to live that kind of life, you need to have money at hand, good health, and a clinic full of psychological counselors at the ready. It is a good-time philosophy for comfortable people living in the most powerful, rich nation on earth. Will it work in hard times? Some doubt is in order.

Hard times require self-sacrifice and altruism—but there is nothing in an ethic of moral autonomy to sustain or nourish those values. Hard times necessitate a sense of community and the common good—but the putative virtues of autonomy are primarily directed toward the cultivation of independent selfhood. Hard times demand restraint in the blaming of others for misfortune—but one outcome of moral autonomy as an ideal is to make more people blameworthy for the harms they supposedly do others. Hard times need a broad sense of duty toward others, especially those out of sight—but an ethic of autonomy stresses responsibility only for one's freely chosen, consenting-adult relationships.

Whether suffering brings out the best or the worst in people is an old question, and the historical evidence is mixed. Yet a people's capacity to endure suffering without turning on each other is at least closely linked to the way they have envisioned, and earlier embodied, their relationship to each other. When one's perceived and culturally supported primary duty is to others rather than to self, to transcendent rather than private values, to future needs rather than to present attachments, then there can be a solid moral foundation to survive pain, turmoil, and evil. Naturally, that set of values can, and often does, have its dark side. Many nations and cultures serve as unhappy examples of communities that stifled and killed individuals. Tight families and kinfolk systems can run roughshod over liberty, and totalitarian states are all too ready to capitalize on the willingness of their citizens to give their lives for some higher cause.

What we have not had, until recently, are cultures that have systematically tried to forswear communal goals; that have tried to replace ultimate ends with procedural safeguards; that have resolutely worked to abolish the most profound questions of human meaning to the depths of hidden, private lives only; and that have striven to sanctify the morally autonomous agent as the cultural ideal. Can that kind of a culture survive hard times? Or better, if it is to survive—mere size and residual power may assure that much—can it do so without the wanton violence, moral indifference, and callous self-interest that are the growing pathologies of life in the United States? It would be foolish to give a flat answer to that question. Our cultural experiment is not over. Only now it is faced with a shift in those material circumstances that as much or more than articulated values made it possible in the first place, and that will pose a severe test.

I want to define one set of moral values that emerged during our recent decades of affluence, and try to show how peculiarly ill suited they are, and even dangerous, for the hard times ahead. For lack of a more graceful term, I will call those values a "minimalist ethic." I have already hinted at some of the features of that ethic, but will now try to be more specific. That ethic can be stated in a simple proposition: *one may morally act in any way one chooses so far as one does not do harm to others.* The accent and some of the substance of John Stuart Mill's "On Liberty" are familiar enough in that proposition. But, as I will argue below, something has gone awry in the way Mill's thinking has been appropriated by our culture. What he understood to be a principle that only ought to govern the relationship between the individual and the state has been wrongly construed to encompass the moral life itself.

I call this a "minimalist ethic" because, put crudely, it seems to be saying that the sole test of the morality of an action, or of a whole way of life, is whether it avoids harm to others. If that minimal standard can be met, then there is no further basis for judging personal or communal moral goods and goals, for praising or blaming others, or for educating others about higher moral obligations to self or community. In the language of our day: the only judgment we are permitted on the way others make use of their moral autonomy is to assess whether they are doing harm to others. If we can discern no such harm, then we must suspend any further moral judgment. Should we fail to suspend that judgment, we are then guilty of a positive violation of their right to privacy and self-determination.

The pervasiveness of this ethic has had a number of consequences:

1. A minimalist ethic has tended to confuse useful principles for government regulation and civil liberties with the broader requirements of the moral life, both individual and communal.

2. It has misled many in our society into thinking that a sharp distinction can be drawn between the public and the private sphere, and that different standards of morality apply to each.

3. It has given us a thin and shriveled notion of personal and public morality. We are obliged under the most generous reading of a minimalist ethic only to honor our voluntarily undertaken family obligations, to keep our promises, and to respect contracts freely entered into with other freely consenting adults. Beyond those minimal standards, we are free to do as we like, guided by nothing other than our private standards of good and evil. Altruism, beneficence, and self-sacrifice beyond that tight circle are in no sense moral obligations and, in any case, cannot be universally required. My neighbor can and will remain a moral stranger unless and until, as an exercise of my autonomy, I choose to enter into a contract with him; and I am bound to no more toward him than the letter of that contract. Although I ought to treat my neighbor with justice, that is because I may otherwise do harm to him, or owe it to him as a way of discharging the debt of former injustices, or because it seems a rational idea to develop a social contract with others as a way of enhancing my own possibilities for greater liberty and the gaining of some primary goods.

4. A minimalist ethic has deprived us of meaningful language to talk about our life together outside of our contractual relationships. The only language that does seem common is

that of "the public interest," a concept that for most translates into the aggregate total of individual desires and demands. The language of "rights" is common enough (though not of putatively archaic "natural" or "God-given" rights). But it is to be understood that the political and moral purpose of both negative and positive rights is to protect and advance individual autonomy. It is not the kind of language that can comfortably be used any longer to talk about communal life, shared values, and the common good.

5. A minimalist ethic has made the ancient enterprise of trying to determine the inherent or intrinsic good of human beings a suspect, probably subversive activity. It assumes no one can answer such lofty and vague questions, that attempts to try probably pose a threat to liberty, and that, in any event, any purported answers should be left resolutely private.

6. Unless I can show in a demonstrable way that the behavior of others poses some direct public harm, I am not allowed to question that behavior, much less to pass a public negative judgment on it. The culture of a minimalist ethic is one of rigid and rigorous toleration. Who am I to judge what is good for others? One is—maybe—entitled to personal moral opinions about the self-regarding conduct of others. But a public expression of those opinions would contribute to an atmosphere of moral suppression in the civil order, and of an anti-autonomous moral repression in the private psychological order. One question is taken to be the definitive response to anyone who should be so un-civil as to talk about ethics *tout simpliciter:* "But whose ethics?"

In some quarters, a minimalist ethic has gone a step further, to a de-listing of many behavioral choices as moral problems at all. Thus abortion becomes a "religious" rather than a moral issue, and it is well-known that all religious issues are private, arational, and idiosyncratic; questions of sex, and

most recently homosexuality, become matters of "alternative lifestyles" or "sexual preference"; and the use of pleasure-enhancing drugs becomes an amusing choice between two valued-soaked (and thus subjective) norms, "psychotropic hedonism" or "pharmacological calvinism."[1]

7. Under the terms of a "minimalist ethic" only a few moral problems are worth bothering with at all. The issue of liberty versus justice is one of them, and that of autonomy versus paternalism is another. The former is important because distributive justice is required to finally enthrone a community of fully autonomous individuals. The latter is vital because it is well recognized that paternalism, even the beneficently motivated and kindly sort, poses the most direct threat to individual liberty. A lack of informed consent, decisions taken by experts, and a failure to observe due process will be high on the list of evils of a minimalist ethic. Anything less than a full egalitarianism—equal decisions made by equally autonomous moral agents—is seen as an eschatological failure.

I have drawn here an exaggerated picture of a minimalist ethic. It fits the views of no one person precisely and, to be sure, cannot be taken to represent any single, coherent, well-developed ethical theory. Not all those who favor a perfect egalitarianism would equally favor (or favor at all) a moral delisting of matters of sex and drugs. There is no necessary incompatibility between favoring a civil-libertarian political ethic and holding a view of the community that affirms the value of close community ties, of seeking transcendent values, and of recognizing duties over and above those of self-realization. Permutations of and exceptions to this general portrait

---

[1]Gerald L. Klerman, "Psychotropic Hedonism vs. Pharmacological Calvinism," *Hastings Center Report*, September 1972, pp. 1–3.

are then easy enough to find. Nonetheless, I believe it sufficiently accurate as a composite portrait of a mainstream set of values in American culture to take seriously, and to reject. A society heavily composed of those who aspire to, or unwittingly accept, a minimalist ethic cannot be a valid human community. In times of stress, it could turn into a very nasty community.

I suggested above that a minimalist ethic sounds very much like a close relative of John Stuart Mill's position in "On Liberty" (1859), but also that it represents a pressing of that position beyond the limits he intended. Is that true? I think so, but it is instructive to look at the way Mill tried to find a good fit between principles of public morality, narrow and limited, and the demands of a broader private and communal morality. It is not easy to find that fit, and Mill's troubles in doing so foreshadow many of our own in trying to do likewise. Although Mill is by no means to be held responsible for what has transpired in Anglo-American culture since the nineteenth century, his thinking has remained powerful in civil-libertarian thought, either as a foundation or as an important point of departure for revised theories.

Recall Mill's famous principle and point of departure in "On Liberty":

> the sole end for which mankind are warranted, individually or collectively, in interfering with the liberty of action of any of their number, is self-protection. That the only purpose for which power can be rightfully exercised over any member of a civilized community, against his will, is to prevent harm to others.[2]

Mill goes on to reiterate and embellish that principle in a

---

[2]John Stuart Mill, "On Liberty," in *John Stuart Mill: Selected Writings*, ed. Mary Warnock (New York: Meridian Books, 1962), p. 135.

variety of ways, stressing not only that society ought to be solely concerned with individual conduct that "concerns others," but also that "over himself, over his own body and mind, the individual is sovereign."[3]

Nor is it sufficient that the individual be protected "against the tyranny of the magistrate." Protection is also needed

> against the tyranny of the prevailing opinion and feeling; against the tendency of society to impose, by other means than civil penalties, its own ideas and practices or rules of conduct on those who dissent from them. . . . There is a limit to the legitimate interference of collective opinion with individual independence: and to find that limit, and maintain it against encroachment, is as indispensable to a good condition of human affairs, as protection against human despotism.[4]

With an even more contemporary flavor, Mill wrote that:

> the principle requires liberty of tastes and pursuits; of framing the plan of our life to suit our own character; of doing as we like, subject to such consequences as may follow: without impediment from our fellow creatures, as long as what we do does not harm them, even though they should think our conduct foolish, perverse, or wrong.[5]

Nevertheless, despite the firmness of those statements, Mill apparently had no desire to reduce all of morality to his "simple principle," as if the moral universe can solely be encompassed by the relationship between the individual and the state. As long as we do not compel anyone in those matters that concern himself only, there can be "good reasons for

---

[3]Ibid.
[4]Ibid., p. 130.
[5]Ibid., p. 138.

remonstrating with him, or persuading him, or entreating him."[6] So, also, Mill states that

> It would be a great misunderstanding of this doctrine to suppose that it is one of selfish indifference, which pretends that human beings have no business with each other's conduct in life, and that they should not concern themselves about the well-doing or well-being of one another, unless their own interest is involved. . . . Human beings owe to each other help to distinguish the better from the worse, and encouragement to choose the former and avoid the latter.[7]

Mill's intention, then, is not to promote a society of amoral atoms, each existing in undisturbed isolation from the moral community of others. There are standards of right and wrong, good and bad, in our self-regarding conduct and in our relationship with our fellow creatures—"cruelty of disposition," "malice," "envy," "pride," "egotism," "rashness," and "obstinacy" are all vices for Mill. Yet he is walking a delicate line. He wants to exclude legal pressures in that which concerns ourselves only, and exclude as well "the moral coercion of public opinion." Yet he also agrees that so long as the individual is the final judge, "considerations to aid his judgment, exhortations to strengthen his will, may be offered to him, even obtruded to him, by others"[8]

I find it difficult to see as sharp a distinction as does Mill between exhorting and obtruding upon others, and allowing them to be free of "the moral coercion of public opinion." It is just that exhortation by others that may and probably will represent public opinion. What if I am allowed in the end to

---

[6]Ibid., p. 135.
[7]Ibid., p. 206.
[8]Ibid., p. 207.

be my own moral judge? If others insist upon their right to harangue, bother, and even condemn me with their moral sentiments, my life is considerably less well-off—on one reading of Mill—than if they would just let me alone. Moreover, that is just what many now say in our day: "It is not enough that you grant me the legal and civil liberty to act as I see fit. You must also grant me that private equality that will lead you to stop judging altogether my moral actions."[9]

Much of what Mill says in "On Liberty" would seem to reject that latter extension of his "simple principle." For him, the problem of his day was not that of too much individuality, but too little. One can only read with a kind of wondrous bemusement a passage like the following:

> the danger which threatens human nature is not the excess, but the deficiency, of personal impulses and preferences. . . . In our times, from the highest class of society down to the lowest, everyone lives as under the eye of a hostile and dreadful censorship. . . . It does not occur to them to have any inclination, except for what is customary.[10]

If one worked at it, I suppose, one could still find many in our society who have no inclination except for what is customary. There are allegedly one or two people like that on my street and many more, I have been assured, living in the Sun Belt, Palm Springs, and Scarsdale. But how do we determine what counts as "customary" any longer in a society that allows any and all moral flowers to bloom?

Mill is by no means unaware of the possibility that the kind of liberty he seeks can lead to some undesirable outcomes:

[9]Anonymous, circa 1981.
[10]Mill, p. 190.

I fully admit that the mischief which a person does to himself may seriously affect, both through their sympathies and their interests, those nearly connected with him and, in a minor degree, society at large.[11] . . . But with regard to the merely contingent, as it may be called, constructive injury which a person causes to society, by conduct which neither violates any specific duty to the public, nor occasions hurt to any assignable individual except himself: the inconvenience is one which society can afford to bear, for the sake of the greater good of human freedom.[12]

In another place, he writes that "mankind are greater gainers by suffering each other to live as seems good to themselves, than by compelling each to live as seems good to the rest."[13]

That is too confident a utilitarian conclusion. What societies did Mill have in mind when he came to that judgment? Apparently not his own or any other extant society; in the passage quoted above, for instance, those societies were characterized as repressive and conformist. He could only, presumably, have been extrapolating from some parts, or circles, of his own social world to have reached such a universal judgment. Yet only in our day have we actually begun to see an approximation, on a mass scale, of the kind of society he had in mind. Lacking other historical examples, it is those we must judge. Whatever its other failings, Mill lived in a time and a culture that could take many if not most western moral values for granted. He did not have to specify or defend the standards by which his countrymen should judge the self-regarding behavior of others, or the moral principles to be inculcated in children, or the norms on which the moral exhortations he countenanced were based.

[11]Ibid., p. 212.
[12]Ibid., p. 213.
[13]Ibid., p. 138.

Increasingly, no such background—tacitly held and almost superflous to state—can be assumed. Precisely because that is so, and because a minimalist ethic has been one outcome of the train of thought that Mill helped set in motion, we are now forced to reexamine the relationship between public and private morality. Can they, in the first place, be sharply distinguished as Mill though possible?

The evidence provided by the emergence of a minimalist ethic is hardly encouraging. It would have us not only obsessively make such a distinction; it would also have us go a step further and eschew moral judgment on the private lives of others as well. In response, I want to argue three points. The first is that the distinction between the private and the public is a cultural artifact only, varying with time and place. The second is that only a thoroughly dulled (or self-interested) imagination could even pretend to think that there can be private acts with no public consequences. The third point is that the effort to sharply distinguish the two spheres can do harm to our general moral life.

What kind of human nature, and what kind of society, would be necessary to viably and sensibly separate the private and the public sphere? As for human nature, the individual would have to exist in total isolation from all others, dependent upon them for nothing at all, either food, shelter, culture, or language. If there existed a universe that made possible that kind of individual, one might then speak of a wholly private, inward world. But in that case the concept of a "public" world would then make no sense. There would be none of those interconnections and interdependencies, past, present, and future human relationships, that characterize what is ordinarily meant by "public." In such a universe, it would also be hard to make much sense of "human nature." It would lack those traits, language and culture in particular, reason-

ably thought necessary to distinguish the "human" from other forms of nature.

If we leave that never-never universe, and ask what kind of society would have to be imagined to support a sharply separable private and public space, our task might seem a bit easier. Do we not, after all, have our secret thoughts, and do things that others never hear about or see? Of course; but what does that prove? As Mill himself acknowledges, actions have their cause in internal dispositions,[14] precisely within the hidden self. Although our behavior can bely our secret thoughts and feelings some of the time, it is difficult to imagine a constant discrepancy between the inner and the outer self. One way of coming to know our inner self, it often turns out, is by observing our outer self, that self which acts and responds in the company of others; and it is normally impossible to say just where the one begins and the other ends. It was not an unperceptive observation on Aristotle's part that virtue is a habit; nor is it any the less consonant with general experience to suggest that inner habits of thought, our feelings and dispositions toward others, have a direct bearing on observable conduct, on our behavioral habits.

One need not turn to the complicated relationship between an inner and an outer self to wholly make the point. Our more recent historical experience indicates that the distinction between the public and the private is at the least a cultural artifact and quite possibly a matter of the sheerest ideology. I earlier pointed to a "de-listing" phenomenon in our society—the attempt to remove whole spheres of behavior from moral scrutiny and judgment. That point needs a complementary one: a number of activities once thought to be private only in their moral significance are now judged to be

[14]Ibid., p. 209.

of public importance. The common moral wisdom at present tells us, for example—in a way it did not tell Mill's generation—that we have, among others things: no right to pollute the water and the air; to knowingly procreate defective children or even to have too many healthy children; to utter private slurs against females, ethnic, or racial groups, or to ignore the private domestic life of public officials. Family planning was, in the days of Margaret Sanger, an entirely public and proscribed matter. Then, with the triumph of the family-planning movement, it became an issue of wholly private morality. And then, with the perception of a world population explosion, it became once again a public matter. The frequenting of prostitutes was once legal in many places, and thought to be a concern of private morality only. Not many feminists, aware of the degradation of women that has been a part of prostitution, are likely to be impressed with a private-morality-consenting-adult rationale any longer. They are hardly keen on pornography either, and for the same kind of reason.

If it is so hard in the end to separate the private and the public, why does the idea continue to persist? One reason is that, on occasion, it can serve to buttress our personal predilections or ideologies. I know that I cannot make a good moral case to myself about why I continue to smoke in the face of all that distressing health evidence. Yet I do not have to try quite so hard when I can persuade myself that the issue is between myself and myself and is no one else's affair. (That others ordinarily believe it necessary to cite potential harm to others as the essence of their moral point against me only confirms the power of a minimalist ethic.) Think also how much more arduous it would be morally for the "prochoice" group in the abortion debate to have to admit that abortion decisions are fully public in their direct implications, and then to be

forced to make the case for the public benefits of abortion. It is an argument that, perhaps, could be made in some cases—but it is much, much easier to relegate the whole issue to the private realm, where the standards of moral rigor are more accommodating.

There are other, less self-serving reasons for the persistence of the distinction. We need some language and concepts for finding a limit to the right of the government, or the populace, to intervene in our lives. That was Mill's concern and it is as legitimate now as it was in his day. In groping around for a solution, our legal system stumbled on a "right to privacy." That concept represents a latter-day reading of the Constitution, and has resisted efforts to give it a clear meaning. Even so, it has its heuristic uses and no better formulation to get at some kinds of civil-liberties issues has been proposed. Yet to say that it is useful does not entail that we need to go so far as to reify, as if it represented reality, a sharp distinction between private and public life. A loose, shifting, casual distinction, taken with a nice grain of salt, may be equally serviceable.

The problem we now face is twofold. Do those of us who want to protect civil liberties have the nerve at the same time to recognize and openly admit the possiblity that our society is paying an increasingly high moral cost for isolating the"private" sphere from moral judgment? We have certainly gained a number of valuable civil liberties as a result. But there is growing evidence that the diffuse and general consequences of that gain have been as harmful as they have been beneficial—the multiple indignities of daily life in large cities, for example. Mill was prepared to recognize that a price could well be paid for the liberty he proposed. But, without offering any specific evidence, he simply asserted that it was a price worth paying. We have less reason than he did to

remain confident about that equation. He was not speaking about the realities of his own society but projecting one yet to be. Not until our own day have we seen, in actuality, what he had in mind. We can thus make a far better judgment than was possible for him. My own observation, however, is that defenders of his "simple principle" in its revised and extended "minimalist ethic" form are resolutely unwilling to look some unsavory reality straight in the face.

If that was done, we would be driven to grapple with the need to set some kind of limits to those liberties that, in balance, produce an intolerable level of moral nihilism and relativism as a cultural outcome. It is not, and ought not to be, just the Moral Majority that worries about violence and more-tolerant-than-thou sex on television; or about children neglected by parental quests for greater psychological fulfillment; or about casual stealing, cheating, lying, and consenting-adult infidelity; or about rising assault and murder rates. Whatever the gain to liberty of the private standards and dispositions that tacitly support those developments, they all point to the emergence of an intolerable society, destructive as much to private as to public life. A legitimate respect for civil liberties does not require a forgoing of standards by which to judge private behavior any more than respect for freedom of speech requires a suspension of judgment on the contents of free speech.

Mill's problem was to find a "limit" to "the legitimate interference of collective opinion with individual independence."[15] Although our task may not exactly be the opposite, the weight of inquiry may now have to shift. What ought to be the limits of liberty, and how can we identify those points at which "collective opinion" ought to hold sway against

[15]Ibid., p. 130.

claims of private moral autonomy? To even ask that question implies that we must be prepared once again to judge the private lives of others, the way they use their liberty, and that the standards of judgment ought to be more demanding than those required by a minimalist ethic.

Why should we believe that the sum total of private, self-interested acts that do no ostensible harm to others will add up to a favorable societal outcome? Those who would be the first to declaim against a pure market economy, guided by an "invisible hand," seem quite willing to tolerate a moral market economy, as if the result in the moral realm will be more favorable than in the economic. (There is an equal irony on the other side of course: those who rage against a government-controlled economy seem quite prepared to accept a government-controlled morality.) There is equally no reason to believe that the good of the individual is necessarily the good of society, as if any free act is, by virtue of its freedom alone, a social contribution. That is especially true if the good is defined simply as moral autonomy and, to make matters worse, is combined with a systematic agnosticism about the morally proper uses of that autonomy. We are then deterred from passing moral judgment on our neighbor (which he may well need and deserve) and, still more, harmed in our capacity as a society to determine what individual virtues, dispositions, and behaviors we want to promote and publicly support. Under a minimalist ethic that discussion cannot even begin. It is ruled out in principle.

The strong tendency in our society to confuse legal standards with moral principles has become a major part of the problem. When it is assumed that, under the aegis of liberty, moral judgment cannot be passed on private life, then the only general moral norms become those supplied by the law. On occasion, to be sure, the law can be a powerful and pos-

itive moral educator. The civil rights legislation of the1960s gradually served to change moral attitudes as well as specific discriminatory practices, whatever the local bitterness it occasioned at the time. But just as frequently a change in the law—particularly a change that sees inhibitory laws removed from the books—can suggest that the matter has been removed from the moral order as well.

The proper relationship between law and morality is an old and difficult question. Yet it can only be a fully meaningful question when there are some generally accepted moral standards against which the law can be measured. Or, if that is too strong a statement, then there must at least be an expectation that explicit limits will be recognized within the private moral order; that is, put in the starkest terms, behavior not controlled by statute will at the very least be controlled or modulated by the power of public opinion. And by "public opinion" I mean the direct and strong moral judgment of others. If (as I believe) the law should be minimal in publicly enforcing moral standards, not going beyond those necessary for civil order, that ought not mean a parallel shrinking of the moral realm. But that is precisely the kind of conclusion a minimalist ethic entails. The inevitable result is that, by default, law is left as the only standard by which to measure and reliably control behavior. It should thus be no surprise that, when cries of moral decline are in the air, many will immediately rush to the law to fill the vacuum. What else does a minimalist ethic offer to put in the place of law? Nothing, and by definition.

Is there an antidote to a minimalist ethic, one that could avoid the moral anemia and casual ethical relativism that are its inevitable outcomes, but avoid as well a reactionary reimposition of restrictions on hard-won civil liberties? I am not at all certain; and it will not be easy. Mill could make a strong

case for his "simple principle" in the relationship between the individual and the state because he could assume a relatively stable body of moral conviction below the surface. Can we make a similar assumption? I think we must. There are no new and better values on the moral horizon than those we already possess: liberty, justice, human dignity, charity, benevolence, and kindness, and that is not a full list. A minimalist ethic cannot endure a serious attempt to deploy all of those values, not just liberty and justice. Nor could it survive a new willingness to pass public judgment on conduct that the law may and should still permit.

Civil tolerance is hardly tolerance at all if one moral choice is in principle as good as another. It can only make sense, and show its full strength, when there are standards against which to measure behavior. Then, within limits, we can allow others to speak and act as they see fit. But we owe it both to them and to morality to let them know when we think they are behaving badly, whether to themselves or to others. We do not have to ban tawdry television programs, or publications, or obnoxious viewpoints. We just bring to bear all the private and public opinion we can against them. Will that work? It had better, for the next step will be far worse, and there are already many who would have the law do what ought to be the work of morality.

INDEX